AF685661

100 PRINCIPLES OF
GAME DESIGN

WENDY DESPAIN, EDITOR
KEYVAN ACOSTA
LIZ CANACARI-ROSE
MICHAEL DENEEN
ZACH HIWILLER
JEFF HOWARD
CHRISTINA KADINGER
CHRIS KEELING
CASEY KUCZIK
NICOLE LAZZARO
TOM LONG
MICHAEL LUCAS
DAVE MARK
DOUGLAS OBERNDORF
PATRICIA PIZER
MICHAEL PYNN
BRIAN STABILE
JASON VANDENBERGHE

NRG

100 PRINCIPLES OF GAME DESIGN
Wendy Despain, Editor

New Riders
www.newriders.com

To report errors, please send a note to errata@peachpit.com

New Riders is an imprint of Peachpit, a division of Pearson Education.

Senior Editor: Karyn Johnson
Copy Editor: Rebecca Rider
Production Editor: David Van Ness
Proofreader: Scout Festa
Illustrator: Ray Yuen
Composition: Danielle Foster
Indexer: Valerie Perry
Cover design: Aren Straiger
Interior design: Claudia Smelser
Cover photo: www.studiodespain.com
Contributors: Wendy Despain, Keyvan Acosta, Liz Canacari-Rose, Michael Deneen, Zach Hiwiller, Jeff Howard, Christina Kadinger, Chris Keeling, Casey Kuczik, Nicole Lazzaro, Tom Long, Michael Lucas, Dave Mark, Douglas Oberndorf, Patricia Pizer, Michael Pynn, Brian Stabile, Jason VandenBerghe

ISBN-13: 978-0-321-90249-8
ISBN-10: 0-321-90249-1

9 8 7 6 5 4 3 2 1

Acknowledgments

A ton of thanks need to be heaped into three piles, so in no particular order, I would like to acknowledge that our "inspiration" for this book is another book used the world over by great game designers; it is called *Universal Principles of Design*, by William Lidwell, Kritina Holden, and Jill Butler. So many great game designers I know count this as a valuable part of their professional library.

However, when we started introducing this book to students in the Game Design program at Full Sail University, we discovered that this classic was in some ways too advanced for them. Their inexperience made it too hard for them to make the leap from architecture or art to game design. We initially tried to write a book that bridged the gap between these wider, classic universal principles and the process of game design. But we soon found that we wanted to add a few game-design-specific principles here and there. And then we found that "a few" had turned into 85 or so, and there was no end in sight. So now there are a few principles in this book that are also covered in *Universal Principles of Design*, but not very many. In my opinion, these two books are great companions on the bookshelf of any game designer.

And the next acknowledgment goes to the person who deserves undying thanks and delicious home-made baked goods every holiday for the foreseeable future. Ray Yuen, the illustrator, who I swear has a collection of gnomes under his back porch sketching adorable, funny characters doing wacky things like bringing a gun to a knife fight, did great things for this book in an insanely short amount of time and did an admirable job of adding zombies. Thanks, Ray. I hope you share the cookies with the gnomes.

And third, but not last, is the long list of contributors who went off this cliff with me. Thanks so much, everybody—you know what for. Specifically, I think Keyvan Acosta gets credit for the original idea for this book, Chris Keeling gets credit for being a temporary figurehead, and Ricardo Aguilo gets credit for being with us in spirit but having finally learned how to say "no" when asked to volunteer for something. I'd better stop now before I get any more teary-eyed about all the great contributors (and the amazingly wonderful editor at New Riders, Karyn Johnson, who tells me I have no more room on the page). So I'll just say I love every one of you, and your baked goods are in the oven right now.

Contents

Introduction xiv

1 Universal Principles for Game Innovation

- A/Symmetric Play and Synchronicity 4
- Aces High; Jokers Wild 6
- Bartle's Player Types 8
- Cooperative vs. Oppositional 10
- Fairness 12
- Feedback Loops 14
- Gardner's Multiple Intelligences 16
- Howard's Law of Occult Game Design 18
- Information 20
- Koster's Theory of Fun 22
- Lazzaro's Four Keys to Fun 24
- Magic Circle 26
- Making Moves 28
- MDA: Mechanics, Dynamics, and Aesthetics 30
- Memory vs. Skill 32
- Minimax and Maximin 34

- Nash Equilibrium 36
- Outcomes: Pareto Optimality 38
- Payoffs 40
- Prisoner's Dilemma 42
- Puzzle Development 44
- Rock, Paper, Scissors 46
- Seven Universal Emotions 48
- Skinner Box 50
- Social Ties 52
- Tragedy of the Commons 54
- Transparency 56
- VandenBerghe's Five Domains of Play 58
- Volunteer's Dilemma 60

2 Universal Principles for Game Creation

- The 80/20 Rule 64
- Brainstorming Methods 66
- Consumer Surplus 68
- Core Gameplay Loop 70

- Define the Problem 72
- Design by Committee 74
- Environmental Storytelling 76
- Experience Design 78
- Flow 80
- Four Ways to Be Creative 82
- Game Genres 84
- Game Pillars 86
- Game Tropes 88
- Gestalt 90
- House Rules 92
- Iteration 94
- Magic Wand 96
- Metagames 98
- Objects, Attributes, States 100
- Ooh, Shiny! 102
- Paper Prototyping 104
- Pick Two: Fast, Cheap, Good 106
- Play Testing 108

- Problem-Solving Obstacles 110
- Prototyping 112
- Risk Assessment 114
- Supply and Demand 116
- Synergy 118
- Theme 120
- Time and Money 122
- User-Centered Design 124
- Wayfinding 126

3 Universal Principles for Game Balancing

- Addiction Pathways 130
- Attention vs. Perception 132
- Balancing and Tuning 134
- Details 136
- Doubling and Halving 138
- Economies of Scale 140
- Errors Players Make 142
- Errors Without Punishment 144

- Hick's Law 146
- Interest Curve 148
- Learning Curve 150
- Loss Aversion 152
- Maslow's Hierarchy of Needs 154
- Min/Maxing 156
- Punishment 158
- Sandbox vs. On Rails 160
- Ten Minutes of Sustained Attention 162
- Variable Rewards 164

4 Universal Principles for Troubleshooting

- Advance Organizers 168
- Affordance Cues 170
- The Buster Principle 172
- Cognitive Biases 174
- Dominant Strategy 176
- Fitts' Law 178
- Fundamental Attribution Error 180

- Golden Ratio 182
- Griefing 184
- Hype 186
- Instant vs. Delayed Gratification 188
- Krug's First Law of Usability 190
- Music and Dopamine 192
- Pacing 194
- Problem-Solving Approaches 196
- Satisficing vs. Optimizing 198
- Sense of Accomplishment 200
- Spatial Awareness 202
- Time Dilation 204
- Working Memory 206
- Zero-Sum Game 208

Appendix 210

About the Contributors 215

Index 218

The 100 Principles

An alphabetical listing

The 80/20 Rule 64

Aces High; Jokers Wild 6

Addiction Pathways 130

Advance Organizers 168

Affordance Cues 170

A/Symmetric Play and Synchronicity 4

Attention vs. Perception 132

Balancing and Tuning 134

Bartle's Player Types 8

Brainstorming Methods 66

The Buster Principle 172

Cognitive Biases 174

Consumer Surplus 68

Cooperative vs. Oppositional 10

Core Gameplay Loop 70

Define the Problem 72

Design by Committee 74

Details 136

Dominant Strategy 176

Doubling and Halving 138

Economies of Scale 140

Environmental Storytelling 76

Errors Players Make 142

Errors Without Punishment 144

Experience Design 78

Fairness 12
Feedback Loops 14
Fitts' Law 178
Flow 80
Four Ways to Be Creative 82
Fundamental Attribution Error 180
Game Genres 84
Game Pillars 86
Game Tropes 88
Gardner's Multiple Intelligences 16
Gestalt 90
Golden Ratio 182
Griefing 184
Hick's Law 146
House Rules 92
Howard's Law of Occult Game Design 18
Hype 186
Information 20
Instant vs. Delayed Gratification 188
Interest Curve 148
Iteration 94
Koster's Theory of Fun 22
Krug's First Law of Usability 190
Lazzaro's Four Keys to Fun 24
Learning Curve 150

Loss Aversion	152
Magic Circle	26
Magic Wand	96
Making Moves	28
Maslow's Hierarchy of Needs	154
MDA: Mechanics, Dynamics, and Aesthetics	30
Memory vs. Skill	32
Metagames	98
Minimax and Maximin	34
Min/Maxing	156
Music and Dopamine	192
Nash Equilibrium	36
Objects, Attributes, States	100
Ooh, Shiny!	102
Outcomes: Pareto Optimality	38
Pacing	194
Paper Prototyping	104
Payoffs	40
Pick Two: Fast, Cheap, Good	106
Play Testing	108
Prisoner's Dilemma	42
Problem-Solving Approaches	196
Problem-Solving Obstacles	110
Prototyping	112
Punishment	158

Puzzle Development	44
Risk Assessment	114
Rock, Paper, Scissors	46
Sandbox vs. On Rails	160
Satisficing vs. Optimizing	198
Sense of Accomplishment	200
Seven Universal Emotions	48
Skinner Box	50
Social Ties	52
Spatial Awareness	202
Supply and Demand	116
Synergy	118
Ten Minutes of Sustained Attention	162
Theme	120
Time and Money	122
Time Dilation	204
Tragedy of the Commons	54
Transparency	56
User-Centered Design	124
VandenBerghe's Five Domains of Play	58
Variable Rewards	164
Volunteer's Dilemma	60
Wayfinding	126
Working Memory	206
Zero-Sum Game	208

Introduction

This book is a toolbox of possibilities. It is not a how-to manual. It contains at least four principles (I'm not telling which ones) that insist or imply there is only one true way to begin designing a game, and if it is started in any other way disaster will ensue. They cannot all be right ... can they?

Well, I'm sure I don't know, and I'm not going to try to convince you one way or the other either. What I do know is that these ways/principles/philosophies are all coexisting in the current game industry. Different companies, rock-star designers, and schools of thought all use them and swear by them. Maybe there's a Master's thesis in there somewhere, but I'm not interested in digging it out and ranking the schools of thought according to some value of success.

I'm a collector, not a competitor. I go through life picking up ideas and adding them to my mental list of "Hey, that's interesting, I might use it someday." And when I stumbled into game design as a profession, I discovered every game designer does this same thing. They have a mental toolbox they have collected over the years, which they bring to bear on whatever problem faces them.

And this is one of the reasons it is so hard to teach game design. The tools of the trade are vast and strange. This book is a download of my own mental toolbox with additions from the collections of my professional colleagues. I find it liberating and exciting to have it out in front of me instead of floating around in a jumble in my grey matter. It's even organized into the four times I find myself reaching for these tools: when I'm trying to innovate, when I'm hacking out the "cruft" in the middle of game creation, when the nearly finished work has to be balanced, and ultimately whenever I have to troubleshoot a specific problem.

How This Book Is Organized

Did I just make a book that needs its own instruction manual? I think I did. I'm not sure if this is a good thing or not! It's certainly very meta. The fact is, this isn't like any other game design book out there, so maybe you do need a bit of help text up front to get you oriented (see Advance Organizers).

This book is riddled with phrases highlighted in orange type (like the one in the previous sentence) that reference other principles of game design. If they look a bit like web links, it's because that's what I wish they were. I wish you could poke them with your finger and have the pages turn to show you that there's a whole section right over there expanding on this idea. Maybe the digital version will work that way one day.

At any rate, they're kind of like footnotes, but I'm not a footnote kind of person. I'm a digital kind of person, so when some part of this book skims over, or touches on, or mentions in passing an idea that is explored in more depth somewhere else in this book, you'll find the principle cross-referenced in orange. Blue type is used to highlight the name of the designer who created or popularized the principle.

So let's look at the parts of this book. As mentioned earlier, these core principles of game design are organized by four themes: innovation, creation, balancing, and troubleshooting. Each page describes a different fundamental principle that may or may not come up in the process of designing games. If you open this book randomly in the middle, you'll see this: On one side is a text explanation of a principle, and on the facing page is an image that helps illuminate or illustrate the ideas. Go ahead and try it. I'll wait.

No, really. I'm not going anywhere. Take a look; then come back here when you're ready.

. . .

Welcome back! I hope you were intrigued by what you found. You now see how the book is set up, and you've also now used it in one of its intended ways.

How to Use This Book

Don't get too hung up on why a principle is categorized into one section rather than another, though (see Hick's Law). They can all be used at any point in game development. The categories are just there to help bring order to the chaos and to guide you in the right direction when you're feeling a little lost.

Here are just a few ways you can use this book:

- **Looking for random inspiration.** Different people learn better in different ways (see Gardner's Multiple Intelligences). Opening this book to a random page is a great way to kickstart a stalled brainstorming session.
- **Brushing up on the fiddly bits.** Some of these principles are convoluted, crazy ideas with lots of parts. Use this book as a reference when you just can't remember what the Fourth Key to Fun is, for instance.
- **Learning something new.** This book is the collective unconscious of many people. Even the contributors themselves were eager to read up on the sections they felt they weren't qualified to write. There's a lot of great information in here.
- **Running diagnostics.** When something in a game is just not working out, this book can suggest avenues to explore. Links between principles can help get you to the root of a problem.
- **Solving problems.** There's an entire appendix with a list of many ways to approach solving a problem. It's not a how-to manual for any particular problem, but it does suggest ways to get started.

Keep in mind that there is no way to completely cover any of these complex ideas in one two-page spread. Contributors to this book complained about how few words I allowed them to work with, and some of them blew past the restrictions altogether (see Griefing and House Rules—not as examples, but as explanations), and I had to cut out a lot of great stuff.

So think of each page of this book as an introduction to or quick summary of the topic it covers. There should be enough information, jargon, and name-dropping in each one that rudimentary Google-fu will get you falling down a deep, deep rabbit hole on any of these principles. In fact entire specific books are sometimes recommended in the text. At any rate, don't think of yourself as an expert on a topic once you've read the one-page description here.

And don't even begin to think that these are the only principles or even the most important ones. There are many we couldn't fit into this book, which are being catalogued at www.gamedesignprinciples.com, so come join the discussion there, and tell us which of your favorite principles we left out!

1

UNIVERSAL PRINCIPLES FOR GAME INNOVATION

A/Symmetric Play and Synchronicity

Symmetric gameplay occurs when players experience the exact same thing at the same time when they are playing a game together. Chess, an analog game, is one such game (with the exception of Chess by mail, where one player knows the move well in advance of the other). Pong is the quintessential symmetric gameplay example in the video game world. Both players experience each move in tandem, perfectly synchronized; each sees exactly what the other sees on their screen.

Many console game that are multiplayer show players the same thing at the same time. In Mario Kart, players see the same "overhead map" of all the players' progress while each "window" shows each player a close-up of their particular vehicle so that they can manipulate their own vehicle accurately. In this case, the play is both symmetrical, because of the overhead map, and asymmetrical, because the players are not watching identical actions simultaneously.

Asymmetric gameplay occurs when two or more players see different things simultaneously, even though they are playing together. The prototypical example of this is when one player is the Dungeon (or Game) Master (DM) in a Dungeons and Dragons game. Whereas the DM sees what is going on in its entirety, certain knowledge is kept from the other players. In a video game, players may have different skills that enable them to see things (like traps) that other players cannot. These are cases of intentional asymmetry.

Finally, players may see different things due to lag. This unintentional asymmetry may cause a player to think they have made a shot that they have not; in fact, they may get shot by an opponent they cannot see because the server hasn't yet caught up to the real-time player.

This brings us to *synchronicity*. Synchronous gameplay is gameplay in which the players make their moves at the same time. This is common in online games where multiple players are in a play space simultaneously. Players usually see some approximation of the same thing at the same time during synchronous play. Multiplayer console games also feature synchronous play. Again, Mario Kart is perfectly synchronous.

The latest craze in asynchronous play is Words with Friends. In asynchronous play, one player makes a move and then waits for the computer/Internet to mediate the move and for the other player to play their move. This can take moments, if both players are connected, or days, depending on when the second player logs in to make a move.

Aces High; Jokers Wild

Aces high; Jokers wild represents an organizational schema in games in which sets of game objects can be reorganized in terms of their presented value or rank. In the case of playing cards, Aces have been (since the French Revolution) classically understood to be the highest ranking card, even higher than the King, Queen, or Jack (which possess a socially symbolical high rank); they are also considered higher than the other numbers, even though they are often used to represent the lowest card (the number one). Similarly, in a Spanish deck, the King beats the Knight, who in turn beats the Page.

However, at the outset of any game using these cards, players establish which of these pieces (cards) is considered the "high" card, and thus they can reorder the deck and change the distribution of probabilities for particular outcomes without changing the foundational rules of the game or even requiring players to draw a new hand. Calling Aces high modifies the distribution of cards available at any one moment without requiring a reset of the game pieces.

Any game in which the set of elements a player has at their disposal, especially those games in which the known values of game objects can be organized in any way, can contain a quick call to Aces high or Kings high. Some games use this principle by changing the high card halfway through the round, or requiring players to call a new high token based on individual or group goals. This introduces an element of variation or surprise into games where the experience might otherwise suffer from too much repetition.

Adding to the complexity of reordering a specifically organized schema on the fly is the introduction of the Joker as a wild card or token. *Wild* cards represent any other card or token in play, rather than having their own value. The wild card is essentially an empty variable that the player can set as needed. Since a game object (card, token, etc.) that can change its value is often used to the advantage of its player and the player's personal playing goals, the Joker, or any other card labeled as wild, can even become the highest possible ranking token; it can even become higher than an Ace, even if Aces are high, adding more complexity to the straightforward game mechanic of one token outranking another in an ordered set.

Some games label multiple objects (or cards) as wild, allowing for a *handicap* on the original distribution in any given set of game objects. These wild objects alter and increase the possibility of coming across rare game moments since they can occur more frequently than the original distribution of game objects allowed for probabilistically.

For example, in Poker, calling Deuces wild turns four cards of low and almost wasteful value (the Twos) into the potential for a higher ranking hand; in this scenario, imagine a Two being used with the other face cards of a Royal Flush family, or even turning a Two and a Seven (statistically the worst opening hand) into at least a pair of Sevens. Calling diamonds, or red cards, or face cards wild creates different statistics on the plays available in any game, while all other rules can remain unchanged.

Bartle's Player Types

Richard Bartle was a pioneer of multiplayer gaming—the co-creator of the first virtual world. Called MUD (for multi-user dungeon), the game allowed multiple players to simultaneously explore a virtual world and interact not only with the game, but with each other. By creating MUD, Bartle and his compatriots split the atom in terms of teaching designers new things about player behavior. In a 1996 paper called "Hearts, Clubs, Diamonds, Spades: Players Who Suit MUDs," he attempted to classify the wide variety of player behaviors he saw into four types. Whereas many studies since have helped refine the topology of player types, Bartle's classifications remain popular for their simplicity and reach.

Achievers' (or Diamonds') main focus is "winning" the game. This could be the intrinsic goals of the game or self-defined goals such as "I want to hit Level 80," "I want to be on top of the leader board," "I want one million gold coins," or "I want to beat this game in three hours with just the combat knife."

Explorers (or Spades) like to figure out the system and experience all it has to offer. Game designers often glom onto the Spade role. Collectors are another type of explorer. Pokemon is a game that itches the itch of explorers to explore the world not only topologically (by running around a map), but also mechanically (by making the battle mechanics nuanced and transparent enough to be interesting to learn). Players that fill out spreadsheets of all the possible items in a game are certainly a type of explorer.

Socializers (or Hearts) play multiplayer games because of the interaction with other players. Beyond just the social nature of playing together, they like to leverage things like guilds and teams to further codify their social existence.

Killers (or Clubs) want to impose their will on their fellow players. This can take on two forms: Some killers kill because doing so shows their prowess in the game. However, some players, called griefers, impose their will strictly because they want to disrupt other players.

Bartle classified these player types on two axes: Acting On versus Interacting With and World versus Players. Achievers prefer to act on the world. Explorers want to interact with the world. Socializers want to interact with players. Killers want to act on players.

By changing the number of opportunities for play in each of these four areas, game designers can affect the types of players who become interested in their game. In analyzing a game, try and determine which of the four player types are being best served. Is there something for all four to enjoy? Is something missing? Is there something for Socializers to do? Killers? By segregating players into logical groups, designers can better provide something for everyone.

Cooperative vs. Oppositional

When playing a game with more than a single player, there are two possible configurations for players: cooperative or oppositional. More often than not, play is oppositional or competitive in nature.

In a *cooperative game* (often referred to as co-op play), two or more players share goals and work together to attain those goals. Table-top roleplaying games (RPGs) are an excellent example of cooperative play. Players band together in parties for adventure. In this case, the obstacle to be overcome is that of the world or the world of the game's design or the game master's imagination.

In video games, cooperative play usually involves engaging two or more players against an artificial intelligence (AI) opponent. Players can trade items, heal one another, use complementary play strategies (such as a battle tank joining forces with a ranged-weapon user), or do things as dynamic as physically boosting one another to get on ledges that neither player could reach on their own.

Animal Crossing is an example of co-op play where players can help each other out by connecting their game cartridges to the system in order to unlock content for another player. A number of games have unlockable endings that can only be accessed by players playing cooperatively to solve the final challenge. Console games often offer co-op play to players on the same console and, more recently, have begun to allow two players on the same console to play cooperatively with players over a network connection. Co-op play even exists in single player games where a player can play alongside their previously saved selves.

The place where co-op and competitive meet is the team sport. Within a *team*, play is cooperative with each player playing a position in order to further the game. Teams are then competitive, playing against each other to score. First-person shooters offer this same team-based competitive play (see Volunteer's Dilemma and Tragedy of the Commons).

An *oppositional game* is just that: Players (or teams of players) oppose one another to win. The win condition is predicated upon having a single winner unless a match can end in a draw. Oppositional competition is at the heart of most multiplayer games, and many single player games are even played "against" a previous "best" play or high score.

A golfer may play against other players on a given course, but is always playing against his or her own previous scores on the course. In this way, the player may lose to competitors but win as far as a personal best is concerned. This is also true of bowling, racing, or a first-person shooter (FPS) multiplayer game such as Team Fortress 2.

Keep in mind that individual game mechanics and features may encourage or discourage cooperation or opposition, sometimes in unexpected ways. For instance, many Facebook games display lists of a player's "friends" to encourage socially inclusive interaction, but the list is ranked leaderboard style, which encourages competition, not cooperation. Achieving a certain position on a leaderboard is just as competitive as any other head-to-head play (see Social Ties).

Fairness

Fairness, according to the dictionary, implies something that is free from bias, something that is just. And fairness in game design is no different; the game must be fair to the player. In other words, the game must always be unbiased and not cheat the player. For instance, if the player has been told that they will receive *X* for action *Y*, it is unfair to give the player *Z* for action *Y*. In this instance, the contract with the player has been broken. When making any contract with the player, it must be honored to be fair.

Fairness becomes particularly important in games of chance. A slot machine that is weighted to give particular results is not fair. Randomness and the guarantee thereof is part of the contract with the player. To renege on that contract is to be unfair to the player.

In a game such as Tetris, part of the contract with the player is that the next piece will be a randomly chosen one of seven piece configurations. Players often perceive the randomness to not be random at all; instead they think the game is giving them unwanted pieces on purpose. If this were, in fact, the case, the game would be acting unfairly or not in good faith. Tetris pieces are, in fact, totally random, but players perceive patterns of behavior and will attribute them to unfairness.

In a similar vein, a game that ramps slowly and then takes a sudden jump in difficulty is perceived to be unfair and it is. Difficulty should scale up evenly so the player does not feel cheated or treated in an unjust fashion.

To go beyond this basic understanding of fairness, one might look to Rabin's model of fairness. This model is based on three central rules. The first is that, to people who are being kind, people are willing to sacrifice their own material well being. In other words, if players are being kind, a single player will act altruistically and give up some material gain for those kind players. The second rule is the basic inverse of rule one; a player is willing to sacrifice her own material well-being to players who are being unkind. If a player is intentionally being unkind to others, another player will give up some degree of material gain to punish the unkind player. Finally, the third rule is that, as the material sacrifice gets smaller, both rules one and two are more likely to be followed. Put differently, the less the player is giving up materially, the more likely the player is to engage in altruistic or punishing behavior.

Obviously, Rabin's rules of fairness pertain to multiplayer games where other players are involved. For instance, as it ordinarily costs nothing to send gifts in Facebook games, players are very likely to send gifts to other players who have been kind to them. On the other hand, if there is a severe material penalty in an MMO for killing another player, most players will refrain from killing even the most unkind other player.

Players who feel a game is treating them unfairly are likely to quit the game. Players who feel other players are being unfair are likely to punish those players. Keep this in mind when creating systems where the fairness of play may come into question.

1ST CREDIT WINNERS
2ND CREDIT WINNERS
3RD CREDIT WINNERS
PLAY 3 CREDITS
25¢
1 CREDIT= $0.25
THIS MACHINE ACCEPTS TICKETS
$1 $5 $10 $20 $50 $100 BILLS
WHITE ICE
DOUBLE DIAMOND
TRIPLE STRIKE

Feedback Loops

When playing a game of Monopoly, often it just seems like one player gets stronger and stronger while the others flounder. The player in the lead keeps getting hotels and knocking other players out of the game while another player is just trying to complete their first set. There isn't really a way to come back. It's not fun. And the other players just want to upend the board and play something else.

Colloquially, this problem is called the *rich-get-richer problem* or a *vicious cycle*. In the previous example, when the winning player buys hotels, it means that they get more money when people land on their properties, which allows them to have more money to buy more hotels. *Because* they are rich, they keep getting richer.

This is a feature more generally known in game design as a *feedback loop*. There are two kinds of feedback loops:

In a *positive feedback loop*, achieving a goal is rewarded, which makes it easier to continue achieving goals. Here are some examples:

- In a roleplaying game (RPG), killing skeletons gives the player level-ups, which allow them to kill more skeletons.
- In Chess, capturing a player's pieces makes them more vulnerable, leading to more captures.
- In Dodgeball, a team who has had more players eliminated has multiple threats to deal with, whereas the team with more players has fewer threats.

The other kind of feedback loop is a *negative feedback loop*. In this, achieving a goal makes it harder to continue achieving goals. Here are some examples:

- In Mario Kart, the blue shell targets only the leader of the race. Being in first means that player is likely to be hit with the shell, which may cause them to fall out of first.
- In American football, getting closer to the end zone means that there is less field remaining in which the 11 defenders are spaced, which means there are fewer empty zones in which to pass.
- In eight-ball pool, one player sinking your balls leads them to fewer options and greater chances of your balls blocking their shots.

Designers want to provide rewards that matter to their players, but players are generally only interested in rewards that help them win. This is why positive feedback loops are so prevalent. The problem is that they can lead a game out of balance, where only the first player to succeed will be able to succeed in the future. Although players want to be more powerful, what they really want is an interesting and challenging game. Sometimes giving them more power goes counter to that goal.

Negative feedback loops are sometimes seen as unfair as well. If a game is designed so it rewards losing, it is rewarding behavior that is contrary to its goals! Designers must be careful in implementing negative feedback loops so that performance in the game isn't seen as irrelevant. For instance, many racing games that have a rubber banding mechanic are chided for rewarding sloppy driving.

Fixing a negative feedback loop problem is generally easy: Reward the player for achieving the game's goals. Fixing a positive feedback loop problem can be a bit trickier. Designers may want to scrap positive feedback entirely, but they must be careful to make sure the player still feels an intrinsic reward for completing the game's goals. Designers may wish to pair the positive feedback given with a kind of negative feedback. Or they may wish to find a reward that doesn't contribute to the player's efficacy, like cosmetic rewards such as new skins or animations.

Gardner's Multiple Intelligences

In 1983, Howard Gardner, a developmental psychology professor at Harvard, came up with a theory of multiple intelligences. This theory states that all of us, as individuals, have strengths and weaknesses in the way we learn. As an example, some take to learning math in school very easily whereas others struggle. This does not necessarily mean they cannot learn it, but that the traditional ways in which math is taught in schools may not be the correct approach for these students.

Through his research, Gardner found that there are eight different intelligences or ways in which people learn; he broke them down this way:

- **Logical-Mathematical:** The process of learning through critical thinking and using logic. This is what may be vaguely referred to as left-brained learning.
- **Spatial:** The process of learning by using the mind's eye to visualize items in space. This is how professional Chess players are able to visualize the moves not only they can make but that their opponent can make in turn.
- **Linguistic-Verbal:** The process of learning from words, whether they be aural or written. Those strong in this intelligence can learn from listening to speeches or reading books.
- **Bodily-Kinesthetic:** The process of learning from moving one's body and the physical world around them. These learners do better if they can stand up, move around, or have physical contact with items they are learning from.
- **Musical:** The process of learning through the use of all things musical; tone, pitch, rhythm, and sound. A learner of this type can learn from childhood rhymes or anything posed to them in a lyrical fashion.
- **Interpersonal:** The process of learning from interactions with other people. This person might be a caring sort or a social butterfly.
- **Intrapersonal:** The process of learning from oneself. These are the quiet people who are always looking within themselves for answers.
- **Naturalistic:** The process of learning from relating to one's natural surroundings.

If designers keep each of these intelligences in mind when designing a game, they can open it to an infinite number of players. These intelligences have been used in games before. Eve Online and Dungeons and Dragons appeal to those with logical and mathematical minds with all of the stats that players have to keep up with. A Rubik's Cube and games like Lumines appeal to those people with a shine for spatial learning. Dungeons and Dragons and most text-based roleplaying games (RPGs) appeal to those who learn linguistically. Games like Red Light, Green Light and any of the new motion-controlled games excite those keen on kinesthetic learning. Musical Chairs and Legend of Zelda: Ocarina of Time utilize music to bring in those who learn this way. The advent of the Internet's online play and group play in Dungeons and Dragons appeals to those who learn interpersonally. Solitary games such as Solitaire and some RPGs help those who are self-reflective learn more about themselves intrapersonally. Scavenger hunts and hidden items games allow those who learn from their surroundings in a naturalistic way to excel.

Many games utilize two or three of these intelligences, but how many of them touch on a little bit of each?

Howard's Law of Occult Game Design

Howard's Law of Occult Game Design (or just The Law of Occult Game Design or Howard's Law) can be expressed as a formula: "Secret Significance ∝ Seeming Innocence × Completeness." Translated into everyday speech, this equation means that the power of secret significance is directly proportional to the apparent innocence and completeness of the surface game. In this case, *innocence* refers to a surface that appears simple, cheerful, even carefree. *Completeness* means that players can experience the game naively as a conventional platformer, shooter, or other standard game genre without being aware of any thematic depth. Sudden knowledge of the game's depths transforms players' experiences. The Law of Occult Game Design is often connected to a sense of the esoteric, of occult significance in both the connotation of dark magic and the original definition of occult: hidden.

The Law of Occult Game Design is why many indie game designers with emotive and thematic design goals tend to work in retro genres with simple mechanics and art styles. Indeed, many successful independent games could be boiled down to "the game seems like a simple platformer (or shooter/adventure game/puzzle game) but then. . . ." Retro genres and styles bring with them nostalgic expectations of simplicity associated with the early history of games. A metaphysical meditation on unseen cosmic forces is more unexpected, and therefore more powerful, in a sidescrolling shooter with eight-bit graphics and a chiptune soundtrack.

Often, a particular mechanic has an unusual twist that operates in both the narrative and gameplay universes of the game, thereby exemplifying excellent narrative design. For example, Braid is a sidescrolling platformer in the style of Super Mario Bros., but Braid's time-reversal mechanic encodes a reflection on the nature of love and loss. Eversion appears to be a platformer into which Lovecraftian cosmic horror gradually intrudes, revealed partially through the player's ability to *evert* (shift between dimensions). Terry Cavanagh's Don't Look Back appears to be a simple platformer, but the player is not allowed to move backward as he emerges from the underworld in the second half of the game. This gameplay rule mirrors a narrative rule attached to the hero, Orpheus, when he tried to rescue his lover, Eurydice, from the underworld: He could never look back, or her spirit would be pulled back into the land of the dead.

All of the games mentioned here create a similar transformative experience for the player, in which a seemingly ordinary game is revealed to have concealed thematic depth the entire time (see Theme), much like a Magic Eye picture from which a secret design suddenly emerges. Howard's Law suggests that the intensity of this transformation will be greater to the extent that the game initially seemed to function as a one-dimensional, self-contained experience.

Occult design is also connected to the idea of the *Easter egg* (a secret hidden within the game, such as a designer's initials), but the Easter egg as integrated with the enterprise of world-building. The first Easter egg appeared in the Atari 2600 game Adventure, in which players could access a secret room with the initials of the game's creator, Warren Robinett. Some Easter eggs promise a vast expansion of the original game, as if offering players the opportunity to peer beyond the veil into another world. For example, in the original Legend of Zelda for the Nintendo Entertainment System (NES), players who input the name "Link" after completing the game once revealed a second quest with altered dungeons.

Howard's Law has design consequences in space, time, mechanics, and cumulative experience. In level design, densely packed, interconnected labyrinths with many hidden passageways and alcoves are the most effective ways to hide secrets. Demon's Souls exemplifies this level design principle, which is writ large across the overworld in the game's spiritual successor, Dark Souls. In terms of time, games that contain events that recur at regular, but unexpected, moments are especially powerful, as when black demonic dogs roam the streets after midnight in the cult horror game Deadly Premonition. Occult design can influence obscure mechanics, such as world tendency in Demon's Souls, in which an undisclosed global variable allows an aggregate of player actions on the server to unlock hidden events, areas, and characters. Such secrets function most effectively when they combine cumulatively to reveal larger truths about the world of the game, as when the demonic dogs of Deadly Premonition echo an overarching dog shape in the map layout, as well as the pet dog of the game's disguised cosmic antagonist.

Information

The amount and nature of information that a player has at their disposal at any point in a game can dramatically change the decisions that player makes. For instance, without knowing the rules or the general state of the game, the player cannot reason through the decisions they need to make. Instead, all they can do is make wild, uninformed guesses. So the type and level of information that is available at different points in a game can dramatically change the nature of how it is played.

Information about a game can take several forms and can be categorized for easier consideration.

Structure of the Game

First and foremost of these information types is the game *structure*, including both its setting and rules. Card games, for instance, print the entirety of the rule set for the game in booklets or on the side of the box. Board games like Checkers have strict rules about valid moves.

The playing environment itself should be regarded simply as information. Consider how the board layout and piece set-up for Chess can be communicated clearly as pure information using algebraic chess notation.

Even the random elements in games are clear information when considered as parameters, rather than as specific values. For instance, in Monopoly players can't know exactly how far they will get to move on their next turn, but they do know movement is determined by rolling two dice.

State of the Game

The second category of information is the *state of the game* at any point in time. Broadly, it can be summed up as "what is going on right now?" This information can include positioning of units, scores, resources, and so on. And the state of the game can be broader information than the specific placement of units on terrain. For example, some board games alternate through "movement" phases and "scoring" phases. Information regarding which of these two states the game is currently in determines which player actions are valid.

Game theory goes on to further describe how this information is used in games. Of course, the exact implementation of these principles varies from game to game, but general classifications help to better describe how game designers can manipulate this information.

Perfect Information

The most basic and least restrictive style of information dissemination in games is that of *perfect information*. Perfect information describes an environment where all players know every single thing about the game—the environment, the rules, the current location, and the status of all items as well as the current phase in the game. Simple board games often fall into this category. Certainly Chess, Checkers, Go, and Monopoly are prime examples of games with perfect information. Nothing is kept secret or hidden in these games.

Imperfect Information

In contrast, if some part of a game is hidden from one or more players, it is considered a game of *imperfect information*. Examples of this kind of game include the classic board game Clue, or the party game Werewolf. In both these cases, the fun revolves around finding out information that is kept secret from one or more players. In Clue, the secret information is the who/where/with what weapon of a murder. Werewolf is a village-wide hunt for secret werewolves in hiding. Both of these games and many more use the manipulation and pursuit of information as their Core Gameplay Loop.

Games of imperfect information are further broken down and categorized, but that is covered in this book under the principle of Transparency, since all games of imperfect information revolve around the implications of secrets. Another principle that tackles this topic is Howard's Law of Occult Game Design.

Koster's Theory of Fun

A Theory of Fun for Game Design is a book by Raph Koster, published in 2004. It is a foundation work that all designers should acquaint themselves with. Koster tackles head-on how to make a game addictive, engaging, and entertaining. He also shows how games fail when they are unengaging and, well, simply not fun.

The premise of the book is that all games are actually low-risk learning tools, making every single game a sort of edutainment. Just as animals engage in play to learn things like dominance behaviors, how to hunt, and so on, humans also engage in games to learn. Playful learning releases endorphins, thus reinforcing the learning and bringing pleasure to the player. This endorphin cycle is what brings us back to a game experience. Once the game is no longer teaching us anything, we generally grow bored and stop playing.

To illustrate, let's take a simple game: Tic-Tac-Toe. This game is very basic with a simplistic core mechanic. For youngsters, this is a fun game as they learn to master where to place their X's and O's. For an adult who has played the game most of their life, it's not an interesting game; it has already been mastered and therefore no longer triggers an endorphin response as there is no more learning to be had. An adult (or even a child) who has had sufficient practice will know the moves required to win within the first few moves, or at least what to do to enact a draw. Without the learning involved, the game is no longer fun to play. Now, an adult may enjoy the fun of introducing his/her child to the game and thus derive fun from the teaching. However, this is usually a case of *naches*—pride in a mentee, or child, as they share the experience of learning and joy through the child's eyes. In any case, this type of fun is derived from Metagames.

Koster goes further with his theory, including how to use concepts such as "chunking" to help with game design. *Chunking* is the process by which a complex task is assimilated into something we do subconsciously (see Working Memory). For instance, when learning to drive, the new driver is faced with many tasks: watching the speedometer, the rear-view mirror, the side-view mirrors, the other cars, the traffic controls, and so on. However, by the time someone has learned to drive, they have chunked this information into one unit, so they can process it smoothly and almost without thinking. Obviously, experienced drivers must be engaged and conscious while completing the task of driving, but they don't spend their time focusing on the process of how to check their rear-view mirror safely.

Koster goes on to incorporate biology, psychology, anthropology, and game theory in this work. His idea is that what we experience as "fun" is whatever engages and challenges us through a number of dynamics, most especially learning. He asserts that the mastery of challenges—learning how to achieve the goals of a game—is what makes it feel like fun. He also points out, however, that games are specifically designed to rewire brain patterns, and that this is a serious responsibility. He takes this seriously and cautions new game designers to keep their power and culpability in mind when designing games.

Ten years later, further research has borne out Koster's assertions. In the second edition, he updates the book with these findings and includes related work, such as Lazzaro's Four Keys to Fun and developments in psychology and teaching that reinforce his assertions.

LEARN
PLAY
FUN

Lazzaro's Four Keys to Fun

Lazzaro's Four Keys to Fun is a design tool to inspire designers to develop new ideas for mechanics and that researchers can use to examine the effectiveness of these mechanics. Engagement comes from the way a player's favorite actions create emotions. Game mechanics create emotions in players that, in turn, drive engagement. There are four reasons why people play games.

First, they're curious or they get hooked and are pulled in by a novel experience. This is called *Easy Fun*, like dribbling a basketball or popping some bubble wrap; it's engaging all on its own and doesn't require players to gain points or keep score.

Next, games offer a goal broken into achievable steps. Obstacles challenge players to develop strategy and new skills to create *Hard Fun*. Frustration hopefully increases the player's concentration and when the player succeeds, this type of fun provides them with the feeling of the epic win.

The feeling of winning is more powerful when friends are also playing. With *People Fun*, the opportunities for competition, cooperation, communication, and leadership combine to increase engagement. There are more emotions involved in People Fun than in the other three types combined.

Finally, there is *Serious Fun*, where players play to change themselves and their world. People play a shooting game to blow off frustration at their boss, for instance. They play brain teasers to get smarter and a dancing game to lose weight. The excitement and relaxation they get from rhythm, repetition, collection, and completion create value and drive them to participate so that gaming is an expression of their values rather than a waste of their time.

The Four Keys to Fun focus on the activities gamers perform most in their play. Best-selling games have at least three of the Four Keys. Although they have favorites, gamers enjoy all four of these aspects of play. They typically rotate between these types of play in a single play session. Because each play style offers different things to do and unique emotions, players find that switching between them refreshes and lengthens play.

Easy Fun is the hook that games use to attract curious players and to draw them in. Gamers respond to Easy Fun with curiosity, wonder, and surprise as they experience novel controls, opportunities for exploration, and fantasy. Exploration, role play, creativity, and story all engage without too much challenge for the new gamer. Easy Fun provides various opportunities to experience other emotions when players have become too frustrated by the main challenge. Fun failure states reward the creative adventurer and make the game world feel more complete.

At a certain point, novelty loses its ability to hold the player's attention and they search for something specific to accomplish. The most obvious fun in games is that they are challenging. Hard Fun balances game difficulty with player skill by offering a clear goal, obstacles, and opportunities for players to use strategy to create frustration and then fiero from the epic win. One of the biggest emotions that comes from gameplay, fiero, requires the player to feel frustrated first. In fact, the player has to feel so frustrated that they are about to throw the controller out the window; if they win at that moment, the feeling of fiero is quite strong and their arms punch the sky. Players can't push a button and win the Grand Prix and feel all that good about it. Instead they need to develop skills to accomplish a goal. Fiero requires the opportunity for failure. Hard Fun achieves this by balancing difficulty and skill. If the game does not get more difficult, players leave because they are bored. If the game gets difficult too quickly, players leave because they are frustrated.

The thrill of victory is more fun in the context of friends. Social interaction in and around the game creates amusement and social bonding. People Fun mechanics such as competition, cooperation, caretaking, and communication create social emotions such as amusement, schadenfreude (pleasure at someone else's misfortune), and amici (friendliness). More emotions are involved when people play the same game in the same room, and more emotions come from experiencing People Fun than from the other three types of fun combined. Walt Disney believed that shared experiences are compelling experiences; compelling experiences are more meaningful, which brings us to the last key.

Serious Fun is where the fun of games changes the player or their world. After the fiero from winning fades, the Serious Fun remains to create value and meaning for the player. Collection, repetition, and impact mechanics create excitement, relaxation, and the desire to acquire items of value or status.

For the best results, designers use the Four Keys as a design framework to map out the opportunity space for increasing engagement for their game. A great story and eye-catching art are powerful experience creators in games, but the core value proposition comes from the emotions gamers experience while they are making choices.

For more ideas on how to use the Four Keys, download the free white paper and poster from here: http://4k2f.com

Magic Circle

One of the features of games (indeed one of the essential parts of the very definition of games) is that they exist in a kind of make-believe. No one playing baseball, for instance, should see it as a battle for life and death. No matter the amount of contract bonuses on the line, it is still a game. The inherent assumption is that games exist in a separate reality than the real world.

Early 20th century historian Johan Huizinga pointed out in his *Homo Ludens* that games have their own separate areas for play:

> *The arena, the card-table, the magic circle, the temple, the stage, the screen, the tennis court, the court of justice, etc., are all in form and function play-grounds, i.e., forbidden spots, isolated, hedged round, hallowed, within which special rules obtain. All are temporary worlds within the ordinary world, dedicated to the performance of an act apart.*

Katie Salen and Eric Zimmerman talk about one of the clauses from this quote—the magic circle—in their *Rules of Play* and further expound on Huizinga's idea: that reality is indeed different when play begins. Tiny, red, extruded plastic shapes become "hotels," trees become "base," and a goal line becomes a spot that must be protected without regard to one's own health or safety.

Although to many, it may seem a distinction without a difference, think instead about the freedom this type of play grants. An entire lucrative genre of digital games is centered around the play experience of being the first to murder the opposing player or to accumulate the most murders. This is absolutely horrific unless one is able to say that play itself is a separate reality. Now use this as a lens for creativity: What interactions can people not do in the real world (because of taboos, because of the laws of physics, because of lack of resources) that become irrelevant limitations in game reality?

Also, some games cross the boundary of the magic circle with regularity. A gambling addict is playing a game, but the effects of that game are certainly not limited to the reality of the magic circle. A player who fumes about his loss, which then puts him in a bad mood for the rest of the day, has crossed the membrane between the magic circle and reality. Indeed, griefers (see Griefing) are a type of ne'er-do-well who embrace the idea that the magic circle can be crossed, and use their power as a type of Metagame.

When "it's only a game" is no longer only a game, the magic circle has been left behind.

Making Moves

Games may be Simultaneous or Sequential, referring to the order in which the players make their decisions or "take turns." Distinguishing between Simultaneous and Sequential games is important because each requires different strategies and design considerations.

In *Simultaneous* games, players must consider what decisions other players will choose while making their own, but without knowing for certain what they will do. Each player also knows that the other players face the same dilemma. This crucial information—of what the other players are doing—will influence the outcome of any turn, but players don't have access to it while making decisions (see Information and Transparency).

In *Sequential* games, each player has more information available to them. They can consider the decisions of players who just made their move and make reliable predictions about what players that follow in turn may do.

Simultaneous games may be literally simultaneous, like Rock, Paper, Scissors, or players may make decisions at different times, but without actually knowing the decisions of any other players (making them effectively simultaneous). These kinds of games are most easily presented using a Normal Form table to show their Payoffs. Simultaneous games may be solved by a Nash Equilibrium (in which all players have a single best choice and will not do better by changing their strategy based on common knowledge of the possible outcomes of all choices). Prisoner's Dilemma is another example of a Simultaneous game (see its Normal Form table on its description page).

Sequential games require that players make their decisions in turn, as in Chess, and also that they know at least some of what decisions were made by other players previously (they may have Imperfect Information—see Information). In multiplayer games, it is also essential to understand whether there is a first-move advantage (or disadvantage) in the game, and at what point in the sequence the player is making their own decision; that is, who has already made their decision.

These kinds of games are most often presented using Extensive Form (or Decision Trees) to show their Payoffs. *Extensive Form* represents all of the options for each player for every decision at each opportunity based on every combination of available information and the payoff for each result. These can be highly mathematically complex for even the simplest game.

Sequential games are generally solved through *Backward Induction*. This is the process of determining the desired outcome, then working back through the Decision Tree to find those choices that will lead to that eventual outcome. Ideally, the player will also determine their best course of action for any branch in the tree based on the outcome of other players' previous decisions. This allows them to make the most optimal decision at any point in the game. This kind of reverse planning is generally based on an assumption of *Rational Self-Interest* (each player moving toward a goal that provides the best result for that player), and is considered to have been brought into game theory by **John von Neumann** and **Oskar Morgenstern** in the mid-20th century.

MDA: Mechanics, Dynamics, and Aesthetics

Mechanics, Dynamics, and Aesthetics (MDA) is a systemized approach to analyzing and understanding games. It comes from the work of designers Marc LeBlanc, Robin Hunicke, and Robert Zubek. They assert that all games can be broken down into the following components:

- *Mechanics* are the rules of the system. This element refers to how the system handles player input and what the player sees and does. In a board game, the mechanics consist of the rules and presentation. In a digital game, the mechanics are the rules vis-à-vis the source code of the game. The source code tells the machine how to interpret what the player does and how the game should react.
- *Dynamics* are how the actors in the system behave when the game is being played. This can be the hardest of the three to fully understand. Take the "game" that is played out when you are competing for an eBay auction. No rule says you need to bid as close to the close of the auction as possible. Yet the vast majority of bids happen in the closing seconds of an auction in bidders' attempts to not signal to the other potential bidders (players) what their interests are (often using sniping software). This dynamic occurs because of the mechanics; the players can see the current high bid and have to stop bidding at a specified time. If this was not the case, people would bid differently. Dynamics are an explanation of the runtime effects of the mechanics.
- *Aesthetics* are the emotional output of the game due to the dynamics. In the aforementioned eBay example, because of the "sniping" dynamic, there is a lot of tension in the closing of an auction for the current leader, the potential bidders, and the seller. There is no catalog of viable aesthetics in games, but challenge, fear, tension, fantasy, social interaction, and exploration are common game aesthetics.

There are two ways to look at MDA. In the first, you, the game designer, starts the design process by defining the desired aesthetic output of a game. You then decide what dynamics the players would engage in that could produce that aesthetic, and finally, you choose mechanics to set up those dynamics. In the second way, the game player experiences MDA from the other direction and interacts with the mechanics. Those mechanics result in certain dynamics, which produce a certain aesthetic response.

This is just one way to approach the task of creating a specific emotional reaction through games. It has its limitations. For instance, what a player experiences as an emotional response isn't just a function of the dynamics that the game creates, but also a function of the player and his or her background. Imagine a child, a teen, and a grandparent playing Resident Evil. The child may find it extremely scary, the teen may find it exhilarating, and the grandparent may find it repulsive. Additionally, culture and time period affect this reaction. Few people would get disgusted at the sight of Death Race 2000 nowadays, but in its day, it created quite a stir.

Nonetheless, MDA can be an incredibly useful tool when you are taking a step back and analyzing the mechanics planned for a new game. Here are some questions it can help you answer: What behaviors will these mechanics create? Do these behaviors match the desired behaviors of your game? If a rule is changed, what change will that make to the dynamic? What is your game about? What mechanics align with what the game is about and what mechanics work against what your game is about?

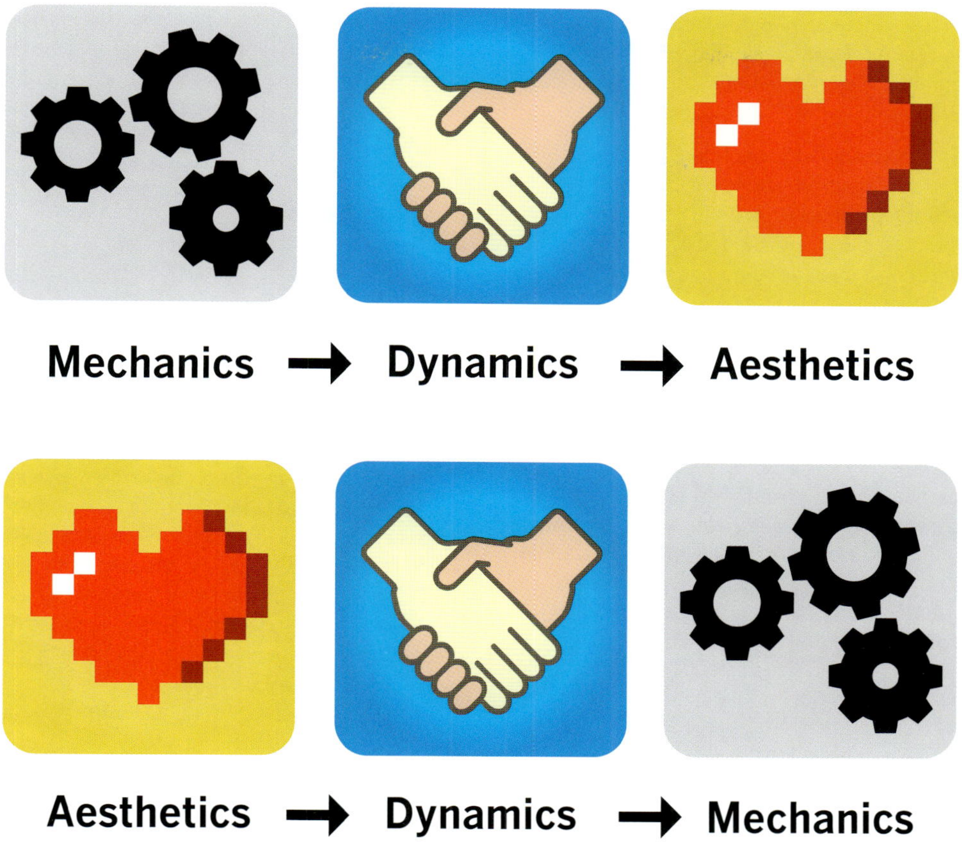
Mechanics → Dynamics → Aesthetics
Aesthetics → Dynamics → Mechanics

Memory vs. Skill

In game design there are various types of game categories, such as first-person shooters (FPSs), roleplaying games (RPGs), and the like. Although those niche markets are great, much broader category classifications for games are memory games and skill games.

Memory games contain elements that need to use trial and error, memory recognition, reflexes (platformers), and knowledge of the game itself. Games of skill contain elements that need physical or mental strength and conditioning in order to progress through them. Many games contain aspects of both in specific scenarios.

Let's take a look at a few examples of memory games. A player in an FPS game becomes more successful in the game once they have played it several times; at this point, they remember where the elements are, where the item-ups are, and how the level is laid out. In a sidescrolling platformer, the player needs to remember where items are and how they move in order to use their reflexes to get through the levels. A racing game has elements of both, where the driver needs to remember the race track and use reflexes to maneuver around it.

Here are a few examples of skill games. The game of Pool, or Billiards, even in a video game format, takes math to calculate the angles of the shot and takes knowledge of how a 3D sphere will interact with other 3D spheres on a flat plane with six possible outcomes. In an RPG, the player might get information from a non-playable character (NPC) about how they can only beat the boss of the area with a specific combination of weapons and magic. This leads the player down a mental path to map out their next move and to evaluate how to get the items their character needs to pass the level.

Whereas a smaller casual game played on a smartphone can focus on remembering where to place a finger or where to aim a flying object, a larger game might have elements of both memory and skill. Good examples of this are the "coin crunchers" from the late, great arcade games. Players needed excellent memories to beat any part of these arcade game since they never changed, and they needed a lot of game-specific skills like using a limited number of bullets wisely, using the correct button combination to throw a super uppercut, or learning the timing on a jump.

When it comes to the two types of games, memory games tend to bore the player after a while because they play the same game, in the same way, in the same areas, and with the same tools or weapons. One method of solving this issue is to add in randomization so that the game mechanics, story, and outcomes stay the same, but the enemies spawn in different locations, the platforms move at different speeds or in different directions, or item drops or where items are dropped in the level change. Games of skill tend to make the player more frustrated if they have not developed the skill set to surpass a certain part of the game. When this happens, a designer can help the player out using different methods. One recent method appears in Super Mario Wii, where Luigi helps show Mario the way to the end of the level if he dies quite a few times. In the same game, Mario can also fly back to the first world to watch videos of tips, tricks, and hidden items that keep the player playing and help the player progress through the game. A designer can also have the game offer tips, and create glowing items to show the player the way or which items they need to pick up. Designers can hide extra items around the level that can help the player in some way, and enemies can help the player as well; for example, maybe jumping on an enemy to hurt him can project the player to a higher level so they can reach a platform that they couldn't reach before.

Memorization techniques in games are also being used to advance skills in the real world. In the simulation industry, soldiers, doctors, students, boat captains, and many more are learning such things as how to field strip a weapon or how to perform a certain type of surgery.

Minimax and Maximin

Not to be confused with Min/Maxing, *Minimax* refers to the concept developed by John von Neumann that says it is rational for each player to choose a mixed strategy that maximizes their own payoff, and that the resulting combination of strategies and payoffs is the most Pareto optimal for that zero-sum game (see Payoffs, Outcomes: Pareto Optimality, and Zero-Sum Game). Minimax can also be used to reduce the opportunity cost (also known as regret) in economic game theory.

According to von Neumann, this theorem is the underpinning of all modern game theory. *Maximin,* the other side of the same coin, but applicable to non-zero sum games, is for players who focus on preventing the most catastrophic consequences and want to protect themselves from the worst outcomes of bad decisions. In general, the two ideas of Minimax and Maximin are nearly identical forms of *rational self-interest*, in which each player believes that they are making the right decisions to ensure their own success.

- **Minimax.** The Minimaxer is an opportunist or optimist, making decisions targeting the minimum possible payoff for the other player. Taking the option with the best success result isn't always a likely choice, since it may not sufficiently reduce the gain for their opponent. Their choice will always be the Nash Equilibrium.
- **Maximin.** The Maximiner is a worrier or pessimist, making conservative decisions to avoid negative payoffs for themselves. Taking the option with the least-horrible failure result is a likely choice. The Maximiner is the kind of person who puts their money in a savings account instead of risking it in the stock market or even hides it in their mattress to prevent its loss in case of a bank collapse. Their concern is maximizing their minimum gain.

Mathematically, a Minimax algorithm is a recursive algorithm for making the next decision in a game with a specific number of players, normally two. A value is defined for each possible state of the game for each player and is computed using a position evaluation function that indicates how successful a player would have to be to reach that position. According to the function, a rational Minimaxer would make the decision that maximizes the minimum value of the position based on their opponent's potential subsequent decisions and values set by the player (i.e., based on predefined goals).

The Minimax theorem is also used for decisions where no other player is involved, but for which the results depend on unpredictable events. This may be approached as a decision made in the face of nature, chance, or environment, such as determining whether to invest in a risky stock, which could provide great profit if the company is successful, but which could fail utterly if not. In this case, the expected outcomes are similar to a two-player zero-sum game.

Nash Equilibrium

The Nash Equilibrium is named for its discoverer, John Nash, who based his research on previous work concerning Zero-Sum strategies (see Zero-Sum Games) by John von Neumann and Oskar Morgenstern. According to Nash, there is a set of strategies for each player in any mixed strategy game with finite choices that provides no incentive to unilaterally change their strategy because such a change would always result in a lower Payoff than if that player had continued with their present strategy.

When all players have a single best choice and will not do better by changing their strategy, this is a Nash Equilibrium. A Nash Equilibrium does not have to be the Pareto-optimal outcome (see Outcomes: Pareto Optimality) for that game. Examples of games with a Nash Equilibrium include Tic-Tac-Toe (for which the Nash Equilibrium results in a draw) and Prisoner's Dilemma (in which the Nash Equilibrium results when both players keep silent).

The Nash Equilibrium can be used to predict the outcome of interactions between players based on their optimal strategies. It cannot predict the results of a decision without taking into account the actions of the other players, so it is not useful unless all of the players have common knowledge of the game's possible decisions and the results. In this case, each player must know all of the possible outcomes and payoffs for all players so that they know which decision is best for them and which decision is most beneficial to other players (see Information and Transparency).

A Nash Equilibrium can be found mathematically through a payoff matrix. Such matrices are convenient only for games with few players and few strategies, however. If the first payoff number in the cell is the highest for that column and if the second number is also the largest for that row, then the cell contains a Nash Equilibrium. For example, in a two-player game with four possible strategies, the payoff matrix may appear as follows (with the Nash Equilibria italicized and results scored for Player 1, Player 2):

As long as the ordinal relationship between the two values in a cell doesn't change, and the two values remain the highest in the column and the highest in the row, the Nash Equilibria will remain stable. In the example shown, values of 11, 12 for BA, 12, 11 for AB, and 16, 16 for CC and DD would retain the equilibrium of the matrix. On the other hand, changing CC or DD to 10, 10 would remove them as Nash Equilibria since there would be a higher value in either column or row for one of these payoffs.

Of course, errors, complexity, distrust, risk, and irrational behavior may influence player strategies, causing them to choose a strategy with a lower payoff, but one which they may feel they have good reason to select. Player communication (outside agreements and credible or non-credible threats) can also influence the selection, particularly in sequential play of the same game, leading to Metagaming strategies (see Metagames) such as Tit-for-Tat, often found in series play of the Prisoner's Dilemma.

The Nash Equilibrium has been used to analyze political and military conflict (including the Arms Race of the Cold War), economic trends such as monetary crises, and the flow of ordinary traffic in congested areas. The application of the Nash Equilibrium to the environment has even supported another game theory called the Tragedy of the Commons. Iteration of games with Nash Equilibria has shown that repeated interaction between players can provide a basis for long-term strategies that may supersede any statistically predicted outcome, including a greater likelihood of cooperation in many cases, especially when players are allowed to communicate freely.

	Player 2 - A	**Player 2 - B**	**Player 2 - C**	**Player 2 - D**
Player 1 - A	0, 0	*20, 15*	0, 10	10, 0
Player 1 - B	*15, 20*	0, 0	10, 0	0, 10
Player 1 - C	10, 0	0, 10	*15, 15*	15, 0
Player 1 - D	0, 10	10, 0	0, 15	*15, 15*

Outcomes: Pareto Optimality

Many game theory examples are presented as Zero Sum propositions—that one player's gain is another player's loss. Certainly, in games, this is often the case. Especially in games where players claim resources—for example, the board game Risk—and in cases when one person's improved position through capturing a territory, by its nature, detracts from someone else's position.

However, there are also situations where a person may improve their own position without negatively affecting any other players. Italian economist Vilfredo Pareto studied these relationships in areas such as wealth and income distribution. The concepts that he developed from his observations have been named after him.

Rather than view improvements solely related to the individual, he analyzed them in the scope of the whole system. For instance, a *Pareto shift* occurs if one is given an allocation of goods, money, land, and so on, and a change from one allocation to another (e.g., through a sale) occurs. Naturally, a zero sum transfer from one party to another is not an improvement of the system as a whole. However, a shift that improves one party's situation without directly making another's worse is called a *Pareto improvement.*

One example of a Pareto improvement is when a roleplaying game (RPG) character upgrades their abilities and spells. In typical game worlds, these actions do not depend on another character having something reduced. On the other hand, a situation in which a character steals another character's equipment is, obviously, *not* a Pareto improvement since the shift impacts the second character negatively.

Often, Pareto improvements can be made by both sides—even multiple times. Once a system reaches a point where no more Pareto improvements can be made, it achieves *Pareto efficiency* or *Pareto optimality*. Any further shifts in the system would be zero sum—that is, the shift would be detrimental to at least one of the parties.

It is an important distinction that Pareto optimality isn't necessarily a fair and equitable distribution. It also doesn't imply any judgment on whether or not the distribution is the best possible arrangement. It only states that the choices have expanded to the point where neither one can be improved without impacting the other.

Additionally, it is interesting to note that a Dominant Strategy doesn't always align with a Pareto optimality. For example, in the Prisoner's Dilemma, the dominant strategy (betray) differs from the Pareto optimal solution (both players cooperate). This occurs because each player "staying silent" amounts to a pair of simultaneous Pareto improvements—each prisoner's position gets better without making the other's worse. At this point, however, neither one can improve their own position (by betraying the other player) without making the other person's position worse.

In cooperative games or systems, Pareto optimality can be a desirable goal. In competitive games, however, when Pareto optimality is achieved, it often results in stalemate or inevitable conflict. In a strategy game such as Civilization, for example, players often expand their territory until their borders meet those of other players. In a general sense, these expansions are Pareto improvements as long as they don't take territory from anyone else. However, once players have claimed all the territory, a Pareto optimality has been reached. The only way for one player to increase their holdings is to take territory from another.

Also, Pareto improvements (and, therefore, optimality) are often used as a resource-balancing game mechanic. For example, a game that involves decisions regarding what types of units to produce (through limited money, time, space, and so on) often deals with Pareto improvements. When given a finite number of resources, for example, a player might be given the decision to create offensive or defensive units. The increased ability to construct either one is a Pareto improvement as long as it doesn't slow the production of the other. Once the maximum creation capacity is reached, however, a decision to increase one necessarily decreases the other. Again, there is no implication of what the "right mix" is—only the recognition that all resources are being used efficiently.

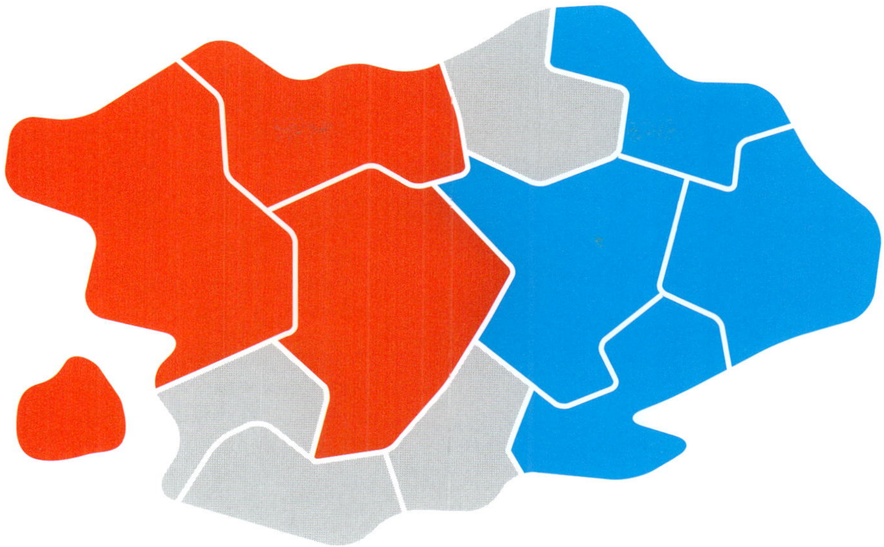

Pareto improvements possible: Either player can improve their position without having any impact on their opponent.

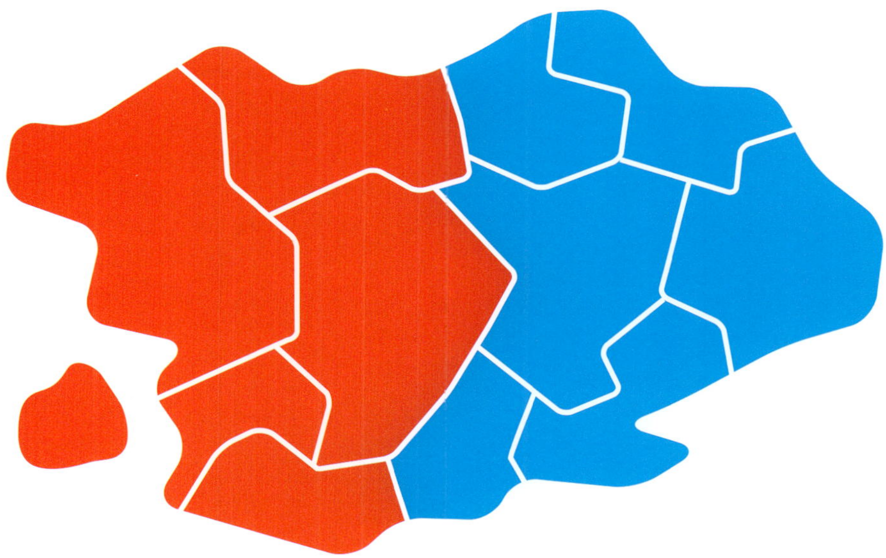

Pareto optimality: Neither player can improve their position without negatively impacting their opponent.

Payoffs

A Payoff is the outcome (see Outcomes: Pareto Optimality) or result of a decision in a game, whether positive or negative, no matter how it is measured. That could be in score, profit, or some other form of perceived value that serves as incentive and motivates a player (see VandenBerghe's Five Domains of Play).

It is important to note that not every player (see Bartle's Player Types) is motivated by the same Payoff. Some players will fight to get to a higher score or level while others are more interested in how many flowers they can plant (see Metagames).

Rational self-interest is assumed among players of games in general, which means that everyone is expected to move toward the Payoff that is best for them, and everyone will try to maximize their Payoff (see Minimax and Maximin). Decisions are rationalized in terms of their effect on the player, based on the player's own internal system of values. This sometimes results in a player doing what they think is best for the group, in hopes that it also improves their own situation (see Volunteer's Dilemma), but usually rational self-interest means that decisions are made solely in the interest of the player, regardless of the impact on other players.

Game theory points out that Payoffs can be classified as either Cardinal or Ordinal.

- **Cardinal Payoffs** are those that represent some identified value of money or points or whatever is being used as a unit of measure. Cardinal Payoffs are fixed, specific numbers, which can be set at varying levels to provide a variety of relationships between outcomes. The key to Cardinal Payoffs is a specific number such as 1 or 0, yes or no. A reward is given or it is not.
- **Ordinal Payoffs** describe outcomes in which the value of the Payoff is of less interest than the relative order in which they occur. Ordinal Payoffs are relative, comparative values, ranked from best to worst, as in a race, where order of merit is more important than time or distance. The key to Ordinal Payoffs is order, such as 1, 2, 3, 8, and 12. The winner is the one at the top of the rank, not associated with a particular number.

Payoffs are generally presented in a *Normal Form* table when play is simultaneous (see Making Moves); that is, when one player must move without knowing what the other player will do. The results of each player's choice can then be compared. The table that accompanies the Rock, Paper, Scissors principle shows an example of a Zero-Sum Game with Cardinal Payoffs. This is made obvious by the possible outcomes, which consist solely of win/lose scenarios rather than a scale from success to failure with multiple points on it.

However, in a full match of Rock, Paper, Scissors—where the same participants play several games—the winner is decided not by who wins the final game of the match (this would be Cardinal), but by which player wins *the most* games. The players can be ranked on a continuum, in order, so the payoff in this case is Ordinal.

One thing to note about balancing payoffs in a game: The application of rational self-interest to the decision-making process (without credible commitments by other players) will often result in the worst possible outcome for the player. As an example, consider the Prisoner's Dilemma, where two players who cooperate with each other (not using rational self-interest) will each receive the second-best outcome. However, when both choose the option that could result in their freedom—betraying each other—then both are instead sentenced for a longer period. Note that even though this game shows Cardinal Payoffs, they are essentially Ordinal, as it is only important that they remain in the order shown (-10, -4, -1, 0), with any values for those numbers acceptable as long as they remain in the same sequence (see the table that accompanies the Prisoner's Dilemma).

Prisoner's Dilemma

The Prisoner's Dilemma is a simple game that demonstrates why two players may make individual choices that are not in their own best interest instead of cooperating for a better result. It models mutual trust in a Synchronous Non-Zero-Sum (usually a Symmetrical) game of Ordinal Payoffs in which rational self-interest is generally assumed (see A/Symmetric Play and Synchronicity and Zero-Sum Game), although cooperative behavior is frequently noted (even though communication between players is forbidden) and heavily rewarded, with mutual cooperation in the Pareto-Optimal Outcome (see Outcomes: Pareto Optimality). The game may be played classically, as a single decision, or iteratively, resulting in patterns of behavior based on previous outcomes. In the table at the right, when a prisoner cooperates, that person is staying silent in support of the other prisoner. When that individual betrays his partner, he is implicating the other prisoner to the authorities.

When two players play the Prisoner's Dilemma multiple times in succession, and each forms an opinion of the other player based on previously exhibited behavior, each will begin to form strategies based on the other's behavior. The most rational decision when playing a known (*N*) number of games in sequence is to betray the other prisoner every time. However, in practice, most people are not so superrational as to realize that the greatest benefit to them is to cooperate every game and then betray on the last play; by supposition, this leads them to infer that the other player is also equally rational and would do the same, and so they betray on the next to last round, ad infinitum, back to the beginning. In a series of an unknown number of plays of Prisoner's Dilemma, this is no longer the game's Dominant Strategy, but only its Nash Equilibrium.

In fact, several strategies develop among actual human players that are not as rational, but are more successful. The most basic of these strategies is known as *Tit-for-Tat*, in which the player does each round whatever their opponent did on the previous round and begins the first round cooperating. Robert Axelrod, one of the early researchers of this game theory, developed four conditions that a player's strategy must have to be successful:

- **Nice.** Do not betray before your opponent betrays (cooperate as often as possible).
- **Non-Envious.** Never try to gain more than the other player (optimal balanced score).
- **Retaliating.** Punish your opponent when they betray you (do not always cooperate).
- **Forgiving.** Return to cooperation after retaliation (as long as your opponent does not betray you).

Unorthodox methods, based on techniques such as random betrayal (the player chooses cooperation or betrayal at random, which results in a slight gain against nicer players), Pavlovian reward (the player cooperates whenever the opponent does the same thing as the player did on the previous turn), and team competition (Min/Maxing by having designated teammates lose so that others can win, communicated through a Morse Code–like cooperate/betray scheme), can sometimes gain an advantage over more traditional strategies. The game can also be played with a single player (balancing among outcomes, each with its own advantages and repercussions), with multiple players on each side each controlling a portion of the outcome, or even with multiple teams managing cooperation and refusal (or resource allocation) between the different teams. This can sometimes result in a Tragedy of the Commons. Additional variants allow for Asynchronous play (see A/Symmetric Play and Synchronicity), Cardinal Payoffs, or Voluntary Transparency and distinctly change the nature of the game.

Recently, a new approach by William Press and Freeman Dyson has emerged called *Zero-Determinant Strategy*, which holds that one player can control the game by causing their opponent to believe that they are going to make a specific choice, giving them some advantage over their opponent through the use of disinformation, but only if they can determine the strategy that their opponent is using. Although common in games that allow communication (for example, bluffing in Poker), this type of second-order analysis has not been done with Prisoner's Dilemma until now, primarily due to the enforced lack of communication between players. Even though it has been shown to offer only a temporary advantage, particularly against other players who also know the Zero-Determinant Strategy, this heavily probability-based method has at least reopened the investigation into Prisoner's Dilemma and may lead to further understanding of Metagames strategies for this particular game theory model.

The Prisoner's Dilemma was originally developed by Melvin Dresher and Merrill Flood in 1950 (although it was named by Albert Tucker). It is frequently used in the study of economics (for business development and advertising campaigns), the military decision-making process (when escalation or disarmament could each result in war), in psychology (as a determinant for addiction models), and in evolutionary biology theory (in investigating whether genetic or social desires can overcome individual wants and needs). It provides a useful paradigm that can compare rational expectations with irrational behaviors to determine potential motivators outside the scope of mathematical probability.

The Prisoner's Dilemma comes down to this: Do you betray your partner (in crime) or do you cooperate with him (to foil the cops)? It goes to the heart of how players decide to cooperate or compete with each other.

Prisoner's Dilemma Chart

		Prisoner 2 (P2)	
		Cooperate	**Betray**
Prisoner 1 (P1)	**Cooperate**	Each receives 6 months (A:A)	P2 goes free P1 serves 5 years (C:B)
	Betray	P1 goes free P2 serves 5 years (B:C)	Each receives 2 years (D:D)

As long as B > A > D > C and they are proportional, the game need not be symmetrical.

Puzzle Development

Puzzles are a very interesting subset of game development. Designer Scott Kim relates this definition of a puzzle: "something fun with a right answer." Squishiness of the definition aside, this does provide at least one useful element of a puzzle: It can be solved. A few additional requirements make for an effective puzzle.

A good puzzle must be neither too easy nor too hard for its audience. A perfect puzzle is just the right difficulty so it challenges the user, but not so difficult that they give up in frustration. A good technique to bumping puzzlers into this flow state is by using *breadcrumbs*. These are hints, either internal or external to the puzzle, that allow players to progress. For instance, in Sudoku or crossword puzzles, as the puzzle is partially solved, the remaining unsolved blocks get easier and easier. Whereas a player may not have known 48 Across when they started the crossword puzzle, by filling in nearby Down clues, they can unlock letters that partially solve 48 Across. Breadcrumbs allow hints to be revealed to the user to gradually ease the puzzle closer and closer to the player's natural difficulty tolerance.

A good puzzle must involve a clever, intellectual effort to get from unsolved to solved. It must not require simple brute force. Consider this example: "I'm thinking of a number from 1 to 10. What is it?" "1?" "No." "2?" "No." "3?" "No." This is not a good puzzle. A maze with just a couple of obviously false paths is not a good puzzle. Because of this, quizzes and some riddles make for poor puzzles in general, because the solver either knows the answer or does not and cannot break the puzzle down into steps.

A puzzle can be generated randomly but must be deterministic once the player encounters it. For instance, a board of Sudoku can be generated pseudo-randomly, but once the player starts the puzzle, every player that makes the same moves will experience the puzzle in the same way. If two players get the same Minesweeper board and uncover the same squares in the same order, they will have identical experiences. Conversely, if two people play tennis and make the exact same movements, they will have a very different game experience. Chess, unless played against an artificial intelligence (AI) specifically designed for this purpose, is not deterministic. If a player makes the same five opening moves, five different players may play it in five (or more) different ways. Chess can be made a puzzle if a set of moves and deterministic rules are provided. Examples of chess problems in puzzle magazines show readers how to get to mate in *X* moves with rules for how the opponent will move.

Finally, a good puzzle must let the player know what the goal is and what they need to manipulate to reach that goal. Some puzzles are confounding simply because the player is never told the rules. Many old adventure games had this problem—a room would have some elements that were obviously a puzzle, but the goals of the puzzle and what pieces had to be manipulated and how were never described to the user. Designers of these "puzzles" used rule obfuscation to increase their difficulty to "challenging," but they never actually developed a puzzle that was fair. "Players have to solve how to solve the puzzle" is an intellectual cop-out used to avoid making interesting puzzles.

To sum up, when designing a puzzle ensure that it

- Keeps the player in a Flow state according to difficulty
- Requires clever intellectual effort to get from unsolved to solved
- Is deterministic
- Is clear and fair as to the goals and mechanics

OPPORTUNITY
ERROR

Rock, Paper, Scissors

Rock, Paper, Scissors, also known as *roshambo,* is a synchronous, semi-random, zero-sum game played only with hand gestures (see Zero-Sum Game). On the surface, it is a very simple game with attributes that are referenced and reused continually in game design. Its simple surface hides some complex ideas, however.

The game uses three symbolic gestures which are balanced against the other two, as shown here:

	Rock	Paper	Scissors
Rock	Draw	Paper Wins	Rock Wins
Paper	Paper Wins	Draw	Scissors Win
Scissors	Rock Wins	Scissors Win	Draw

As you can see from the table, each gesture—Rock (fist), Paper (open hand), and Scissors (two fingers, spread apart)—beats one other gesture, and yet it can be beaten by one other gesture as well. This game is perfectly balanced, with the gestures forming a circular pattern of supremacy: Rock > Scissors > Paper > Rock and so on.

Matches of games are normally played, such as "best two out of three," to prevent cheating and to allow for the formation of strategies. Draws are not counted against the total. National and international championships are played in this game, sometimes for very high stakes.

Skilled players can win more frequently than the default one-third of the time through an understanding of the game's patterns and how other players are likely to react. Strategies may be used, such as ploys to confuse the opponent, including yelling the names of gestures other than the one the player is using, or goading the other player into making an invalid move (neither Rock, nor Paper, nor Scissors) to force them to forfeit (see Metagames). Some players plan out all three of their selections for a match in advance, which can prevent confusion or hesitation, but can also result in predictability when competitions allow players to watch each other perform. Computer programs have also been developed that can "play" Rock, Paper, Scissors against other computer opponents and can select "gestures" using algorithms based on player patterns and trends, Markov Chains, strategic prediction, and random numbers.

The concept of a circular chain of supremacy has been used in other games to prevent the evolution of a dominant strategy and allow each type of unit to hold an equal value in gameplay (see Dominant Strategy). For example, in a modern war game, tanks may beat infantry, while infantry beat artillery, and artillery beat tanks. Usually, these advantages are set up as weaker attacks and specific defenses against the other units, but the direct causality can be modified and obfuscated by attributes (see Transparency) and triggers like weather, terrain, tactics, and other influences (see Objects, Attributes, States).

Tabletop card games frequently use Rock, Paper, Scissors approaches to level the playing field and balance power-ups (see Balancing and Tuning). Some games even go so far as to increase the number of units in the chain to five or more, or create webs rather than chains, causing a more complex and varied set of strategies to emerge.

One note of caution, however: Rock, Paper, Scissors is sometimes used as a crutch for lazy game designers who are not interested in coming up with a more interesting, innovative, or unique method of balancing. Be very careful if Rock, Paper, Scissors is the only strategy ever proposed for how a feature should function.

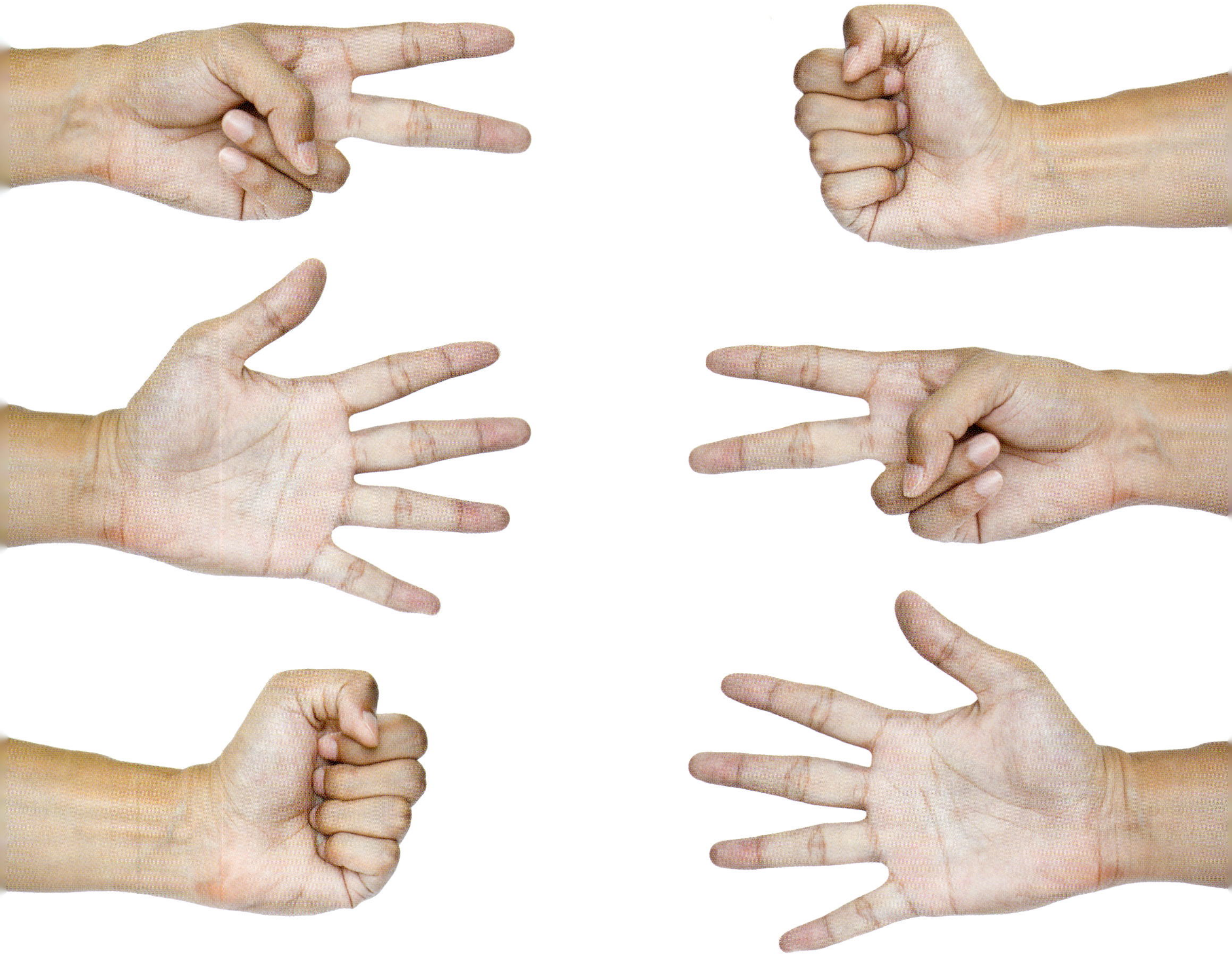

Seven Universal Emotions

Game designers often focus on evoking emotions in their players, and it takes up a great deal of energy and enthusiasm as they pore over Interest Curves and struggle with keeping players' attention. Facial expressions can tell us a great deal about the emotions and feelings of another person and can communicate to others the current emotional state this person is in.

Emotions are a very individual, private experience, and people raised in different cultures may feel different emotions for different reasons. On top of that, people express their emotions differently from culture to culture. In some cultures, remaining quiet is a sign of submission, fear, or shyness; in others, it's a show of force and an implied threat.

So studying human emotion can be very tricky. Yet, humans do share a lot in common with each other, and some emotions truly are universal. Scientists hit upon the idea of studying facial expressions and comparing them across cultures. What they found was that there are seven universal emotional expressions that are recognized worldwide in every culture.

These seven emotions are:

- Surprise
- Contempt
- Anger
- Joy
- Fear
- Sadness
- Disgust

These seven universal emotions were first described by Paul Ekman, a former U.S. Army psychologist and a professor of psychology at the University of California, San Francisco. He found that emotions are unconscious and fleeting, but can be easily readable via the changes in people's faces. This is a marked difference from moods, which last longer than a fleeting emotion and can be hidden or lied about.

Some of these emotional expressions have been used in older games, such as the player character's image front and center in the heads-up display (HUD) of the original DOOM. The basic expressions shown are contempt and anger, and this conveys to the player their character's emotions during the game in an easily recognizable and visual way.

As graphics have improved facial expressions, they have also become better at communicating the in-game characters' emotions through the use of the universal expressions. The game L.A. Noire utilizes this theory to make a very full and enriching story with characters who are easily readable overall just from the fleeting expressions on their faces. As the game characters' faces change, the player is able to learn more about the characters as well as connect with the characters on a basic human level due to the specific use of these universal emotional expressions.

The seven facial expressions common across all cultures are surprise, contempt, anger, joy, fear, sadness, and disgust.

Skinner Box

Game designers have a fundamental need to anticipate player behavior. This makes the world of psychology of immense interest and value to them. One overly abused school of study, Behaviorism, was popularized by B.F. Skinner in the middle of the 20th century. One way Skinner tested Behaviorist theories was by putting a rat in a cage and rewarding it with food pellets for different kinds of actions; he then measured the efficacy of those actions.

Skinner tried the following:

- Give a rat a food pellet every time it presses a lever.
- Give a rat a food pellet every *X* times it presses a lever.
- Give a rat a food pellet the first time it presses a lever after *N* minutes.
- Give a rat a food pellet after a random *X*th press of the lever.
- Give a rat a food pellet the first time it presses a lever after a random *N*th minute.

It turns out the rats clearly responded to different types of reward cycles. Some of the reward cycles caused the rats to feverishly press the lever again and again in the hopes of getting more pellets. Others were more tempered and caused the rats to press the lever fewer times.

If the purpose is to get the rat to press the lever as often as possible, the best reward schedule is what is called a *variable ratio*. This is when the reinforcement is based on how often the rat presses the bar, but the rat can never be certain exactly how many presses it will take since it is based on a random variable.

Some game designers have taken this finding to its more applicable conclusion. They reason that interaction with the game equals value, and therefore, the way to elicit the most interaction with the game is to give players rewards based on a variable schedule. Roleplaying games (RPGs) show this in action. If the player "kills" a skeleton, sometimes a magic jewel drops out. But the player doesn't really know which skeleton will provide the drop. Players don't know when they are going to win, but they reason that the more skeletons they kill, the better their odds, so they go on a skeleton pogrom.

Designers are split on the normative repercussions of this. Are players just rats in a box that can be manipulated into doing a designer's bidding? If yes, then there is really no need to actually make a game fun, the designer just has to make it so that rewards are compelling enough to force the desired actions. Many Facebook games and massively multiplayer online games (MMOs) fall into this trap. Interview players and they are ambivalent about how "fun" the game is, yet they still admit to being drawn to playing.

In small doses, however, Behaviorism can simply be used as a neat trick to drive engagement. Perhaps instead of giving a player a gold coin when they win, give them a chance at a number of gold coins (variable versus fixed)? Perhaps instead of rewarding players after a fixed or variable interval of time invested, reward them instead for interactions with the system (ratio-based instead of interval-based)?

Some kids have to mow the lawn every weekend. Some of these yards are fairly large by kid standards and as they start, they dread the chore. In the hot summer sun, pushing a lawn mower doesn't rank very highly on a kid's list of preferences. But then they notice something: As they get closer to finishing the lawn, the task gets easier, they complete rows of mowing more quickly, and they become more thrilled about the $5 they will get for completing it.

This phenomenon is called the *goal-gradient effect*. Researchers Ran Kivetz, Oleg Urminsky, and Yuhuang Zheng found that as humans get closer to a goal, they became more motivated to complete it. They found that people participating in a coffee buying program (buy 10 cups of coffee and get the 11th free) would buy more coffee as they got closer to the goal of the free cup.

This works even if the progress is illusory! The researchers found that people bought more coffee if the program was called Buy 12 and Get 1 Free and the first two punches were free than if the program was called Buy 10 and Get 1 Free. Even though both groups still need to buy 10 cups to get the free one, the first group felt that they were closer to their goal because of the free punches.

What implications does this have for game design? Imagine an RPG with a leveling system. The player is at 100 XP and needs 150 XP to reach the next level. You can represent the character's experience growth in one of two ways: a bar that is empty at 100 XP and filled at 150 XP, or a bar that is filled at 100 XP and filled at 150 XP. The goal-gradient effect says that the player will be more motivated to reach the next level with the latter example.

Furthermore, if a player knows a reward is coming, they will be more motivated to complete the task that will get them that reward. If you find that your players are petering out at a certain point in your game, perhaps that is the best time to show them the reward they will get if they just keep at it?

Social Ties

Not all games are designed to be social or include interaction with other players; however, many game designs are built around the significance and importance of play that includes social elements. For a majority of players, games are enjoyed as a group activity, whether it's a board game, a card game, or a video game. Solitaire versions of card games do exist, but those requiring four to six players are far more common and varied. In video games, the traditionally popular, but alienating, multiplayer "frag-fests" have given way to a boom of social gaming with the rise of Facebook and mobile platforms. These social, cooperative games have proven that social ties in game design are highly effective at increasing audience interest, engagement, and satisfaction (see Interest Curve).

Most modern games and their designs require designers to at least consider activating a player's social network. To understand social game design, designers usually need to begin with the psychology behind human interpersonal relationships and interaction, and while this topic is its own entire field of academic study, a good place to start is with Dunbar's Number.

Named for the British anthropologist **Robin Dunbar**, the theory maintains that any one person's entire social network is made up of roughly 150 network connections; that is, relationships. This is the number of relationships that the average person is able to maintain stability with, actual knowledge of, and benefit from. Trying to maintain a network with more than this number weakens all relationships in the network. The idea behind Dunbar's Number centers on the concept of maximizing "network externalities," or network effects (see Minimax and Maximin). This refers to the benefit derived by each included individual in the network—whether through favor brokering, access, or other means of helping one another.

The field of mathematical sociology adds in concepts like strong social ties, weak social ties, positive social ties, and negative ones. Additionally, there are ways of predicting the nature of social ties where the developer has no information; they do this based on very little information they glean from related social ties. So, for instance, a mathematical sociologist could reliably predict if Person A and Person B are friends with each other based on the nature of A and B's individual relationships with Person C. They can also map out how one person's personal network of 150 people overlaps, intersects, and connects with another person's personal network of 150 people. It's even possible to prove that the Six Degrees of Kevin Bacon game is true for everyone, not just Kevin Bacon.

Moving beyond the purely anthropological and psychological aspects of social ties and back to gaming, you can begin to imagine how finding compelling reasons for players to socialize within their network may provide a benefit—compelling players to consistently engage with games over time.

Social mechanics can be active, passive, or somewhere in between. Leader boards promote competition. Gifting mechanics allow for collaboration (see Cooperative vs. Oppositional). Both promote a game's potency by creating a positive feedback loop between the player and their friends. This in turn can reinforce play and enhance a game's stickiness while reducing churn. There is a real phenomenon known as "Fear of Missing Out," and it is a compelling reason for individuals to seek experiences that promote their inclusion in a group.

Without being unscrupulous, game designers should consider how activating social ties through competition or collaboration (see Cooperative vs. Oppositional) can benefit the games they are making, especially in Web, Social, or Mobile game platforms where players are more accustomed to these types of mechanics. Designers need to evaluate whether their designs can benefit from friend requests, game rating prompts, gift loops, competitive high scores, asynchronous player versus player challenges (see A/Symmetric Play and Synchronicity), or the more traditional mechanisms of player vs. player tournaments or cooperative play modes.

Keep in mind that a target audience's preferences and comfort zones all affect the general approach for designs relying on social ties. For example, some players strongly prefer to collaborate instead of compete (and these players have been largely underserved in the past). Or, consider that a chat function in a game intended for children under 13 has to take into account legal privacy issues. Researching audience preferences and being savvy about the methods of social design included can add a layer of complexity and enjoyment and ultimately set a game apart from the competition (see User-Centered Design).

Tragedy of the Commons

The *Tragedy of the Commons* is that if a resource is available for everyone to use, then that resource must ultimately be depleted—to everyone's detriment. The long-term tragedy and loss outweighs the short-term advantage gained by users of the resource, but since no one person sees themselves as responsible for the loss, they often don't acknowledge their part in it or moderate their use of the resource.

The Tragedy of the Commons assumes that the increased use of the resource is within a finite system (that is, the population using the resource grows and the resource does not). In spite of any apparent similarity, the Tragedy of the Commons is not based on any specific economic or political system, not even corporate greed. It certainly is a principle that can be used reliably in game design, however.

In generalized terms, the Tragedy of the Commons presents people with a difficult choice: Strive for material gain at an eventual cost to both themselves and others—hoping that the short-term gain made is sufficient to offset the long-term loss—or cooperate with others to conserve resources for the benefit of all, at the potential cost of losing out to someone who has better personal resources or who lies and over-uses the common resources (see Cooperative vs. Oppositional).

In games, either player strategies or game mechanics may lead to a Tragedy of the Commons. A set sequence of play may allow the players who go first to take a lion's share of the available resources, while simultaneous play (see Making Moves) may end with all players trying to grab the most they can because they assume that the other players will do the same, thereby reducing all players' resources to an equal level. In either case, it would take some kind of agreement (or specific rules rewarding players who use less) to prevent the players from using up all of the resources available to them.

The theory of the Tragedy of the Commons was first put forth by Garrett Hardin in the 1960s; he based it on a series of agrarian philosophers from ancient Greece through the 19th century. As his example, he used a common grazing area for cattle that anyone in a town could use. All the cattle owners use this land first, both because it's free and because it allows them to purchase more cattle, which they can graze on their own lands. When the commons become overgrazed (as actually happened on the Boston Common), the cattle owners have to move their cattle back to their own pastures, which then become overgrazed in turn due to the additional cattle purchased while the owners were using the commons. Hardin likened this to our similar overuse of limited natural resources such as forests, water, fuel, and air.

As Hardin also pointed out, individuals seeking to maximize their personal consumption contribute to the exploitation of the world's common resources. However, it is also true that people who want to save all human lives, cure all diseases, eliminate all human suffering, guarantee universal rights, and provide equal opportunity for all do the same by helping to increase the number of people using these common resources.

There are two common—and oppositional—solutions for the Tragedy of the Commons, but neither provides an optimal solution. Equal redistribution of resources (communism) means that many who are incapable of using the resource effectively still receive it, leaving much of it to be wasted or used up quickly. Monopolizing the resources (government control), on the other hand, means that the efficient use of the resources comes a distant second to corruption, legislation, and special interest groups.

In 2009, Mark Van Vugt outlined several ways to reduce the impact of the Tragedy of the Commons in the real world. He suggested providing enough information about resource overuse for people to value conservation, ensuring strong attachments to communities to reduce selfish hoarding and misuse of collective property, creating trustworthy institutions to manage critical shared resources fairly, and providing incentives for responsible use of resources while punishing irresponsible overuse.

Many games are built around interesting, difficult choices, and the Tragedy of the Commons is just such a case. Without an obvious, easy solution, players encounter more challenges and have opportunities to explore areas that are not well-traveled.

GRASS

The Tragedy of the Commons: A shared grazing area allows all cow owners to increase their herds beyond what their personal resources will support. Unfortunately, the shared resource is depleted from common use over time and cow owners find themselves in an insupportable position.

Transparency

Many games revolve around the discovery of hidden information. They take the human love of learning (see Koster's Theory of Fun) to the next level of intensity by tapping in to the human love of discovering someone else's secret (see Howard's Law of Occult Game Design). Exploring and experimenting are part of the Core Gameplay Loop in these games.

Game theory classifies these kinds of games, where information is not transparent, as *games of imperfect information*. This transparency (or lack thereof) applies to all types of game information, both the game's structure and the game's state (see Information).

An example of the concealed *structure* of a game is the "fog of war" conceit so many video games and some board games use to hide part of the map and to encourage exploration (see Bartle's Player Types). Similarly, complex algorithms in video games sometimes obfuscate the exact nature of cause-and-effect relationships, such as in morality or affiliation systems. In both these cases, it's the underlying structure of the game that is being hidden from the players.

The other type of information—the *state* of the game—allows for even further subdivision within the games of imperfect information category. The distinction is based on how much and what kinds of information players have at their disposal—in other words, how transparent various kinds of information are.

- **Complete Information.** The subset of imperfect information games where the player has access to all the information about the environment and the rules, but not necessarily to the state of the other player's actions, are said to be ones of *complete information*. A game such as Battleship, where the locations of the opponent's forces are hidden, is one of "complete but imperfect" information. Both players know they each have five ships of specified sizes, but they don't necessarily have access to the current state (location/orientation) of those ships on the map. Similarly, most card games such as Gin, Hearts, Bridge, and Poker have complete but imperfect information. Players know the game is using a familiar, finite deck of cards and that the other player has a specified number of them, but the location of specific cards at any time during play is not known.
- **Incomplete Information.** A game of imperfect information where a player cannot ever make assumptions about the unknown is considered one of *incomplete information*. A game of Magic: The Gathering would be an example because the basic assumptions about the composition of the cards that a player holds cannot be made in the same way they can in games using a standard 52-card French deck. Another comparison would be that of Stratego—where the exact number of each type of piece is known—or Starcraft—where no such information is known about the composition of the enemy forces.

One way to think of the distinction between these may be to say that it's possible to "count cards" in a game of complete information. A player knows all about all the pieces currently in play in a game, and if they have sufficient mental fortitude, they can know the probability that a specific piece or card is the one being hidden by their opponent.

However, in games of incomplete information, there is no way to "count cards" because there is no way to know for sure exactly which types and kinds of pieces are in use. Players simply do not know what cards their opponents may pull out, because it could literally be anything, not just one of 52 known possibilities.

A final key to understanding just how robust this idea of transparency can be for game designers is to remember that being transparent can either be voluntary or involuntary.

- **Involuntary Transparency.** To go back to the game of Clue as an example, remember that part of the rules state that a player must sometimes reveal to another player one of the cards in their hand, which they are otherwise keeping secret. This is involuntary transparency. The player may get to choose which card to reveal, but they don't get to choose whether or not a revelation must be made. They are forced into confessing part of their secret.
- **Voluntary Transparency.** On the other hand, a game like Werewolf allows some roles like the "seer" to choose if they reveal their role—when everyone else must conceal the role they are playing. Usually, game designers set up this dynamic to encourage bluffing, double agents, and a general sense of distrust. After all, if someone is not being forced to confess a secret, but they do so anyway, the motivation and veracity of that confession becomes a charged question.

VandenBerghe's Five Domains of Play

Understanding human psychology is fundamental to game design. In many ways, the functional goal of games is to invoke in players the desire to take action—and right there we're talking about a need to understand the way the human mind works.

One reputable, reliable psychological system is called the Big 5, or O.C.E.A.N. Based on an ongoing collaboration of numerous international researchers, the Big 5 system contains vast data from reliable studies and has proven predictive enough that game developers can comfortably use its findings.

Game designer Jason VandenBerghe has done a lot of work to show how to apply the theories in the Big 5 directly to game development.

The foundational theory behind the Big 5 suggests that there are five domains of human motivation into which human action can be classified and inclined toward:

- Openness to Experience, which separates creative, imaginative individuals from down-to-earth, more predictable ones.
- Conscientiousness, which is concerned with how individuals control and moderate their own impulses.
- Extraversion, which makes distinctions between individuals who seek stimulation and the presence of others and those who do not.
- Agreeableness, which deals with behavior around the rules of social harmony.
- Neuroticism, which reflects an individual's tendency to experience (or not experience) negative emotion.

What distinguishes the Big 5 from other systems like it is the degree of detail within these domains. Each domain is broken up into six facets that address far more specific motivations. For example, Openness to Experience comprises the following facets: **Imagination**, which separates those whose inner world is more interesting to them than their outer world from those individuals who feel the opposite; **Artistic Interest**, which deals with how a person experiences beauty; **Emotionality**, which indicates the degree to which a person is consciously aware of their own internal emotional state; **Adventurousness**, which makes a distinction between individuals who desire to explore and seek new things and individuals who prefer the known and a routine; **Intellect**, which deals with the amount of satisfaction an individual gains from solving puzzles in their heads or engaging in complex mental puzzles; and **Liberalism**, which measures a person's preferences in terms of the desire for society to push into the future, stay static, or return to the past.

There are six such facets for each domain of the Big 5, leading to 30 total. Jason VandenBerghe has given talks at major game industry conferences about this concept and has shown how game designers can correlate a player's score in these 30 facets of motivation with a preference for specific game elements. Two important examples include

- Imagination correlates with a preference for fantasy or realism. Someone with a high score in Imagination will tend to prefer games that take place in exotic worlds unlike this one, while someone with a low score will prefer games that take place in a world much like ours.
- Adventurousness correlates with a preference for exploration as a mechanic and a desire for encountering new things (for high scores), and with a preference for building, farming, or other "local" play styles that do not involve leaving the boundary of the known (for low scores).

These correlations continue all the way down the line, through the whole Big 5. They point us to an uncomfortable yet inevitable truth that has been backed up by multiple studies, and is the first piece of application of this kind of psychology to game design: *People play for the same reasons they live.*

It's important to understand that fully. The idea that we play to be someone else is common, yet false. In cases where an individual's personality is different in a game than it is in real life, without fail that "other" personality will still show up in personality scores in the Big 5 test. Often, such people do not have a way to express a particular part of their personality in their normal life, and so use play as an opportunity to let it out; yet, that motivation is still part of who they are. We play for the same reasons we live.

There are many other psychological systems that exist, and many of them can teach game designers a lot. When starting out in understanding humans at play, however, the Big 5 is a great place to start.

Volunteer's Dilemma

The volunteer's dilemma is a special case of a group game theory similar to the Tragedy of the Commons. In the volunteer's dilemma, a person is faced with the choice of committing a small amount of something for the betterment of the group with no additional reward for doing so. If the person does not commit, and *no one else does so either,* there is a significant disadvantage. The choice, of course, is to either commit the small amount of time, effort, money, and so on or take the risk that someone else in the group will do so instead.

One classic example involves a shared public utility such as electricity. If an outage occurs in an area that affects an entire neighborhood, only one call to the utility is needed to initiate repairs for the entire neighborhood. However, if a cost is associated with making that call (either through money, time, or both), people might be reluctant to do it. Instead, they may think to "let someone else do it," thereby saving themselves from incurring the cost. However, one caveat is that if *no one* makes the call, the entire group suffers. Another related caveat is that, by making the call, the cost is incurred regardless of whether anyone else has made the call already (or will do so shortly). In that case, the cost is wasted as a duplicate. The choice a person faces is whether or not to trust their neighbors to make the call or whether to simply take on the cost of making the call themselves.

In an example payoff matrix, the 0 represents no one making the call and, therefore, no one receives any benefit. The 5 shows the maximum benefit of someone else making the call and the player benefiting by having their power restored. The two 4s show that the payoff (the power being restored) minus the commitment (cost of the call) is the same whether or not someone else makes the call as well.

	At Least One Other Person Cooperates	All Others Defect
Cooperate	4	4
Defect	5	0

The volunteer's dilemma is similar to the *free rider problem*, where individuals in a group commit to each pay a portion of the cost to undertake a task that benefits the group as a whole. In this scenario, some people may elect to not pay their portion assuming that the action will be undertaken regardless. These are the free riders. If the cost of the undertaking remains fixed, the per-person burden of paying for it is increased—providing an even greater incentive for the free rider to not pay their share.

Both of these scenarios are common occurrences in online co-op games. For example, a player in a team-based shooter game such as Team Fortress 2 may decide not to participate in dangerous but necessary activities and, instead, perform more self-serving ones. The assumption is that the team will take on the responsibilities of the tasks necessary for team survival and victory. If the strategy is successful, it encourages continued behavior like this—and more players may elect to take the no-risk route—thereby transferring more and more responsibility onto those who are still willing to perform the dangerous tasks. Obviously, if the trend continues, the entire team (including the free rider) fails.

2

UNIVERSAL PRINCIPLES FOR GAME CREATION

The 80/20 Rule

The 80/20 rule, sometimes called Pareto's Principle (not to be confused with his other breakthroughs—see Outcomes: Pareto Optimality), is one that many development teams should keep in mind in order to focus their development efforts on those features that will provide the highest returns and help avoid detrimental feature creep.

The theory essentially states that 80 percent of any resource is controlled or driven by just 20 percent of the controlling factors. This was first observed by Vilfredo Pareto in 1906 when he noticed that 80 percent of the land in his home country of Italy was controlled or owned by just 20 percent of the population. He then found this ratio held true in most other countries. Even today, 80 percent of the wealth in the world is controlled by just 20 percent of the population. The rule extends even beyond wealth and property—Pareto found this out when he realized that 80 percent of the peas in his garden were produced by just 20 percent of the pods.

This correlation is evident in games as well. For example, during 80 percent of the game experience, only 20 percent of the features are used.

Although many flashy features are touted in reviews and press releases, the players will spend the majority of their time (about 80 percent) interacting with some of the essential features (usually about 20 percent of them), such as jumping, fighting, upgrading, or scoring (see Core Gameplay Loop). Developers need to be cognizant of this and focus on polishing and bug-fixing these core features.

As an example, the original Legend of Zelda had very few features when compared to today's games, but players primarily interacted with the world of Hyrule: specifically the way Link moved about and the way he attacked enemies. If we look at all the items that Link must collect in his quest for the Triforce, many extra little items, secret doors, hidden life, and other Game Tropes do help Link complete the game, but he only uses them for a very short time. Take, for instance, the Candle, Bombs, and Silver Arrows. In Legend of Zelda, all of these items are crucial to completing the game, but the player spends much more time in their play experience moving Link around the world and swinging his sword to either kill or deflect attacks from enemies.

A development team should be aware of the relative impact these features have on the overall play experience. If they spend all their time polishing the Candle, Bombs, and Silver Arrows and hurry through the construction of the game world and combat, the player could suffer through a rough, buggy experience for 80 percent of their time with the game.

The same can be seen in much larger games that have been developed in recent years. World of Warcraft is a prime example of using the 80/20 rule in their expansions. In its original release, World of Warcraft (WOW) was somewhat slow and difficult to move about in. This caused players who did not want to spend 10 minutes running across an area to turn in one quest much grief.

Just as with The Legend of Zelda, the movement balance of the player characters should have been a higher priority to World of Warcraft's development team, even though this was just one feature. In later updates and expansions, the movement speed improved and it became easier for player characters to travel faster. This improvement was essential because the world in World of Warcraft is massive; traversing it is a feature that players use constantly, even though it's not the flashiest, most exciting game element.

Another way to see the 80/20 rule at work is within other aspects of WOW expansions. Take a look at how fast many players reach the endgame and then turn their focus on raids. No matter what new race or flashy feature they add, the new endgame with raid opportunities gets a lot of focus and attention—even though it is only 20 percent of the content, this is where players will put 80 percent of their effort and interest.

Alternatively, in a new game, where players haven't already built up characters and are expected to replay the game multiple times, the beginning of the game will be experienced far more often than the end and should have a proportional amount of development attention—probably approaching an 80/20 split.

Brainstorming Methods

Brainstorming is a term everyone should be familiar with. Basic methods are taught in schools to students who are facing the task of writing their first research paper. Writers use brainstorming to give their characters more depth or to fully entwine their reader in their plot. The same sort of brainstorming goes into games. From plot points to unique mechanics, brainstorming methods can assist designers in creating all pieces of a game.

Some of the most basic brainstorming techniques can come naturally if one has access to a writing utensil and a blank slate—this is referred to as the *idea space*. This is always the best starting point, no matter which techniques are used; the only limit that one might have while brainstorming is the amount of space with which to produce and record thoughts.

Freethinking Methods

These types of methods are good to use when there is no need to have a specific structure to the ideas. The idea is to create an open forum that allows free-flowing thought and has no pressure to produce a specific outcome.

Word bubbles and *idea webs* start with one or more ideas written down. From each of these starting points, more words and ideas are added that connect back to the starting points. As the ideas grow outward, ideas connect not only back to the starting point but also to other ideas on the idea space, creating an interconnected graphic of ideas that typically resembles a spider's web. These techniques work best for the beginning stages of game development when the designer has only a basic concept for a game or the base plot for a game story.

Structured Techniques

Although open freethinking can be extremely fruitful at the beginning stages of development, later on, developers need some structured brainstorming.

Flow charts and *tree diagrams* start in a similar way to word bubbles and idea webs; they begin with a starting idea, and from this point the ideas and words added during the session are done so in relation to the starting point.

Flow charts are useful for the areas of game development that need a sequential structure. Each idea leads into the next with very little variance and few offshoots. Tree diagrams are useful in game development when designers need to create a hierarchy of items or actions.

Physical Techniques

Brainstorming doesn't have to be limited to writing down the ideas; designers should act them out as well. *Bodystorming* is a fairly new term, but the process of it should be familiar to gamers who have played any live-action roleplaying game. Bodystorming uses the body's movement to assist in the creative process and is useful in planning out complex character movements or (with the advent of motion controls) newer control mechanics.

All of these techniques can be used in conjunction with the others, and each should be used in the process of game development.

Consumer Surplus

If one paid attention to the games industry around 2008, they would have seen a remarkable shift in business models take place. Seemingly overnight, the old model where a consumer would walk into a store, buy a $60 game, and then play it until they tired of it was challenged by a model where games were very cheap (or even free!) and players would pay for consumable or durable in-game items.

Why this model became more attractive to game makers goes back to an economic idea popularized in the 19th century called *consumer surplus*.

Imagine that the 50,000 people who want to play a new game are really just 10,000 copies of the same five people:

- Abe is a poor college student. He likes games but generally doesn't ever buy them. He doesn't want to pay anything for them.
- Bill likes games and is curious about this one. He may buy it for $1 but wouldn't pay more.
- Cathy likes the game and would pay up to $30 to play it forever.
- Dave really likes the game and would pay up to $60 to play it until he is tired of it.
- Ed is a fanatic. He would pay $500 over the lifetime of playing the game.

Now, in a game maker's perfect world, they would be able to go up to each of these groups and offer them the game for the maximum they are willing to pay. The Bills would each give $1, the Cathys would each give you $30, the Daves would each give $60, and the Eds would each give $500.

But game makers can't do that in the real world. Game stores generally set one price that everyone has to pay. If the game was set at $60, the Daves and Eds would buy it, but the Abes, Bills, and Cathys would be priced out. If the game was set at $1, Bills, Cathys, Daves, and Eds would all buy it, but the game makers would be leaving huge amounts of money on the table. Ed would give them up to $500, why would they sell it to him for $1? This amount of money left on the table is called *consumer surplus*.

What Free-to-Play (F2P) models allow game makers to do is allow all groups, Abes through Eds, a chance to play the game and also the opportunity to pay as much money as they desire. They do this by not charging anything for access to the game and then they *monetize* by selling in-game items and privileges up to the gamer's maximum willingness to pay. By capturing that consumer surplus, the game maker can compete economically in a crowded marketplace.

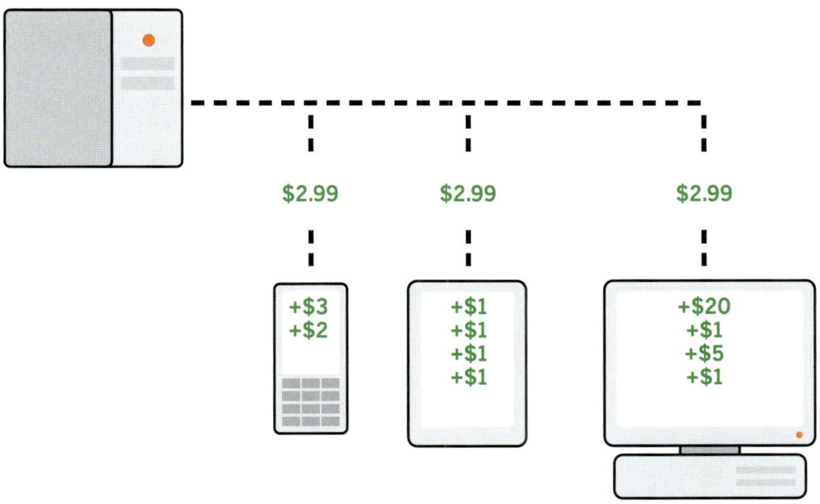

Traditional retail distribution of games only allows consumers to pay a single price for a game, even if they would have been happy to pay much more. This results in unused consumer surplus. Digital distribution and modern payment methods allow consumers more flexibility to invest as much or as little as they like in their favorite entertainment. The creators then have access to the consumer surplus to use for further development.

Core Gameplay Loop

Repetition is one of the fundamental aspects of play. When people enjoy something, they want to repeat it (see Addiction Pathways). Children exhibit this to an extreme degree as they watch a movie over and over or ask for the same short storybook to be read to them five times every night before bed. It's the same with games and play, even into adulthood. This becomes clear in video games where a few select mechanics repeat over and over throughout the experience. Almost all of the moment-to-moment satisfaction comes from diversity in these few core mechanics' results. Fundamentally, game designers need to whittle down big-picture design goals into granular components that the audience will be compelled to complete under a variety of gratifying circumstances. *Core Gameplay Loop* is the principle that video game designers must clearly, carefully define, and then they must refine the central, recurring mechanics that provide the foundations of the play experience.

The core gameplay loop is the central building block of a game's design. Usually, it consists of verbs—usually the more specific the better. Steering, Shooting, or Sneaking are just a few random verbs that start with S, but each could provide the core loop required to build a game. A superior core gameplay loop can be described in just a few words and should clearly illustrate the fun and engaging part of the experience (see The 80/20 Rule).

The "loop" of core gameplay loop comprises an action on the player's part, the result of that action, the player's reaction to the result, and the game requiring the player to repeat the original action to progress (see Feedback Loops).

Consider Super Mario Bros. circa 1985. Its core gameplay loop is "Jumping." The entire game is based on jumping. Jumping interpolates movement or incorporates actions like crushing enemies, breaking blocks, navigating terrain, and more, but the repetition of jumping is the core gameplay loop. In Super Mario Bros., the jumping gameplay loop remains "fresh" throughout the experience because a variety of challenges are introduced and the player experiences new combinations and results while jumping (see Synergy).

A more refined approach to the core gameplay loop is the "30 Seconds of Fun" concept associated with the Halo franchise. To summarize, 30 Seconds of Fun seeks to expand the core gamplay loop beyond the 5 to 10 seconds of only a couple of mechanics. It proposes that a number of well-designed systems, rather than just mechanics, can be the basis for repeated play, as well. Systems of mechanics can then be transported over the entirety of the game, repeated and expanded upon, and still engage players. The 30 seconds of Fun in Halo games centers around the sequence of firing weapons, tossing grenades, a close-in fight, and a short period of recovery before facing another encounter that follows a similar formula. However, by introducing new weapons, new enemy types, new terrain, and other external influences, the combat loop of Halo remains strikingly poignant.

It's fair to say that many people consider *repetitive* to be a negative word. However, the art of creating video games must involve embracing repetition and providing circumstances that keep it interesting, compelling, and rewarding (see Koster's Theory of Fun).

With this in mind, here are some time-honored tips for designing a strong core gameplay loop. It should include designing actions that are

- Easily understood
- Easily performed
- Enjoyable
- Able to provide direct feedback
- Flexible enough for multiple scenarios
- Extendable with additional actions
- Combinable with other actions
- Evolvable to provide support of other play loops

Ultimately, the core gameplay loop is key to long-term audience satisfaction. If the loop at the heart of your experience is flawed, it will be extremely difficult—and likely impossible—to use all the other elements incorporated in the game to make the experience feel fun. A core gameplay loop without depth and flexibility won't hold up over any significant amount of time.

Finally, keep in mind that not all games have a huge scope for ambition, like Halo, that seeks to hold attention indefinitely. It is entirely possible to build a small experience that succeeds in being fun. Consider how much repetition is involved in simple games like Bejeweled. Again, it comes down to the strength of the core gameplay loop. Often a small game is a great tool in Prototyping the loop that will end up being central to a bigger experience.

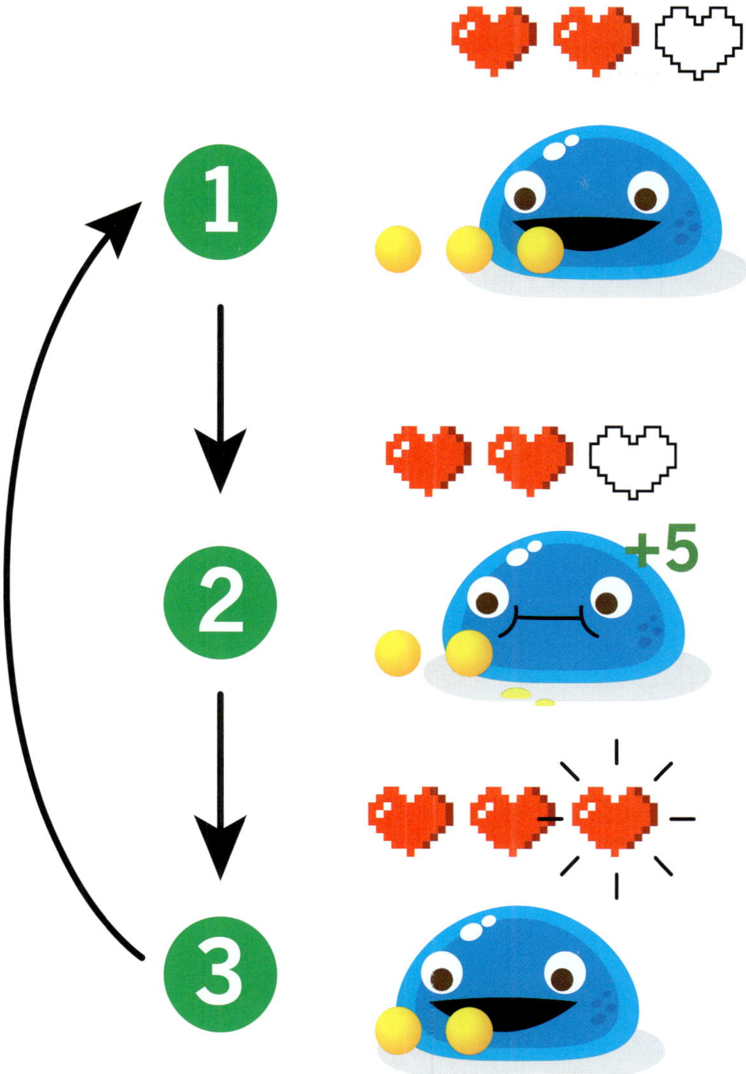

A core gameplay loop is based on a player-driven action that feels fun and encourages repetition.

Define the Problem

Defining the problem is one of the first, and potentially most impactful, steps in the initial creative process for a game designer. By pursuing a poorly considered or constructed problem a designer may find themselves choosing an inappropriate starting point from which to achieve the design goals, solving the wrong problem, or performing unnecessary work. Begin to define the problem by structuring your curiosity into the form of a problem statement that will enable you to pursue an ideal solution. (Note: Effective problem statements are a good practice for problem solving in general [see Problem-Solving Approaches], not just for game design). This is an established method of defining the core approach for designing a new game.

Most effective problem statements adhere to a format that consists of common parameters, which are widely practiced and regarded as helpful in problem solving. These include the following:

- Set a specific focus with an appropriate scope.
- Provide for measurable results.
- Ensure the problem statement is clearly communicable.

Bear in mind that these parameters are suggestions, not rules (see House Rules). Use discretion in framing a problem statement in the most effective fashion, given the preferences and circumstances of the situation.

Start creating the problem statement by identifying the issue to be solved. When the design team has a specific focus in defining a problem, their best efforts are aimed at the most crucial elements of design. Is the goal to design an entire game, a system, or a specific mechanic? Each is possible, but what is the focus in this instance? An accurate, clear focus makes it easier to avoid distractions and dead ends.

Problem statements can still be quite general, such as, "How can I design a turn-based strategy game for a mass audience?"; they can be more specific, such as, "How can I design a revival of the sidescrolling beat 'em up games from the eight-bit era for tablets while including a Free-to-Play business model?"; or they can be even more specific, as in, "How can I create an advanced enemy patrol AI?"

Pinpointing the correct focus is difficult; being overly broad or narrow can have negative consequences either way. If focus is too broad, the results may be too unspecified to integrate. Starting the solution in the wrong place may waste a great deal of time, or a solution may seem correct when it is not specialized enough to solve the issue under investigation. If focus is too narrow, it may not be possible to implement the solution within the context of the existing designs, and by ruling out nonconventional solutions, creative potential may be hamstrung.

When a problem statement's definition and focus include the proper scope, terms will be generated that allow for measuring results. A problem statement that does not uncover actionable data is less valuable to the process of problem discovery and problem solving. So, even if "How do I revolutionize the fighting game genre?" may seem like an OK first question, it lacks a specific focus and it's too broad in scope. This problem statement is not going to provide quantifiable results that indicate a place to start researching, hypothesizing, and designing.

By narrowing the scope to "How can I create a fighting game with light RPG elements and craftable weapons?" boundaries are established and points of insertion open up avenues for drawing logical conclusions. With this second question, there are clear starting points and measurable end goals.

When defining the problem, a good test is to try to communicate it to another person. Usually a fellow designer can be a good sounding board for defining the problem. To be the most helpful, he or she should be familiar with the design issue at hand and familiar with the practice of defining a problem with a problem statement.

Additionally, communicating problems in a team setting can improve teamwork, spur conversation (which may then further refine the problem definition), and contribute to keeping the project's common vision (see Design by Committee) on track. A common vision helps reinforce designers' efforts to maintain consistent goals during development. Shared end goals enable cohesive results while helping designers solve the unexpected problems that will invariably arise.

Clearly differentiating the one problem being worked on from all possible problems in existence allows for a more efficient approach to game design and development. To form a clear problem statement, define scope and include measurable end goals.

Design by Committee

Creating a video game is a calculated and deliberate process of integrating theory into practice while also innovating. It's difficult for one person, or sometimes even a team, to balance the practical concerns of making a game while also creatively pioneering. This tension, and the give-and-take relationship between team members and the final game experience, is at the heart of Design by Committee.

A designer's passion for making games usually exhibits itself as the designer's excitement about all the elements involved in the potential of the medium, especially when they compare them to other channels of culture. An individual's interests may focus on Core Gameplay Loop, Interest Curve, Dominant Strategy, narrative, visual grammar, skill progression, or even music. However, it is unlikely that any one person will become an expert in all aspects of these design elements, and, even then, it is not a comprehensive list of everything that needs to be considered when designing a game. And so the balancing act begins. It is imperative that any individual communicates with and trusts others so they can enter into a partnership to design and build one cohesive experience that is bigger than the sum of its parts (see Synergy).

Diving deep into a specific design focus and becoming an expert there will require sacrificing other areas and curiosities. There are only 24 hours in a day, and if one thing is being studied, another is not. Specializing is essential, and respecting the expertise of others is also essential. Everyone hopes to be part of a team of experts with egos in check where each contribution to the project is just the right scope and integrates seamlessly. Unfortunately, that is almost never how it works out.

Game development teams are a collection of passionate, creative, and driven individuals with diverging motives and instincts. And that's not a bad thing. If a game becomes the collective imagination of a group, then the more diverse the group, the greater the potential for a unique and non-cookie cutter design. The wider an audience it will hit home with, and the stronger their experience, the more likely it is that it will make a bigger impression. However, there is also a risk that the game will feel like an awkward patchwork without enough consistency or cohesion—all because of the amalgamation of personalities involved. Design by Committee can be a blessing for creativity, but a curse for organization and execution.

Best practices to limit the down sides of Design by Committee have been studied extensively in other industries. In game development, a production approach, such as *Waterfall* or *Agile*, can promote consistency, schedule accountability, and planning. Assigning reliable, experienced management in the form of Leads, Producers, Project Managers, and Executives is also a way to organize the chaos of game production. This also highlights the importance of leadership.

Many teams need a leader—a person who can communicate the final vision, make tough and fully informed decisions, and champion the cause of quality and standards. Common vision helps to hone the game's Theme and speed up design decisions.

Common vision helps curb the chaos inherent in Design by Committee as it allows for the group to feel ownership and to know how to provide useful contributions. Used effectively by a trusted leader, common vision can motivate, unite, fix expectations, and answer questions before they're asked. It acts as a touchstone of game design in written or oral form.

Leadership and Design by Committee are not inherently at odds, although conflict can result. Again, it's a matter of moderation. Some projects need a single firm hand to be created, and games are no exception. *Auteurship,* or a single person's vision, is possible in making games, but this might not be the best approach to take and can be a miserable experience for the rest of the team, depending on how the auteur treats coworkers. Ultimately, the best teams of game makers rely on honest, effective communication.

Every position on a team can make good use of skills like constructive criticism, sincere listening, and even something as mundane as holding effective meetings. How well these are implemented impact Design by Committee for good or ill. As in most types of creative pursuits, communication is paramount. Be fair, be accurate, and consider the point of view of the whole team or audience whenever delivering news, good or bad. Usually everyone in the room has a stake in what's being discussed, so acknowledging this can show understanding. Empathy is important.

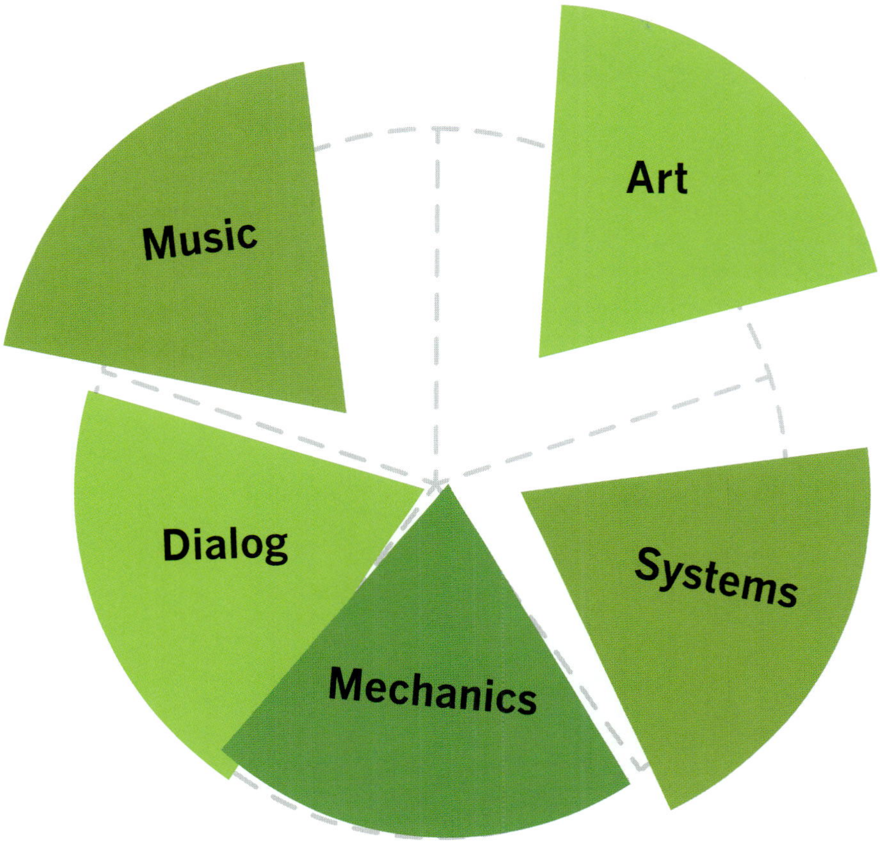

A group of experts working together with a common vision can create a cohesive whole, which is a better end result than anything an individual alone could produce.

Environmental Storytelling

The setting for a story communicates important ideas and information to the audience. In a story with a particularly strong setting, the world itself becomes as important as any of the characters. This is an idea writers have known about and employed for some time; it is often described as treating the setting as a character, giving it the same amount of attention and development any person in the tale is given. This process is often referred to as *world building,* especially in the context of fantasy and science fiction.

In video games, players sometimes have the ability to explore a world beyond the limited scope required by its narrative. That's why games should always treat their settings as living environments in which to play. The more detailed and interesting the world is, the more compelled to explore the player will feel. However, even in games that don't offer large territories of open space to explore, the setting is a crucial part of the narrative.

Imagine a world in which two political forces have reached the point of violent conflict. Such a situation requires a fair amount of explanation (what writers call *exposition*) before the player can fully understand the reasons behind and potential consequences of the conflict. Explaining those reasons and consequences can become burdensome to the narrative, perhaps even boring the player and diluting opportunities for entertaining gameplay. Designers need ways to show the player those ideas and facts, thereby keeping players informed about important aspects of the fiction, without using long cutscenes or blocks of text the player has to read.

This is where environmental storytelling becomes incredibly valuable to the writer. Graffiti on the walls might show us that one side in this conflict represents the interests of the lower classes or offer ominous warnings about the dangers this conflict creates on the streets. Boarded up windows and doors could suggest fear and perhaps evacuation by the world's civilian inhabitants. A voice over a loudspeaker could, without interrupting gameplay, indirectly convey which of the warring parties is currently in power and what their goals, interests, or prohibitions include. People passing on the street might grumble about limited access to an important resource, providing a glimpse at the origins of the conflict.

From just those few bits of environmental storytelling, the player learns a lot about the world they're playing in. They know who's in charge, who supports them, who opposes them, what each side wants, and why they're fighting in the first place. That's a significant amount of exposition that the setting provides without even a single cutscene.

This same principle can supplement character development, as well. Character behaviors and dialogue go a long way toward helping players understand a person's motives and abilities, but getting a look at the place in which they live adds to the player's understanding. If a house is filled with books about philosophy and nature, for instance, the player knows that the character living there has an academic interest in those subjects. This fact may come in handy later in the story, or it might just supplement the development the player sees in their interactions with the character.

When designing a setting for a game, designers must remember to let the environment tell the story, too. The players will feel more deeply immersed in the narrative, more of the story will emerge during actual gameplay, and the whole experience will be more enjoyable for player and writer alike.

Dead
STAY
AWAY

Experience Design

The idea of *Experience Design* is to recognize that there is a higher purpose other than merely assembling play mechanics to make video games. To affect an audience in a meaningful way requires more than just clever play. It demands considerable resolve. Think beyond the restrictions of "I want to make a great video game," and welcome the chance to proclaim, "I made a fascinating experience."

Again, understand that there is more to making games than play mechanics. Integrating advances in fields like usability and user experience design are increasingly the norm; video game play competes against other hobbies, and it's necessary to make an easy, enjoyable experience that can trump simply turning on a movie.

Both experience design and game design now demand that designers have fully conceived their audience's game interaction from purchase to final credits. With the rise of mass-market game consumption that has resulted from the burgeoning casual audience and the higher adoption of social and mobile games, designers must consider a full range of topics that are part of experience design; these can range from the desktop icon image and how tutorials are paced, to shop flow and purchase friction, to end game credits and social connectivity features like leader boards or achievements.

Designers now need to design the overarching experience from tip to tail. The more ancillary, but important, aspects of the game designers make that they can align to their goals, themes, and designs, the better their product stands to become. Think about successful brands and how their stores, packaging, and products are aligned. It's cliché, but for years now, Apple design has been consistent and is distinctly Apple. Furthermore, cultural relevance should also be encouraged.

A game that does a good job of experience design is Dead Space. From its box art, prerelease webisodes, and comic books to its in-game HUD-less presentation and endogenous navigational elements, Dead Space seeks to transcend classification as merely a game, and instead wants to position itself as an experience that evokes horror, the cruelty of space, and religious zeal. Branding, transmedia aspirations, big-picture themes, and a consistent, team-supported vision are what can spur the game into becoming a memorable experience.

Remember, video games are irrefutably modern culture—a multibillion-dollar form of globally confirmed culture. And, although they are not yet as revered as other popular formats of culture like literature or cinema, games have unique, inherent qualities that satisfy their audiences and players. Specifically, the uniqueness of games comes from a couple of factors that are exclusive to their play experience.

Among these, the following are the most influential: the potential for non-linearity so that the experience differs between participants, or even time over last; greater freedom of choice—the player decides whether it's a well-constructed morality system or a branching dialogue; and active audience engagement—the player must actually play using thought and action and they must overcome challenges to continue.

Designers are called to develop an appreciation for the total game experience in contrast to the deliberation they must perform to construct simply the individual parts. Keep in mind that most of a designer's audience isn't playing the game merely because the designer is innovative in the way they approach physics-based puzzle design or the story's plot twist; it's a combination of all elements. The designer's experience grows from the process of making the game, but it needs to become greater than the sum of its parts (see Synergy).

An easy rule to embrace is this: Focus on the player. The game designer, while a participant in the game's development, is not the exclusive enjoyer of the end product (see User-Centered Design). Although the designer has vision and passion, someone else will eventually spend time or money to enjoy what the designer created. As long as the designer remembers the end-user, they are apt to round design into an offering with greater experiential impact.

Focus on emotions and create tension. One method for doing this is to expressly plan that "this game is about unexpected delight," or "crude humor," or "satisfying stealth," or "feeling like a professional athlete" (see Theme). When the designer takes the time to identify the goal of the entire experience, the path to great gameplay starts to appear.

If performed successfully, experience-focused game making will mature the medium of games; it should be actively considered in game development efforts, even if the game being made doesn't have such lofty ideals. So, the struggle is that designers can be singularly occupied by making games that are the sum of their interactive systems to encourage fun, but fun alone will not resonate beyond the play session. Designers need to make sure the focus remains on the merit of the medium and advancing it. Use the designing experience as an opportunity to challenge broader thinking, to engage unique themes, and to delight and surprise the gamer. Remember, making games is manufacturing culture, and designers need to accept the responsibility that comes with it.

Flow

Flow is the idea that at the apex of intrinsic motivation, the mind transcends its physical perception and enters a state of performance ecstasy. It is achieved when the individual's skills are perfectly in tune with the task or challenge at hand. The principle Flow was described by Mihaly Csikszentmihalyi in the book of the same name. It is characterized by enjoying the process of the activity, being fully involved, and being fully immersed in a feeling of energized focus. Other terms for this include being "in the groove," "in tune," and "in the zone."

Often, humans experience flow when performing in a sport. For instance, if a skier is swooshing down a hill that is the perfect level of difficulty for their level of mastery, they will experience flow, ideally. During this experience, time will dilate and become seeming irrelevant; the activity will be consuming of all of the skier's focus.

Everyone has achieved a flow state at some point or another. Writers who are on a roll, craftsmen who have become completely absorbed in their task, or a game player who has become entirely absorbed in the game are all experiencing flow.

The key to flow is that the individual's concentration is fixed and the difficulty of the challenge matches their skill level. A beginner may have laser-focused concentration but will not achieve flow because the task is generally too challenging for their skill level. When making games, this is what designers develop tutorials and introductory levels for. By making the game easier up front, designers are preparing the player to achieve flow at a later stage in the game; they slowly introduce the beginning player to the mechanics of the game.

Game designers often underestimate the importance of those beginning levels of play. Because the new player has virtually no skill at the game (unless it is a genre that the player has a great deal of experience with already and they are merely picking up the particular controls of the new game), the challenge will almost universally exceed the skill of the player. In order to entice the player to higher, more sophisticated levels of play, designers must adjust the difficulty downward to match the player's skill level. This is not to say that it should be made ridiculously easy; the player will still need some challenge or they will become bored and abandon the game.

On the flip side, if the game immediately jumps to a mastery level of play, the player will be too frustrated by the experience and give up. Ideally, the player should be in a constant state of flux in the range between frustration and boredom. Straying too far to either end of that range will result in the player ceasing play.

One of the tools game designers can use to enhance flow is game aesthetics. Riveting graphics, a charming story, and attention-grabbing themes can help the player move through the introductory phase of the game to a greater level of mastery. At this point, the aesthetics are the reward the player gets for dealing with a new challenge. The aesthetics may pull a player in initially but they will not keep them long. To get to the meaty center of the game, the player must pass the beginner phase and make it to the practice phase.

This second phase of gameplay is when the task at hand is still a little beyond the skill of the player, but the challenge and aesthetics of the game have effectively pulled the player in. Players may spend a great deal of time in the practice phase; the game's aesthetics, dynamics, and mechanics will pull them through this phase of learning until they reach the level of mastery required to experience flow.

Finally, when the player has reached the mastery phase, flow will keep them there. The fine balance between frustration and boredom has been achieved, and exquisite attention to the riveting content will keep the player engaged for many hours.

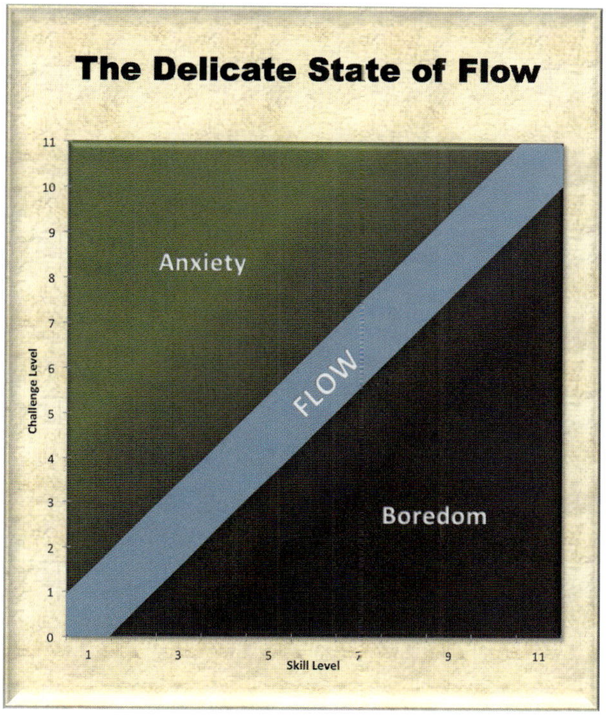
The Delicate State of Flow
Anxiety
FLOW
Boredom
Challenge Level
Skill Level
0
1
2
3
4
5
6
7
8
9
10
11
1
3
5
9
11

Four Ways to Be Creative

Many people believe that creativity is a natural talent and not necessarily one to be learned. A professor of psychology named Arne Dietrich argues, however, that all individuals can be creative in their own ways, and in some respects creativity can be a learned skill. His theory states that creativity can be

- spontaneously cognitive
- spontaneously emotional
- deliberately cognitive
- deliberately emotional

Some forms of creativity are very spontaneous; the "light bulb" in the shower or the fantastical dream that in time leads to the production of something great. Whether the ideas are acted upon or not, everyone has access to these forms of creativity and participate in them on a constant basis. Artists, writers, and those people most of us consider to be very creative types tend to have more strength in spontaneous creativity.

Then there are the forms of creativity that come from building upon and evolving a learned set of skills such as solving a problem by using current knowledge of the situation and taking the risk to find alternate solutions. This is deliberate creativity. Nikola Tesla and Steve Jobs were innovative creators that utilized their education and knowledge to create amazing products and solve problems.

So, if these are the ways in which everyone can be creative, how can we access or spur ourselves into using these forms of creativity and how is it useful to game development in particular?

By nature, games are creative. In order to get and keep the attention of the players, the game must have a hook, flow, and playability (among other aspects). Each of these pieces has a differing level of creativity applied to it.

Games that tell a story or are art heavy need the spontaneous creativity that comes naturally within visions, dreams, or daydreams. This is the spark. After the spark has taken hold, it needs to be molded into a hook. This is where learned writers and artists come in and take the time to sculpt the spark into something accessible to the players.

All games should have a Flow. Multiple types of creativity are needed to produce a game flow that does not put off or bore players. This mainly requires accessing and utilizing deliberate creativity and using current knowledge about the game—subjects, mechanics, and content—to create the flow and be able to experiment as well.

Where deliberate creativity is a conscious focusing of knowledge and is changed and experimented on, spontaneous creativity can be spurred into action by breaking away from the project for a time. Taking lunch, playing a different game, or taking a power nap can be one's best tools in being creative.

Game Genres

Genres are categories of endeavors in the arts that have a particular form, content, technique, or similar characteristic. Game genres are wide and varied and are used to differentiate games by their *interaction* rather than by visual or artistic differences. So it's not quite accurate to call "zombie games" a genre, as this is a description of the setting or story, and not the type of interaction players can expect (see Theme).

Game genres shouldn't be seen as rigid templates. In many cases, an element from one genre can be included in another to create a new, fun experience. For instance, the game Portal could be described as a mash-up of an FPS and a puzzle game.

There is also still room for inventing new genres, though this is more likely to happen in the "indie" game development scene or the educational game industry. The large, traditional game companies have a harder time innovating that deeply because they tend to be more conservative about risk. A new genre may become a huge hit, but it may also be a huge flop. Without prior performance metrics to gauge how profitable a game will be, large companies have a harder time committing funding (see Risk Assessment).

The list of genres on the next page should not be seen as comprehensive or restrictive. It is just an overview of the most common genres, provided here for inspiration, for brainstorming, and to foster discussion.

Game Genres

Genre Name	Description
FPS	Probably the best known genre is the first-person shooter (FPS). In an FPS, the player sees a first-person perspective and is trying to shoot enemies with a weapon that appears to be held in their hand. This genre is well known for its level design because levels are key to creating compelling and interesting play spaces in which players can compete. FPSs are highly competitive games ordinarily, though sometimes they are played cooperatively in teams or capture-the-flag sorts of games.
RTS	Another very popular genre in games is the real-time strategy (RTS) game. In an RTS, the player is given resources to manage and allocate in order to build up an empire of some kind. Civilization is probably the best-known game in this genre. The real-time aspect of the game comes from things happening in real time; it takes time to build resources, and moves are enacted in the order they are played.
Adventure	Adventure games have evolved from being heavily story-based interactive fiction to being games in which the protagonist has an adventure, such as Tomb Raider. The protagonist must solve puzzles, encounter enemies, and navigate terrain and mazes and the like to get to the final goal of the game. This might be simply the culmination of the story or they might obtain a fabulous prize.
Action	Action games are a subset of adventure games and have similar qualities. In some cases, the terms are interchangeable or such games may be referred to as action/adventure. Action games are more likely to focus on combat than traditional adventure games are.
Puzzle	Puzzle games, not surprisingly, involve solving puzzles. These may be spatial or logic puzzles and can vary in difficulty from the simple to fantastically difficult.
Sports	Sports games are a very well established genre. Most sports games emulate a particular sport, such as golf, football, soccer, basketball, and so on. These games try to, as closely as possible, provide a sport experience to the armchair enthusiast.
RPG	Next up is the roleplaying game (RPG). This has a subset of JRPG (Japanese RPG). The RPG is a game in which the player takes on a role and plays that role in the game. Usually, it is a heroic figure, though most RPGs allow a player to play either as a good character or as a bad one. JRPGs are singled out as they tend to be very heavy on narrative.
MMO/MMORPG	Another subset of the RPG is the MMO/MMORPG (massively multiplayer online game or massively multiplayer online RPG). In an MMO, the player must have an Internet connection to play and will be in a play space with possibly thousands of other players. This sort of RPG most closely correlates to a traditional roleplaying game as players are interacting during play and actually play together (or against one another).
Simulation	Simulation, or SIM, games simulate some real-life activity like driving, flying a plane, building a city, or life itself. In simulation games, the activity is, as in sports games, as realistic as possible. SimCity set the tone for many simulation games as did early flight simulators, which were frequently used by pilots in training and still are today.
Strategy	Aside from the RTS, there are other strategy games, usually centered on military actions or combat. Think of these as chess games taken to their logical conclusion. Strategy games can be set in a particular war if they are historical strategy games, or they can be pure fantasy. All of these games have strategy as their basis.
Casual	In casual games, play sessions are short and gameplay is not particularly deep. Solitaire, Minesweeper, and myriad others fall into the casual games genre. These games are popular on mobile devices and platforms like Facebook that encourage players to fit games in between other activities. Facebook games have grown so fast and become so popular that they have generated their own new tropes (see Game Tropes).
Niche	Finally, a wealth of niche games defy traditional genres. One is the rhythm or music game, something Guitar Hero and Rock Band brought to the fore. Others include the more traditional party games, trivia games, and card or board games. Into this bucket also fall art games, which are more about the aesthetic experience than the gameplay. Aside from these, serious games are defined as a genre unto themselves. These include games that help patients combat an illness, teach surgeons new techniques, and the like.

Game Pillars

A *game pillar* is a high-level, action-centric concept or goal that acts as a development guideline. When you craft a new title, deciding on the game pillars is often the first order of business because they clarify the project's overarching direction to the entire team. Once you have created them, arrange the pillars into a sentence to come up with a synopsis you can use to pitch a game to publishers and the public.

Because games are interactive, it's crucial that the pillars stick to the actions users will be undertaking. Using artistic and thematic elements as inspiration for pillars (see Theme) is appropriate as long as the paramount consideration is the game's specific functionality. To understand why, consider what happens if this isn't the case. If developers focus their game pillars entirely on the art, they wouldn't have a clear direction for making decisions about mechanics, and so they might fall back and borrow an existing game's entire design and change only the art. The result would be a reskin of an old game instead of an interesting new game. That being said, pillars can be used in a nested fashion. For instance, the art team may make their own art-specific pillars, which work to support the pillars that guide the rest of the project.

Clearly defining a project's pillars allows the team to evaluate their efforts in terms of innovation and familiarity. If all of the pillars are identical to those of another title, informed players will recognize the underlying patterns and approach the new game as a clone instead of a stand-alone experience. By extending, improving, and uniquely mashing up pillars found in a variety of games, originality can be achieved without as much risk (see Risk Assessment).

How to Create Pillars

One good method for brainstorming pillars is to ask "what-if" questions:

- What if the best elements of one genre are combined with the best of another?
- What if a failed mechanic from another title is implemented differently?
- What if this specific gameplay mechanic is extended to allow for new actions?
- What if a game replicates the experience found in this other medium?

By continually asking what-if questions, a team is forced to analyze the project, which can lead to discovering uncharted territory in the gaming world.

Restricting the number of pillars is usually beneficial as well. Three pillars is a common practice as it allows for depth without too much complexity. Six pillars is usually too many.

How Pillars Are Used

Defining the pillars at the beginning of development helps determine the appropriate scope, taking into account limitations on available time and people. Clearly defined game pillars at the beginning of a project also prevents contradictory elements from creeping in. For instance, if "accessibility" is a pillar, including a puzzle that can only be solved through trial and error is almost diametrically opposed to the tenet of accessibility. This contradiction will disappoint and frustrate players who were attracted to the rest of the accessible elements of the game.

A well-formed pillar is specifically helpful in that it outlines the requirements for the development team before they begin working. Take the pillar "fluid navigation" as an example. This pillar can dictate the perspective, character design, combat design, world design, and animation workload.

- **Perspective:** Third-person perspective shows off and enhances the benefits of fluid navigation. In comparison, first-person perspective suffers from fluid navigation, as motion sickness becomes a serious consideration.
- **Character Design:** The player's avatar will most likely need to be more slender than stocky, so it makes sense that they navigate their environment in such a fluid manner.
- **Combat Design:** A character navigating their world fluidly should extend to combat as well. Clunky, rough combat will break the player's sense of immersion.
- **World Design:** The architecture and terrain need to visually support everything the player can and cannot do. A visual language for defining climbable and non-climbable surfaces is one example of necessary constructs.
- **Animation Workload:** Fluid navigation requires many animations that have to seamlessly transition and can over-tax hardware if not carefully planned for.

Game pillars guide the development team to create a focused and unique experience. Defining these early can mitigate many problems, make the development process more efficient, and streamline the design process.

Strong game pillars civilize the development process and elevate game design.

Game Tropes

A *trope* is an idea that has been used so often and so consistently across a broad swath of games that it has become accepted as normal and even standard. Some of these tropes are very useful; for instance, many games map the X button on the controller to the Jump command. There's no law stating that it must be this way. Designers could map the Y or the A button to that action. However, it's been used so often, players expect to jump if they hit the X button. If jumping is not an action used in the game, X is often the most-common action (see Core Gameplay Loop) because it is the easiest button to reach.

Again, this is a convention or a trope, not a law of some kind, and there are many more tropes like this one. However, if usability of a game would be improved by having "jump" mapped to some other key, it's important to do that. This X button mapping is convenient and helpful most of the time. Players can pick up a new game and not have to think (see Krug's First Law of Usability) too hard about learning a new control schema every time.

Not all game tropes are as useful as this. Many were started 20 or 30 years ago and may have been useful at the time, but they have outlived their usefulness—sometimes to the point of being bizarre.

The most obvious example of this is murder. In the real world, it is an extreme act to take someone's life. There are serious consequences and problems associated with this behavior. In video games, it is a trope that killing things—people, monsters, animals, ghosts—is the default way to interact with them (see Magic Wand).

From a designer's perspective, tropes can be friends or foes. Sometimes they make a game interface more intuitive. On the other hand, sometimes they can get in the way of a unique theme or experimental gameplay loop. For instance, if a designer wants to portray their main character as extremely honest, they need to subvert the trope that it is OK to pick up random objects from other people's homes or roll the bodies of enemies looking for loot.

As long as designers are aware of tropes in their designs, they can be used to their advantage—either as a way to speed usability or as a touchstone for innovation.

Here are some tropes that have grown up within games:

- **Free Health:** From a design standpoint, putting a white box on the ground with a red "plus" symbol on it instantly tells a player that it is a med pack that gives health to the player in the form of magic healing potions. This is great, but in real life, a first aid box may be available in an office building, for instance, but it only has Band-Aids in it, and it isn't laid out on the floor in public every 10 feet. Med packs are so widely used in video games that many designers litter their worlds with white first aid boxes for no good reason and don't even consider if this is the best way to balance their game.
- **Stealing:** In real life when someone breaks into someone's house to steal something, they get punished for breaking in and punished for stealing. In video games, players are often punished for *not* breaking into someone's house, and for *not* taking an item that belongs to someone else. They can get punished by not obtaining the points they wanted, not getting the upgrade they needed, or not getting the boss kill that gets them to the next level. In games, if it is not nailed down, you are supposed to grab it.
- **Crates:** Just as the real world is generally not littered with first aid boxes, it is also not usually littered with crates. Yet, a very common trope in video games is a world strewn with crates, which players can bash or shoot open; they can then take whatever is inside. An indie game called Super Crate Box has even taken this trope to an extreme; they played with it and turned the ridiculousness of the trope into the core gameplay loop.

  This is an excellent example of how to turn tropes on their head or re-imagine tropes that other people have taken for granted.

The list here is by no means comprehensive, but it should provide a starting point for examining and discovering tropes in the wild.

Gestalt

We have all heard the phrase "The whole is greater than the sum of its parts," but what exactly does that mean and where does it come from? Those are actually the easy questions. The hard question is *how do we use it in game design?*

It is said that the Gestalt principle of the whole being greater than its parts originated in the early 20th century with Christian von Ehrenfels, Kurt Koffka, Wolfgang Kohler, and Max Wertheimer, and that it has been tweaked over the years by numerous scholars. The principle can be found in almost everything artistic and design related, but it can be found in other places as well. The main idea behind the principle is that although everything has value, when you add those items together in a specific way, they add up to even more.

The principle also has a set of rules that go along with it. They are listed here:

- **Closure/Reification:** We see complete objects even if a part is missing.
- **Continuance:** We tend to see continuous figures and not smaller pieces.
- **Similarity:** We group together anything that has similarities.
- **Proximity/Common Fate:** We group elements that are close together or travel together.
- **Symmetry:** We group things based on their proximity to something else, recognition, and balance.
- **Invariance:** We recognize distorted or moved objects.
- **Figure-Ground:** We tend to see one image at a time instead of multiple images. We either see the "foreground" or the "background," where those terms are items in relation to each other.

The Gestalt principle is used in a lot of places other than in art. A simple mathematical example can be found in Algebra: ($x = a + b$), where a and b are variables that are worth something when they are separate, but when they are combined, they form x, which can be drastically different from both a and/or b.

Gestalt artwork can also be used in psychology. When someone looks at inkblots known as Rorschach tests, they use *figure-ground* by seeing different images inside the total image of an inkblot on paper.

The following are some examples that explain how to use the Gestalt principle in game design:

Example #1: A game contains a lot of separate pieces that must work together synchronously to obtain fun game play and maintain a solid game. Each part of a game can be broken down into its own section: UI, HUD, Player, Enemies, NPCs, Levels, Mechanics, Leader Boards, and so on. Each part of the game not only has to work individually but must work seamlessly with all the other aspects to create a solid functioning game.

Example #2: Many designers and gamers have probably heard of a *skill tree*, where gamers can choose how and when to upgrade their skills, weapons, potions, or other abilities. A designer needs to think not only about the economy of the skill tree but also about how the levels, enemies, and artwork will ramp up over the course of the game. The designer needs to see not only how each level of a game relates to all the other levels of the game, but how each must also stand alone. From this, they will determine which levels will be grouped with other levels based on the art, design, story, and/or the mechanic. It is the same with enemies: Some enemies will fly, some will have one or two weapons, some will perform specific amounts of damage, and so on.

Example #3: Another way Gestalt works in a game is from the story aspect (see Environmental Storytelling). There is another saying: "You can't see the forest because of the trees," meaning that one cannot see the big picture because they are getting caught up on the small things. When developers make games, a lot of little pieces can bog them down, but as long as they keep their eye on the big picture of the finished design, they can get through it. At the same time, each piece of artwork inside a game must have the same feeling, art style, and overall look in order for it to match everything else in the game, and all of the pieces need to work together to help with a player's immersion in the game.

Example #4: This example goes into more depth with the art examples. On Level 5 of an example game, the gamer will see two types of enemies throughout the level. After seeing both enemies on Level 2, the gamer understands that one does 5 percent damage to them while the other does 25 percent damage and jumps straight up in the air when the player is close to it. Therefore, the player understands that on Level 5, since the enemies are exactly the same, they will do the same damage as they did on Level 2. Once they get to Level 7, they realize that one of the enemies has now changed its shirt color to a darker, more evil color—from light yellow to dark red. This artwork modification tells the player that this new enemy is grouped with the Level 2 enemy in abilities, but something about it has gotten stronger ... in this case, it could be that the enemy does 15 percent damage instead of 5 percent. This example works well with enemies, environments, and player stats. It is a visual method of explaining details and story to the player. The reason this works so well is because the human brain processes and remembers images faster and more easily than it does text.

House Rules

Everybody knows a game needs rules, but even this Game Trope can be carefully examined and used for innovation.

Rules

To start with, all games need rules, one of the foundational elements in the definition of what constitutes a game. The rules are at the heart of every game and lay out the game mechanics, setting, play instructions, and Core Gameplay Loop. In board games and card games the rules are usually enforced by participants, though tournament situations often have referees and judges. Breaking rules is considered cheating.

Video games enforce the rules through programming. In theory, it's impossible to break the rules in video games since they are hard-coded into the system. Players often take this seriously and feel that if they can make something happen in a video game, then it must be OK (see Griefing). So if they find a bug that allows them to make thousands of coins out of nothing, they go full steam ahead doing so and usually don't feel they are breaking the rules. (The game developers and designers often don't agree, however; see Supply and Demand.)

House Rules

House rules are often not written down. They are the more informal, unique rules added on to a game by participants during unique instances within games. They are often invented by the players, with no input from designers. For instance, in traditional card games, the use of wild cards is often left up to house rules (see Aces High; Jokers Wild). Sometimes younger players are allowed certain advantages, or if a particular rule feels unbalanced, it may be modified by house rules. Even though video games have rules hard-coded in, it's still possible to implement house rules. For example, if the player has three avatars to choose from with different abilities and strengths, the host of a multiplayer match may dictate which avatar is "allowed." In these cases, house rules usually add more rules to those programmed in, rather than modifying them as often happens in analog games.

Guidelines

Guidelines are even less formal than house rules. These are sometimes written down in the rulebook, whether for a card game or a video game. Guidelines usually come from the developer rather than participants. For analog games, they are usually set apart from the formal rules as a way to suggest possible house rules and let players know how to adjust the difficulty of a game according to the unique abilities of the individual players of that individual game. In video games, these kinds of difficulty settings are usually found in an optional menu. It's also possible to see developer-organized video game tournament rules as really guidelines, since they are not hard-coded into the fabric of the game.

Suggestions

At the other end of the continuum from strict, hard-coded rules is the amorphous category of suggestions. Suggestions may be provided either by participants or developers. If they are not followed, nobody cares much. Strategy guides, collections of hints and tips, walk-throughs, and videos can be thought of as suggestions.

The most obvious way for a game designer to innovate with rules is to include guidelines and suggestions when possible, even within the fabric of a video game. Tooltip hints and directions for shortcuts buried in old journals are just a tantalizing taste of what is possible when rules are seen on this continuum from hard-and-fast to up-in-the-air and optional. House rules are an excellent way to experiment with an existing game and learn a great deal about Balancing and Tuning through hands-on play.

Iteration

Iteration is the process of repeating an action while building onto the result of its previous repetitions. That is to say, using the previous repetition's *output* as the next iteration's *input*. It is best to think of cycles or drafts—each step, or iteration, slowly adds to and improves on the one before, bringing what is being built to life through gradual stages of evolution, from bare bones to fleshed-out whole.

More often than not, the development of a game (or any body of work, generally) is an iterative process. A game will start off as a prototype (see Prototyping and Paper Prototyping), with crude graphics (possibly even just shapes or letters) and not a lot of functionality. With each iteration, the team builds more and more features on top of the existing code. More gameplay features are added, already developed mechanics become more complex and robust, and graphics and sound become more representational of what the team's vision is. Iteration is an essential principle to apply to a game's design in order to have a game that is polished, responsive, and—most importantly—glitch-free.

Beyond the internal development cycle, players see more explicit iterations as well. Most of the sports titles that receive an annual sequel are a new iteration of last year's build, adding on newer features and fixing or improving old ones.

Games themselves can also exhibit iterative gameplay traits. Some good examples of games where iterative gameplay can be observed are

- **Any tower defense game.** This is an incredibly blatant example of iterative gameplay. Each wave of enemies is a new iteration: The map stays the same, but the enemies are tougher and more varied, as are the player's turrets.
- **Call of Duty: Zombies.** Similar implementation as other Call of Duty games, but with ZOMBIES! (An improvement? Depends on the player.)
- **The Street Fighter series.** Capcom is notorious for releasing multiple iterations of their fighting games: a few new characters, a few extra features, and, of course, a new prefix or suffix added to the title.
- **Metroid.** As Samus progresses through Zebes (or wherever she's wound up this time), she gradually gains new powers and abilities. These allow her to return to locations she has already traveled to and interact with those locations in new ways (new passageways, the ability to destroy previously impenetrable blocks, etc.).
- **Donkey Kong.** Along with many other '80s arcade classics, once the player beats the fourth ("last") screen, they are warped back to the first screen, but this time, it is a harder iteration—barrels are thrown faster, and now there are fireballs as well.

With the mention of Donkey Kong, it can be argued that difficulty levels can be thought of as iterative gameplay. As the player plays through each progressively harder level, they are presented with a new challenge built on the back of the previous level's gameplay.

This game concept starts out as fairly straightforward. Each iteration sees additions and improvements to features, themes, and art.

Magic Wand

Who doesn't remember playing cops and robbers or cowboys and Indians, gleefully shooting one another and dropping dead when fairly shot, or perhaps remember seeing a sibling or other relative engage in this deadly play? According to the research of ethnologists, this is universal behavior. Where guns don't exist, spears or bows and arrows are used. Children, at one time, practiced hunting behaviors through play and fantasy because one day they would grow up and have to hunt for food. Today, children still engage in this sort of fantasy play even though they no longer have to hunt for food. Why is that?

In his book *Killing Monsters*, Gerard Jones examines the fantasy violence of children and the role it serves. The important word here is *fantasy.* Fantasy play allows humans to practice adult behaviors in a safe way. It allows children to enact their fears and deal with them in an environment, the imagination, which is contained and not dangerous.

It provides them someplace to go with their frustrations. Whether they are mad about having to go to bed or disappointed that a play date is over, fantasy play provides them with a safe tool with which to act out their anger. It is a tool for harmlessly dealing with aggressions.

One of the key elements of fantasy play is that it lacks consequence (see Magic Circle). Lack of consequence is just as much a reward as an actual reward is. In the previous scenario, unless the parent acts disapprovingly, the child has reliably dealt with their fears and feelings of anger.

Similarly, such play provides children with practice at being willing to face life's challenges to get what they want. The willingness to get "shot" and "die" in play leads to overcoming the fear of a job interview or other adult pursuits that we find challenging.

Guns or wands (or bows and arrows or spears) help children feel strong. These props allow them to project destructive power across space to knock down foes with a gesture that is almost effortless. The result is that they feel confident to handle anything that comes at them. All of these projectiles are effectively magic wands. They deliver magic power at a distance to negate foes.

The magic contained in the wand is emboldenment. The emboldenment teaches children "don't be afraid and do what's right."

Remember that as adults, even as teens, we learn to dismiss the intensity of involvement with fantasy that a child has naturally. It allows small children to *become* something other than themselves while adults and teens can merely learn about things in the world.

Video games allow teens to take on their greatest fears (annihilation) and conquer them. Because they are less attached to their fantasies than children are, they revel in games created by someone else, by fantasies created by others.

Many offices participate in an end-of-day or end-of-week ritual of a rousing round of some first-person shooter in which coworkers kill each other. This, like children's play, is without consequence and can allow adults the opportunity to blow off steam from a long week of dealing with the frustrations of the job without actually taking it out on their coworkers in destructive ways. Many adults are still fascinated by power at a distance. Think about all the magic users and ranged weapon users in fantasy games, whether Dungeons and Dragons or the latest fantasy RPG.

Whether it's a magic wand, a gun, or a computer hacker, the appeal of all these ideas is not the violence, but the power at a distance and the inherent confidence this inspires.

Metagames

Many players will say the best part of a game like Magic: The Gathering or World of Warcraft is the hunt for and winning of cards or pets, respectively. Players of these games are interested in growing their collections.

Some players will spend hours upon hours playing in one section of the World of Warcraft universe in order to collect one rare pet and never see the "end game." Similarly, some players will spend thousands of dollars on new boosters or collectors packs of cards for Magic: The Gathering, while rarely participating in other areas of the game, such as tournaments.

Designers may be tempted to think these players are missing the point or playing the game incorrectly, but in neither case are these players breaking the rules. They are just entertaining themselves almost exclusively with something originally designed as a side feature rather than the Core Gameplay Loop. This is the most basic type of *metagaming*. Players are not concerned about making the game developer's dreams come true. Players only care about having fun and they will use whatever they have at their disposal to do so.

Often players will institute their own original and complex House Rules and guidelines for their metagame, making use of the environment and objects provided by the developers, but not using them in the intended way. These guidelines are often a variation on whatever the designer had in mind, but not always.

Developers have tried to get into the act of metagaming, rather than leaving it to be invented by the players, by including things like achievements on the Xbox Live platform. These badges commemorate actions in the game that don't necessarily influence the outcome, such as opening every door in the game, or trying every type of weapon.

There is ample room for innovation with metagames. Take a player's penchant for pet collection in World of Warcraft. There are achievements related to this, but isn't there some interesting way to use this metagame to add to the storyline or theme? Say a player has collected all dragon whelps as pets, and when they return to a major city they've received a message stating that a collector has heard of their feat and would like to see their collection.

Developers who embrace metagaming invented by their player base may find a new use for existing code, or a new target market. Players who get acknowledged for their ingenuity instead of punished for it often become die-hard fans. The tradition of hiding things in games (known as Easter eggs) is another way developers have made metagaming part of the discipline (see Howard's Law of Occult Game Design).

One type of game that takes metagaming to an extreme is the Alternate Reality Game. This genre of gaming uses every aspect of real life as the game platform, layering a metagame on top of activities as mundane as answering the phone.

Objects, Attributes, States

Try taking a step back and looking at games in an abstract, generalized view. Breaking complex things down into essential parts is an excellent route to better understanding them. So consider this: A game can be boiled down to an experience comprising 1) a space for play, 2) a piece (or two) for interaction, and 3) a player (or two) providing inputs

This ecosystem of three essential component categories provides the foundations of all interactive play. Pong, Asteroids, Tetris, Call of Duty, and Carcassonne can all be broken down into these elements.

So, in a very practical sense, designers spend most of their time defining the space and itemizing the "pieces for interaction" that are more universally known as the game's *objects*. Jesse Schell spends some time talking about this idea in his book, *The Art of Game Design: A Book of Lenses*, but in a broader sense, it is the way programming languages function as well.

Objects are elements like the player's character, set pieces, movable items, and more; or, practically, in a game like Super Mario Bros., they are Mario, coins, and goombas. Objects can be as simple as a non-interactive rock used to impede character movement, or as complex as a boss encounter with multiple attack patterns, stages of evolution, and physical manifestations. Fundamentally, objects are the building blocks of play; and typically, they are nouns: box, enemy, door, key, fuel, and everything else interactable in a game. These nouns can be described in minute detail. These coded and codeable qualities or variables of an object, which are open to change or manipulation, are known as its *attributes*.

Consider an object like a clay pot that a player can attack to reveal a reward of gold or health. These could be its attributes.

- **Size:** 0.5 meter × 0.5 meter
- **Animation:** Pot idle
- **Player collision:** Yes
- **Health:** 1 point
- **Affected by:** All damage
- **Item Drop Rate, upon destruction: Time:** 0.5 second spawn delay, **15 percent:** 1 heart health bonus, **8 percent:** 1 gold coin, **2 percent:** 1 bag of 10 gold coins, **75 percent:** no reward

This is a fairly basic object with fully fleshed-out attributes. These attributes describe it in detail, including how often an attack will result in a bag of coins (not very often). Of course, these are not the only attributes it could have. Most game designs list all attributes of every object in the game. This can be an extensive spreadsheet for very large games, or it can be more straightforward for card games and board games featuring fewer objects.

And attributes are not the end of the story. Objects can further be defined as having *states*. States are the ways that objects manifest their attributes. State changes generally result from interaction between the object and player, interactions with other objects, or from the object being scripted into action by a game designer, for instance, with a timer.

Take a look at the clay pot example again; there are really only two states here:

- **Alive:** The base state of the pot simply existing in the game.
- **Dead:** The state the pot is in after it has been attacked.

The change in state is triggered when any damage dealer attacks the pot. The attributes defined earlier indicate that when it receives greater than 1 point of damage, the pot may spawn an item according to the probabilities in the drop table. Then it will enter the state defined as Dead.

This Dead state can then have its own attributes, as seen here:

- **Death Animation:** Pot shatter
- **Size:** Small pile of rubble .1 meter × .2 meter
- **Duration:** Disappears after 3 seconds
- **Player collision:** No
- **Affected by:** No further interaction

These are the basic ideas behind looking at games in terms of objects, attributes, and states. With this method, it is easier to see the moving parts as interlocking gears that can be tinkered with, rather than as a monolithic experience. And indeed, the whole ecosystem is interconnected and complex. One object's change in state can set off a chain reaction, lighting another object on fire, for instance. Or such a change could trigger an enemy to spawn two rooms away. With state changes and attributes, all the complexity of games is possible.

In addition, these words make up a baseline vocabulary for discussing game making during development that crosses disciplines. In conversations that include designers, artists, programmers, and producers, the ability to specifically classify an element within the game and describe its interactivity requires this level of understanding and fluency.

CLAY POT

State: Alive

Attributes:
Player collision – yes
Health – 1 point

BROKEN CLAY POT

State: Dead

Attributes:
Player collision – no
Health – 0 point

Ooh, Shiny!

How does one go about capturing a player's attention? There are, of course, many ways of doing this, but this text focuses on "cheap tricks" designers use to garner a player's attention.

Advertising has to be the king of attention capturing for quite some time, so look to advertising for some of the methods used to capture the audience's attention.

First on the list is sex. As they say, sex sells. It also captures attention quickly. Sexy avatars are nothing new in the field of video games. Frequently, women are hyper-sexualized in games as a way of keeping the player's attention focused on something in particular. For instance, the cover of the original Everquest box featured a buxom blonde babe with minimal clothing. This trope is used quite frequently both in the marketing of games and in the games themselves. Female armor is more like lingerie than armor (after all, who would expose all of their vital organs when doing combat in armor?), crafted far more for the aesthetic experience and sex as attention grabber than for the player's protection.

Tomb Raider specifically featured a skimpily clad Lara Croft so that the primarily male players would have something to look at while running through the game. After all, who wears short shorts to go adventuring in the jungle and tombs?

Another attention grabber is faces. Most humans respond to faces. Babies are hard-wired to recognize human faces, and humans will make faces out of patterns that are not meant to be faces at all. Using a face to get a player's attention is like waving a cookie at them. They can't help but look at it.

Speaking of cookies, food is another attention grabber. In the case of the game Chocolatier, many players would crave the sweets depicted in the game after playing because the artwork was so compelling. Similarly, in Asheron's Call, food items were craftable and catering services sprang up overnight to cater in-game events like weddings or parties. Using food is like playing dirty; by using it, the game maker is appealing to one of the most basic of human desires.

Another inexpensive trick for getting a player's attention is by using movement. The player will eventually click on that little gift box that shakes every so often. A button that has an animation on it will garner similar attention. Blinking, pulsing, and small animations all grab attention easily. Keep this in mind when creating elements in the heads-up display (HUD) or user interface (UI) if the player should be paying close attention to that element.

Finally, surprise is an attention getter. Players become inured to interfaces and experiences that are constantly and repeatedly the same. By changing it up and providing a different response or graphic in a place where a player has built expectations, surprise can be achieved.

Paper Prototyping

Prototyping is a method of designing the product before spending large amounts of time and money developing the idea, and prior to fully understanding it and knowing if it will be successful or even worth developing. By *prototyping* it, the developer can save useful capital and resources while still becoming fully knowledgeable of their product and while gaining more data to research in order to determine if the idea is worth producing.

Paper prototyping is one method of prototyping products and ideas. It is also the easiest, fastest, and usually the cheapest method. You can paper prototype many game-related items from card games, dice games, and board games to puzzle games, user interfaces (UIs), heads-up displays (HUDs), and even button configurations.

So, how does a designer paper prototype? Well, they just grab some paper, a pair of scissors, some type of drawing utensil (crayons, pen, pencil), and *an idea* and then just get to work. If they want even more items to help them, they can try adding dice, cardboard, stencils, stickers, markers, paint, glue, graph paper, and any other crafting item they can find. The main goal of paper prototyping is to get an idea across with as much *detail* as possible, as *quickly* as possible, as *efficiently* as possible, and as *cheaply* as possible. Some of the more popular tools designers use are blank playing cards, blank hexagon cardboard pieces, drawing supplies, and friends to help play test their idea. Some go as far as to record the Play Testing for presentation purposes. In the animation and movie industries, that video presentation of the storyboards can also be called an *animatic*.

Although paper prototyping is efficient and inexpensive, it does have its drawbacks. Some professionals consider it unprofessional and unorganized. Paper prototyping can also hinder the design if the application of the paper does not make sense or the idea does not come across well. There are good ways to circumvent both drawbacks, however. Get creative with paper prototyping and add as many details as possible; as a result, the work will look more professional. For example, use different colored paper with different textures and thickness to separate ideas, menus, windows, backgrounds, and other items in the prototype. Using different styles of writing, drawing, and different colors of ink to write with can also improve the prototype . . . follow basic graphic design principles such as color theory, rule of thirds, grid systems, and so on. When the prototyping starts to become unorganized, find methods of keeping it clean by creating a folder structure to carry the work in, think about the design's Flow, and use more paper prototyping knowledge to create a presentation board to showcase the prototype.

As electronic devices become smaller with touchscreen capabilities and drawing devices, more paper prototyping is being done as digital paper prototyping that can be done at any time from any location without paper, scissors, and so on. Current technology is allowing developers to create, edit, and move items around the screen with the touch of a finger; it also lets the developer take notes directly on top of the design, and then present the design around the world with the click of a button. This way they can showcase their ideas to testers, designers, producers, and anyone else who needs to see the improvements they've made.

Pick Two: Fast, Cheap, Good

The trifecta developers have to balance in every project is fast/cheap/good. In a perfect world, a perfect game would be all three—created quickly, without much expense, and demonstrating super high quality. This is an impossible ideal, however. Almost no team can ever do it and one of the features must always be sacrificed.

To illustrate, the relationship between fast and good is easy to see. Ambitious plans often come into conflict with tight deadlines. This is where the idea of a project's scope comes from. Sometimes by planning a smaller, less ambitious project (a smaller scope) and ruthlessly avoiding feature creep (staying within scope), the quality of the project can be relatively high without taking too much time.

However, quality work is never inexpensive. The usual objection to this is the prototypical indie developer who can single-handedly create a masterpiece. Most people who think of this quintessential figure forget that it takes years for this person to do the work involved in creating something so ambitious. Even if it is good and cheap (requiring a budget for just one person), it will never be fast.

One famous, rigorous work on this subject is the book *The Mythical Man-Month: Essays on Software Engineering* by Fred Brooks. He recommends Prototyping as one way to move production forward, since this is pretty much the definition of sacrificing quality in the above equation. He also points out that "Nine women can't make a baby in one month." Some projects will take as long as they take and can't be speeded up, no matter how much money and how many people are devoted to it.

When faced with making the decision about what gets sacrificed—speed, money or quality—remember that nobody has to sacrifice the same thing in every situation. Different parts of a project can have their emphasis on different elements of the trifecta. So although a game's pre-production phase may have to be fast and cheap, sometimes the production phase can be fast and good (ergo, expensive). And of course, some of the less-important features can sacrifice quality and get done quickly so that the budget and talent can focus on the big features and Core Gameplay Loop (see Details).

Sadly, the inverse of this principle isn't a corollary. Turning this principle on its head doesn't work. It is entirely possible to be all three at the same time: slow, expensive, and clunky.

Play Testing

Play testing is the art and science of playing a game to ensure that it communicates effectively with the player, does what the design planned on having it do, does not confuse or frustrate the player, and ensures a quality experience for the player.

Something that sounds like a good idea in the concept phase doesn't always turn out to be a good idea in practice. For example, think about cooking. Anybody can brainstorm new recipes, but until eggs get cracked, heat is applied, and someone tastes the final result, there's no way to know for certain that the recipe will be as good as it sounds. Even then, one diner may find the new dish delectable, while someone else just isn't impressed. No product can please everyone, but play testing helps find out if it pleases anyone.

The purest form of play testing is just that: Hand someone the game and have them try to play it. This will reveal many incorrect assumptions the developers made during game development as well as the things that the game makers thought were obvious and are entirely opaque to the player. It is during play testing that they find out what they need to put into a tutorial (that shows the player how to use the interface of the game and what they can do in it), places where they might want to add help text, and how the player actually plays the game.

There are many forms of testing. One is called the *Kleenex test.* In this form of testing, a given tester is used only once, like a tissue, and discarded after the play session. This method of testing gets at the concepts and mechanics that need to be communicated to the player, how the game feels to the player, and similar functions. Testers are used only once because once they've learned how to do things in the game, they've lost value as a tester. This type of testing is to examine the first encounter with the game (or sections thereof) and how well the game lets the player know what is going on and how to proceed.

Another form of testing is called *black box testing.* In this form of testing, the player has no idea how the game is *supposed* to work; they simply play the game and see how it does work. This method not only reveals bugs in the system, but also shows the game makers how players actually *play* the game, which is often different from the way the game makers intended. Black box testing should figure into test plans early on to help dispel assumptions the team has made concerning the game. It should be repeated late in the process to ensure that the changes that have been made are in keeping with the actual play patterns of the players.

Another key type of play testing is *white box testing.* In white box testing, the players have some idea of what is supposed to happen in a given circumstance and can rely on test scripts to ensure that the game is doing what the game makers intended. This is where most bugs are revealed; after they are fixed, the game must be retested (*regression testing*) to ensure that something else did not get broken with the fixes to the bugs.

Although not strictly play testing, *load testing* is another form of testing used in online and multiplayer games. In this form, a number of testers enter the game simultaneously and play to ensure that the code and server can withstand the load of packets being moved back and forth. Eventually, this process is automated with simulated players numbering in the thousands.

Finally, the greatest reason for play testing over strict Quality Assurance (specifically looking for bugs) is to ensure that the game experience is fun. Kleenex testers and black box testers can both find out this information and are key to creating good games. If play testers are not having fun, players will not either.

Problem-Solving Obstacles

It can be said that games are just a series of complicated problems that a player needs to solve. The interesting part is that this sounds like a mathematical word problem, and those are usually no fun and are often too complicated. So, how does a game make these problems fun for the player to solve, and why does a player try repeatedly to solve them?

Cognitive psychology focuses on how people acquire and process knowledge (how people think) and store information (how people remember things). It also dives into how people perceive things and how they learn.

When a player comes to a point in a game where they must make a decision, something happens. The player becomes immersed in the game, takes ownership of the character, controls the story, makes a decision based on the issue at hand, and comes to a conclusion based on the surroundings and factors associated with the issue. This process happens in games almost constantly—the player asks themselves, "Do I jump over the object, land on top of it, shoot it, talk to it, kill it, friend it, give it something, unlock it, lock it, bash it, upgrade it, build it, destroy it, summon it, set it on fire, or just save the game?"

Most of the time the problems that need solving are simple and can be conquered very easily, but every now and then, a player just cannot solve an issue. This unsolvable problem can lead the designer to add in a tip, the player to ask a friend for help, the player to skip that part of the game, or the player to stop playing the game forever. When this happens, there are usually up to four reasons why:

- **Functional Fixedness:** A player understands how to solve the problem after doing it a few times, but when the problem is adjusted slightly, they cannot solve it. This happens because they learned the equation, but they do not see the new variables that have been added to it. A good example of this is when a player understands that a brown crate can be broken at any time and with any weapon so they can get an item, but they do not understand what to do with a blue crate. Do they break it, shoot it, stand on top of it, carry it, or blow it up? It is a crate, and the player knows what to do with a crate, but now that it is a different color, what does that mean? The player then must change the way they think in order to figure it out.
- **Irrelevant Information:** When playing a game, the player must understand what is relevant to the problem at hand and disregard the rest. When the player is dual wielding pistols and is not allowed to swap weapons out in the game, then why would they bother to pick up knives or rockets if they can pick up the bullets and ammo boxes? In game design, a game must contain as much detail as it can to maintain the immersion, but some games offer so much detail that the player gets bogged down. A game needs to have just the right amount of information for the player to stay immersed without containing irrelevant information.
- **Assumptions:** Everyone has heard the saying "You should never assume anything." This is true in game design as well. When playing a game, a player might not make a jump because they think it is too far, especially if they would have to start over at the beginning. Some designers could assume that everyone or no one will make the jump and then redesign the jump altogether. In either assumption, this could be poor judgment on the designer's part. A player should never be stopped from playing a game due to false information, and a designer should not assume a design is poor until it is tested. Because games become harder, some designers give save points or save abilities to the players, which leads to fewer assumptions and more death—meaning the players tend to jump in head first when they can save right before they jump so they can start over right before the jump if they mess up. As a designer, consider ways to have the surrounding area of the game warn the player that the jump is too far or that the player will be safe if they make the jump. Designers can accomplish this using visual art clues, sound effects, or background music, or they can introduce a wall jump or wall climb ability or many other methods.
- **Mental Set:** This refers to the ability to learn from experience and have common sense instead of being book smart and only learning one way to do something. Game players are actually great at this and tend to game the game, but sometimes they do need help. A very simple example of this could be when someone is playing a sidescrolling run and gun game like Contra. After pressing all the buttons the player will know how to run and shoot enemies. However, some obstacles in the game require the player to jump and shoot and run and shoot at an angle at the same time. In parts, the perspective of the game even changes completely from a 2D sidescrolling platformer into a 3D third-person shooter game. Some players will learn the first set of game mechanics and then have a hard time switching to the second set. However, experience playing the first set should have taught the player that the down button still lies down, one button still shoots, one button still jumps, and the left and right buttons still move the character from side to side. The only thing that changed was the art, but it was enough to throw some players off.

Assumptions are a common obstacle to solving problems. Approaching a problem with incorrect assumptions can lead to the problem seeming unsolvable, when in reality it is just a different problem than was originally assumed.

Prototyping

Most products developed by a person or company originated as an idea, were sketched on paper (see Paper Prototyping), and were artistically designed over numerous Iterations. The entire production pipeline for product development also includes testing groups, marketing, advertising, mass production, and then distribution into the market (see Play Testing). Games are no different.

Testing and prototyping are valuable tools during every phase of the design process, starting with the initial idea and lasting until the game is in the hands of players. For live environments like social games or massively multiplayer online games (MMOs), prototyping becomes valuable even after players are starting to interact with it.

Prototyping is the process of building a representative model of an idea for the purpose of testing and iterating. It provides opportunities for checking the viability and believability of a new design, and its usability, uniqueness, marketability, and x-factor, without taking on the full risk of developing the idea fully before testing it. Individual mechanics or features may be prototyped on their own before being combined, though most times a prototype is most useful if it is as close to complete as possible.

Data collected on prototypes can be sorted into categories such as things to remove, things to add, issues with current design, new ideas based on testing, new features based on testing, a possible work-around for development, possible changes to the product's design, and more.

Prototyping can come in many forms. In the film and animation industry, a movie is prototyped in the form of *storyboarding,* and this is also quite useful in games. Storyboarding is the process of telling a story visually on a series of pieces of paper.

As mentioned above, another form of prototyping is Paper Prototyping. Other times basic middleware is used to work out the essentials of a design, even if proprietary software is used to plan for the final product. When a game is part of the physical world, inexpensive 3D printing in plastic is often used for prototyping.

In game design, there are several parts that will undergo prototyping. The first prototyping session will be creating a basic game level or area in order to test the game mechanics. This is to see if the idea is fun, within scope (based on the platform and current technology), or even worth pursuing with more resources. It might contain level design elements, characters, weapons, basic programming, and a few other items that are needed for the core game play of the main game idea. Multiple iterations of prototypes are often enlightening.

A large company might have specific teams just for prototyping or play testing. In a smaller company, often the same team works from prototype through final product. There are different philosophies about whether prototypes should be tossed out entirely before starting development of the final game, or if the prototype should be used as the first iteration of the final.

At any rate, the key to prototyping is to do it. When timelines are tight, the temptation is to skip early stages and get right to the final game development. However, prototypes often shorten development time and costs because so many problems can be worked out before a codebase gets large and unwieldy (see Pick Two: Fast, Cheap, Good).

Prototyping can even be used as a brainstorming tool in a game-jam style approach to finding fun. Beginning to build something real, instead of using only words on paper, can energize a project and move it forcefully out of the vaporware stage.

Risk Assessment

Risk Assessment is a foundational game design principle that pits player choice against uncertainty. At a basic psychological level, humans are risk averse. People seek to avoid situations with uncertainty, especially if they cannot determine any benefit from engaging in risky behavior. Consequently, risk assessment determines which choices provide the highest benefits with the least exposure to failure or detriment; it's a cost-benefit analysis (see Minimax and Maximin as well as Satisficing vs. Optimizing and Min/Maxing).

Good game designs compel the player into frequent states of risk assessment. If risk assessment motivates player choice, it becomes an exercise in maximizing benefit or minimizing exposure to harm; and, when the player chooses properly, they are typically rewarded in a satisfying way by gain, or at least by preventing loss (see Loss Aversion). Engaging designs integrate risk assessment directly into gameplay and moment-to-moment interactivity by regularly forcing players to make decisions. In this way, players engage in the behavior of risk assessment almost the whole time they play a game, whether they are consciously aware of this thought process or not.

As a common example, many sidescrolling, shoot-'em-ups provide players with a bomb, or other power weapon, that clears the screen of enemies. When action is intense, this is a valuable weapon for survival, but is it more or less valuable to the player in an upcoming boss encounter? Players must decide whether to use this advantage they've got in the current, urgent situation or hold onto it for later. This circumstance is a nagging instance of risk assessment that helps raise suspense in a game.

As bombs and power weapons are usually strictly rationed to the point of scarcity (see Supply and Demand), players often engage in nearly obsessive risk assessment when deciding how to use them. Sometimes players complete the game without deploying the power weapon at all. During play, they assessed the risk of not having the bomb or weapon as being greater than the benefit of ever deploying it. This is an example of risk assessment driving a hoarding behavior, and it highlights the psychological power of game design.

Jesse Schell talks about risk assessment in terms of triangularity in *The Art of Game Design: A Book of Lenses*. *Triangularity* means providing the player with branching pathways that segment the risk and reward of the challenge awaiting. The idea is for the design to provide at least two choices: One is a lower risk or challenge branch with a lower reward, whereas the other is more challenging and risky but promises greater rewards. Designers can make triangularity explicit with visual indicators, such as signage or atmospheric effects, or they may hide it so that players must rely on trial and error.

To visualize triangularity, imagine the player standing at a fork in a road; one branch is a lower risk/reward option and the other offers higher risk/rewards. The player is free to pick their poison, and, from the player's position, they appear to have two choices, both of which achieve roughly the same progression through to the next stage of the game.

Designers face a couple of notable dangers when designing risk assessment scenarios. Rewards players gain must be meaningful and shouldn't deviate too far from their expectations. If the reward economy (see Supply and Demand and Variable Rewards) is too unpredictable or unfulfilling compared to the implied values a player determines through risk assessment and play experience, then the player will feel a lot of frustration. This is true even if the rewards received are greatly to the player's benefit.

The principle of Risk Assessment has life outside the foundational mechanics of game design and is a practice applied to game development, as well. Similar to players who need to assign value to the risks presented before them, developers need to weigh the risks in game development. Risk assessment is a periodic process that takes the temperature of the game in progress as a way for the player to evaluate the project's health and any outstanding threats and to guide iteration.

Usually game makers practice risk assessment in a rhythm dictated by the production methodology they have implemented; for example, in a traditional Waterfall style of software development, milestones and deadlines are usually good points from which to take a snapshot of the production progress and from which to perform risk assessment. In *Agile* development processes, the risk assessment usually happens during sprint planning meetings. The job of risk assessment can be undertaken on an individual basis but is often more beneficial in a team setting, provided there is a strong structure to support what may become a rigorous conversation.

Part of the attraction of playing games is that they offer an experience where risk assessment can be practiced in a relatively safe environment. The risk of drag racing in a video game is much less than in reality, but the game version can be almost as fun.

Triangularity is the idea that a player is offered two ways to progress to the next level in the game. One is low risk, but also low reward. The other is higher risk, but also higher reward.

Supply and Demand

Supply and Demand is a key component of economics, but it comes into play in games constantly—and not just in massively multiplayer online (MMO) auction houses. The fluctuations of supply and demand show up in the pursuit of rare items, the desire to personalize avatars, and the interplay of dominant races or play styles.

To understand the basics of supply and demand, think about a grocery store heading into the end-of-year holiday season. Most of the time, they sell cans of pumpkin for $1.25 and there is always a full shelf. However, when the holidays start to approach, the store knows demand for this seasonal treat is going to increase, so they know they need to increase their available supply to keep up with demand and to sell as much as they can.

So instead of arranging perhaps six cans on a low shelf, they make a huge display of 200 cans and put them in a prominent place and on sale to catch shoppers' attention. It's exactly the same product as it is every other time of year, but the increased demand—because of the time of year—means cans move off the display at a good clip; they may even need to be replenished from stock in the back room. If they had left it at just six cans, they would have run out very quickly.

Imagine how much two warring chefs would be willing to pay for the last can of pumpkin? Way more than $1.25. The price can increase dramatically when there is a short supply and a high demand.

And yet, this balance is always fluctuating. The holidays will end, and for a while, the store may not be able to sell a can of pumpkin to anybody for any price, since everyone is tired of it and thinks of it as tied closely to the already passed holiday. A huge supply with little demand can cause prices to plummet.

When making a game instead of pumpkin pie, this still applies. Look at the popular card game Magic: the Gathering. In this game, players collect cards that have different values and abilities. Certain cards are worth more than others, and certain cards are easy to find whereas others are very rare. These rare cards are in high demand and yet are hard to find. The combination of a very useful card in limited supply means owners can ask a high price if they are willing to sell.

When designing a game, it is important to carefully plan how the supply and demand of items in the game will work, and it should cover a wide range. Some objects/weapons/spells/pets should be very easy to obtain but have little value while still being necessary to the game. Then some items should be a little tougher to obtain and have an increased value and usefulness. These items shouldn't be as abundant as the lesser items, but they shouldn't be impossible to obtain, either. The last objects are the ones that are few and far between. These rare objects should be very hard to obtain and also hold a high value for the player. This range of different levels of supply and demand mimics a free market and feels natural to players. However, keep in mind that economies of all kinds (in games) require play testing and experimentation to find the right balance (see Balancing and Tuning).

When supply and demand is tuned correctly, a game will have a solid balance that makes it immersive, challenging, and yet still appealing. If either supply or demand is out of control, players usually get frustrated and quit.

The field of economics devotes much research and theorizing to the intricacies of these concepts. From price elasticity to purchasing power and market equilibrium, there is a great deal more to supply and demand than can fit here.

Magic: the Gathering is a game that uses principles of supply and demand to increase engagement and fun.

Synergy

Synergy is when two or more elements combine to produce a new, more powerful impact than either could have had on its own. It's often summed up like this: The whole is greater than the sum of its parts.

When applied to game development, synergy refers to the possibility that the output of many individuals will come together to produce something greater than the output of those individuals independent of each other (see Design by Committee).

Players experience synergy as they see mechanics, art, and technology come together into a cohesive, larger experience. The game is more fun with all of these things combined than it would be with the individual parts. Both types of synergy increase efficiency and productivity.

Synergy Found in Games

In order to understand how synergy is created in games, it's useful to relate it to a chef constructing a new dish. Chefs take their professional knowledge of various individual ingredients and experiment by mixing them together using a host of well-known techniques. Successful mixtures often turn into reusable recipes.

In games, players also create their own "recipes" or insert "ingredients" into an existing "recipe" by experimenting with and combining mechanics and systems, or by crafting inventory items. In both circumstances, synergy is born when the gamer produces a new maneuver or item by manipulating something that was already present. The discovered synergy results in the player progressively mastering their environment. This, in turn, encourages them to search and experiment further in order to feel the happiness that comes from complete mastery.

Combining Mechanics

The most obvious way a game can invoke synergy is by allowing players to discover unique maneuvers from skillfully executing combinations of mechanics. For example, a game that relies on melee combat could allow players to string together light and heavy attacks in specific orders to create new, more powerful maneuvers. Pressing light attack twice, followed by heavy attack once, for instance, could result in a devastating maneuver whose damage values and status effects exceed that of the individual attacks.

Synergy with mechanics is also encountered when players start adding Metagames. Multiplayer instances of games, like the skateboarding simulators in the Tony Hawk franchise, may not be set up with programming or rules to support multiplayer games like King of the Hill or obstacle course races, but players who enjoy a certain virtual environment will often invent new synergies that allow them to play these kinds of metagames with each other, using the game world as more of a toy and finding synergies the designers never anticipated. It's important to note that players are exploring in these ways because they love the experience and want to expand and continue it, not because they are intentionally trying to break the game or play it the "wrong" way.

Crafting

Another way to allow players to feel the surprise and excitement of synergy is through *crafting*. Although this varies from game to game, the core idea involves mixing found or purchased items together to create a new, more valuable or useful one. A simplistic example can be found in early Resident Evil titles, where combining herbs results in more powerful plants that contain unique status effects. More complex examples are evident in Minecraft, Farmville, and most massively multiplayer online games (MMOs).

The first step to creating a crafting system is to list out every permutation of item combinations. Break each item into as many individually useful component parts as possible in order to increase the number of available combinations. From there, figure out what each combo could logically craft. It's important the game makes the player feel like *they* figured out the combination on their own, so obvious mixtures should be common early in the game.

It's OK if certain combinations do not yield any unique items, but crafting works best when all of the *logical* combinations are handled (see Theme). Although separate from crafting itself, it's also important that crafting be rewarding by having benefits outside of the new object created. The aforementioned Resident Evil titles would limit the amount of items a player could carry, thus organically rewarding the player for crafting because doing so would reduce the number of held items and create an open slot in their inventory.

Synergy is the magic that happens when the whole is greater than the sum of its parts.

Theme

Theme can be a tricky idea to comprehend. It's often confused with similar concepts like motif and genre, partly because they all address stylistic decisions that influence one another. However, theme is an especially important part of the design process, whether the focus is mechanical, narrative, or artistic.

Here's why: *Theme* is the central idea your design will convey. It's the one big concept that drives all of the work you do. It's the part of your design that adds substance and makes people see value beyond the fun they'll have or the skills they'll learn. It's also a valuable tool to help guide your design process.

With a theme in mind, there is a clear guide for each design decision. When a designer adds a feature to their game, the first consideration will be whether or not it makes thematic sense. It's possible for a new feature to completely undermine the theme, conveying the opposite emotion or message that the designer intended to get across in the big picture. On the other hand, new features—or particular implementations of features—can echo and enhance the larger theme. Theme can be the razor's edge that helps determine whether a potential feature is a good idea for this game or just a generally good idea.

For theme to be the most useful, it needs to be as specific and targeted as possible. As an example, "war" is simply too broad to be a helpful theme. Is the game about the horrors of war? Or maybe about honoring the soldiers who fight? In looking at just those two thematic ideas, some very important differences dictate significantly different implementations in design.

A game about the horrors of war would highlight the civilian toll, the torment of post-traumatic stress, and other negative aspects of the experience. A game about honoring those who serve as soldiers would focus on acts of heroism, selfless sacrifice, patriotism, and achievement.

It could be disastrous to mix these thematic elements. For example, if the soundtrack to a game about the horrors of war fits better with the theme of honoring soldiers—strident, upbeat, patriotic—the end result is a sense of glorifying the sad scenes you're trying to present as terrible. Not only would this fail to show the horrors of war, but players could be confused or angry.

To find the right theme for a design, focus on what feeling or thought players of your game should walk away with. If they had to try to describe what they experienced while playing this game, what would that be? The thought or feeling that sticks with them is a beginning point for crafting a theme. Consider what players should learn about the situation they've been in and what thoughts are top of mind for events they've just witnessed or created. Putting that into words is the heart of your theme.

It's important to note that theme is independent of any genre, setting, or trope (see Game Tropes). It's possible to have a theme such as "Anything is possible with good friends" set in King Arthur's court, a modern battlefield, or outer space. A theme like "It is worth it to sacrifice one's life to preserve a greater peace" could be set in ancient China, the mythic Mount Olympus, or a modern high school. Having this fully fleshed-out theme will allow the design to be flexible enough to incorporate new ideas, but solid enough to identify when an element doesn't fit.

As theme relates to narrative, in particular, the main character's story arc (the change in a character from the beginning of the story to the end) usually acts out the theme most clearly. In almost every case, whatever the protagonist of the story learns or experiences is what the player will learn or consider. The protagonist who learns to become less selfish teaches the audience the virtue of selflessness. The protagonist who becomes more self-reliant demonstrates the danger in dependency.

A strong theme is the backbone of a good design. It will be a guide throughout the creative process and offer the player meaning and value beyond the fun of gameplay.

Theme: Love Conquers All
Note: Although this theme seems to fit most easily in the 1750s social scene, it's possible—and even a bit more interesting and unexpected—to set it on a modern battlefield instead. The ideas seem deeper and more fresh.

Theme: Courage Is the Most Valuable Virtue
Note: This theme seems tailor-made for a modern battlefield, but if it's set in the social scene of the 1750s, we are able to see the ideas in a whole new light instead of feeling like they are boring and recycled.

Time and Money

Imagine two players:

1. Abe is a ramen-chomping college student. He only has classes three days a week, so he basically lazes about playing online games on his off days.

2. Zack is a high-powered suit-wearing executive. He likes games quite a bit but finds it hard to fit them into his day.

Abe has a surplus of time and is constrained by money; Zack has a surplus of money and is constrained by time. Both players enjoy the games and want interesting stuff to happen, but they have different resources that they can spend to unlock that content. In fact, there is a whole spectrum of gamers between Abe and Zack. Some people have both a moderate amount of money and time that they are willing to spend.

If the up-front monetary price of the game is high, all of the Abes are turned away. They just don't have the money to get in the door. If the time price of the game is high (the amount of time one needs to invest before getting to "the good stuff"), then all of the Zacks and their ilk are turned away.

But if the game allows players to trade money for time and time for progression, the need to turn any player away for lacking either of these disappears. If Abe can get to the good content without ever paying (meaning the game is free to play) and if Zack can pay some cash and get to the best content quickly (meaning the game offers items or progression for real money), then both types of players and all of the spectrum in-between can be satisfied.

What if players have neither time nor money? Riot Games has a solution for this with their League of Legends game. Since the game is very social by nature, they allow players to buy gift cards—for other players. This allows players with surplus money to give in-game rewards to players with neither the time nor money to amass them on their own. Many other games now allow the gifting of useful items via either in-game actions or purchase.

Of course, tying an in-game economy to real-world currency in any way opens up a myriad of complications and problems not yet fully understood or taken into account in public policy and legislation. For instance, at what point does the exchange rate for Interstellar Kredits (the currency in Eve Online) become just as important as the exchange rate for Euros in the real-world economy? And at what point, then, does the game qualify as a bank, with all the regulations required there?

There have already been extended court cases as people accuse each other of stealing objects—furniture, items, jewels—that only ever existed in a game. So although this exchange of time for money in an online, persistent world is an exciting boundary to push for game designers, it also adds a layer of complication to managing the real-world side of the game.

User-Centered Design

At the highest level, *user-centered design* (UCD) is a term applying to user interfaces that take into account the needs, limitations, and desires of the end user of a production at every phase of the design. This is an approach that requires extensive usability testing throughout the process to understand users' actions and predict their behavior early on in the design. Designers need to analyze and predict how users will utilize a product and then test those assumptions with actual users. This real-world testing is critical because designers often have a difficult time predicting what the initial experience of users using their software will be and what each user's learning curve is like.

It is deceptively easy to believe as a designer that the needs and desires of the end user are known and understood intuitively. The chief factor separating UCD from other design methods is making an effort to study and capture how users will want, need, and expect the product to function rather than making the user conform to the designer's expectations.

The International Organization for Standardization (ISO) describes six principle keys to UCD. The design is based upon an explicit understanding of users, tasks, and environments.

- First, users are involved throughout design and development of the product.
- Second, user-centered evaluation drives and refines the design. This is an iterative process.
- The whole user experience is addressed in the design. An understanding of users, tasks, and environments is explicitly understood and taken into account by the design.
- Finally, the design team must comprise multidisciplinary skills and perspectives.

There are many questions that must be answered when creating UCD. Who are the users? Are they middle-aged housewives or hardcore 25-year old men? What tasks and goals are users trying to achieve? Are those tasks and goals clear to the user? What is the user's experience level and what is their experience level dealing with games like the one being created? Also, if it is a totally new genre, the learning curve will be very steep and accounting for that must come into play.

More questions to ask include: What functions do players need and how will they access them? What information and in what form do users need to play the game? How do players think the game should work? What are the extreme environments in which the game will be played? (If it is a mobile game, this is very difficult to answer as the environment could be nearly anywhere.) Is the player multitasking or are they playing the game exclusively? What is the input for the game? Is it spoken, gestural, touch, or orientation? Again, with mobile games for devices like the iPad, this will be very different than for a game that is played exclusively on a PC.

The designer must consider the visibility, legibility, accessibility, and language used in the game for the player. The designer must also account for "who" the user is. This includes age, gender, ethnicity, geographical location, education level, and so on. What is the purpose of the game? What are the cultural and contextual settings for the game? How do these relate to the user?

There are a number of tools available to the designer in UCD. The three primary ones are persona, scenarios, and use cases. Persona is the player's representation in the world. It is the fictional accounting of the player. Scenarios are the settings for the persona and are circumstances of how the world around the player looks when the persona is engaging with the game. Finally, use cases are the careful breakdown of the possible actions and results the player or persona may encounter.

Answering all of these questions can be time consuming and expensive, which is why UCD is often overlooked for games. However, the more UCD is utilized for a game, the better the game will be and the more likely it will be a hit.

Wayfinding

Wayfinding is the process of orienting one's self in relationship to the world and navigating from the current position to the desired destination. Humans instinctively find their way using Spatial Awareness, context clues, landmarks, well-structured paths (see Affordance Cues), and lighting. All of these clues communicate direction for the player without supplying something as overt as a glowing arrow pointing the way. Successful wayfinding dynamics empower players with a sense of mastery over the world.

One way to illustrate this principle is to see wayfinding at its worst; in this case it is used as an environmental puzzle. In the original 1976 text-adventure game Colossal Cave Adventure, the player eventually discovers a part of the cave that the game describes only as "You are in a maze of twisty little passages, all alike."

Every move the player makes, in every direction, is met with exactly the same response: "You are in a maze of twisty little passages, all alike."

There is no way a player can navigate out of this maze using the usual methods of orientation and planning. The wayfinding for a human's brain is completely broken. There are no landmarks, no affordance cues—nothing.

The solution to this classic puzzle is for the player to drop an item in whatever room they are standing in—effectively creating their own landmark. (This has the added benefit of working with the Theme, as the classic way to get out of any maze is to drop breadcrumbs.) The description of the room now looks something like this: "You are in a maze of twisty little passages, all alike. There is a glove here."

So the player moves on to an adjacent nondescript room and drops another object. Continuing in this way eventually lands them back in a room containing an item they dropped previously—a familiar landmark. Now that the rooms have unique identities, the player can map and solve the entire cave.

Unless the environmental puzzle of a maze is the entire point, games should provide clear wayfinding for players so they can focus on the appropriate content (see Attention vs. Perception), rather than spend their time trying to orient themselves.

The basic techniques for good wayfinding in games are as follows:

- **Landmarks.** *Landmarks* are any aesthetically distinctive architectural or geological feature in the game world. Landmarks are exceptionally useful to wayfinding when they are associated with decision points. Mechanically, they serve as a decision node and can also be used as a fixed object for determining one's position in the local game space. The dynamics of landmarks instill confidence in the player's navigation decision. In order for landmarks to maintain value, they should be a scarce resource and serve the game world's larger purpose, as too many may just add confusion to the navigation.
- **Weenies.** Aesthetically, *weenies* are architectural or geological landmarks with a wow-factor. They tend to be large and define a land's region or territory with their presence. These special case landmarks have the tendency to demand the player's attention and make the game's location memorable. Mechanically, they serve as reference points from which to gather one's bearings in the game world. The dynamics of weenies pique the player's interest and beckon them nearer as they anticipate action or the furthering of the game's story arc. Think of it as holding out a piece of hotdog as a treat for a puppy. They can't take their eyes off it and will do anything to get to it.
- **Birth Canals.** *Birth canals* are aesthetically linear, claustrophobic spaces which first funnel, then constrict, and finally release the player into agoraphobic spaces (see Spatial Awareness). The mechanics of birth canals direct the player and clearly delineate game regions spatially. They can be used as safe zones or combat zones. The dynamics of birth canals build anxiety and anticipation in the player and often result in a sense of relief or awe when they are finally over.
- **Well-Structured Paths.** *Well-structured paths* are navigation routes that aesthetically communicate a clear start point, journey, and end point from either direction. Paths can be defined by either the physical (a paved road) or the negative space (a forest clearing) in the scene. A well-structured path serves as a mechanism to guide and move a player through the game space. The dynamics of a well-structured path afford the player with the perception of progress in the game world and the story arc.
- **Lighting.** *Lighting* is the means by which the game's atmosphere and mood are communicated to the player. Lighting can convey feelings and emotions, temperature, direction, and meaning. A warm yellow light is comforting. Cold, blue light can be forbidding. In wayfinding, the dynamics of lighting are akin to a moth to a flame; players instinctively seek the brightest areas, and thus these areas communicate an intrinsic direction they should go. This relationship allows designers to create non-structured paths for drawing the player forward.

Wayfinding at its best: A clear path, checkpoints at unique landmarks, and a dynamic weenie.

3

UNIVERSAL PRINCIPLES FOR GAME BALANCING

Addiction Pathways

One can hardly read a reference to a game without seeing some line about how addictive it is. In fact, we pride ourselves on making addictive games. Unsurprisingly, we also refer to our players as users, just like drug addicts. So, how do we go about making games so compelling that they become addictive? We utilize addiction pathways.

Humans, like other organisms, engage in behaviors that reward them; feelings of pleasure provide positive reinforcement, and so they repeat behaviors that give them pleasure. The behaviors humans exhibit to gain pleasure are linked closely with survival: eating, bonding, and sex. Each of these behaviors stimulates the addiction pathways in the brain (see Ooh, Shiny!), which the brain thinks of as rewards. There are natural rewards as well as artificial rewards.

Natural rewards include the dopamine response a player gets from learning new behaviors and overcoming challenges that games present (see Koster's Theory of Fun). Artificial rewards include loot drops and other "material" rewards that games provide, including leveling, medals, achievements, and so on (see Variable Rewards).

What is known of these addiction pathways is primarily acquired from research with rats and how researchers directly stimulate their brains with electricity, which activates their dopamine response; researchers can then train rats to repeatedly press a lever to continuously stimulate this response. In fact, the rats become addicted to the stimulus and eventually starve themselves to death rather than stop the behavior (see Skinner Box).

Addiction occurs when the subject is unable to moderate their intake of the behavior in question, like the rats in the experiments that let themselves die rather than give up their dopamine fix. Is it any wonder that sufficiently compelling games trigger addiction in players?

Designers can mitigate these addiction behaviors in a number of ways. One method is to use an energy meter that essentially limits how much time a player can spend in one play session, unless they spend real-world monies to extend their play sessions. Another, used in massively multiplayer online games (MMOs), is to decrease the reward players experience over time.

It is said that with great power comes great responsibility. When designing a game, keep addiction pathways and the power of the dopamine response in mind. Try to employ mitigating mechanics that interrupt the dopamine response occasionally to give players a break from the lever pushing. Be responsible for the games being designed and take them to heart. Users will.

+25 Pleasure
-1 Food
Reward

Attention vs. Perception

We perceive many things that do not necessarily grab our full attention. *Perception* is the process of interpreting, identifying, and organizing sensory information we gain from our environment so we can understand it. This process involves stimulating the nervous system's sensory organs and the brain's interpretation of the input it receives from them. This may include light striking the retina, an object coming into contact with the skin, smells, tastes, or sounds. Perception is largely passive. People do not choose to dismiss sensory input; however, they may choose not to pay attention to it.

Attention differs from perception in that attention is somewhat more elective. People actively choose to pay attention to certain input while actively choosing to ignore others. It is a cognitive act to selectively take in certain input while actively ignoring other input. For instance, in a crowded cafe, music might be playing and other conversations may be going on, but people choose which input to direct their attention to at the time, such as their companion or the food you are eating. However, certain circumstances, such as one person nearby talking excessively loudly or during momentary lapses of attention (see Ten Minutes of Sustained Attention), may let through perceptions that were not the original focus.

Obviously, when designing a game, the goal is to grab the player's attention and focus it on the game—specifically on the individual parts of the game that are most important at any given moment. Games include visual and audio cues (and, in some cases, tactile feedback) to communicate with the players and direct their attention. When engaged, the players pay attention to what the game has to offer while perhaps "tuning out" other stimuli such as ambient noise or movement (see Motivation.)

When designing an interface, you must also keep in mind the phenomenon of *inattentional blindness*. This is the inability to perceive something directly in front of you. When an interface is overwhelming the player with information, they will gloss over elements of it because it is simply not possible for them to pay attention to every stimulus input. This inability to see something on the screen or process and listen to the ambient music is the result of inattentional blindness.

When creating the game experience, it is up to the designer to balance the players' attention. Make sure to selectively choose which input the player will pay attention to during play. Beware of overwhelming the player with sensory input unless trying to intentionally evoke in them a certain emotional state. Ordinarily, the designer should introduce elements to the player over time, slowly showing them the elements that require attention. Be wary of introducing too many elements at once, as this may induce inattentional blindness, which will cause the player to overlook key pieces of the game.

Players can only focus their attention on one thing at a time, no matter how much information or distraction impedes on their peripheral vision. Although this information beyond their focus may be perceived, it is not necessarily understood or available to the player's consciousness as something to be acted on.

Balancing and Tuning

Video game *balance* is the hard to define quality of correctness that results when designers skillfully combine all the game design elements and systems that make up the play experience. This includes tangible factors, like character class or level layout, as well as intangibles, like game flow or time dilation. Perhaps more practically, balance is the economy of Fairness and challenge within a game; and when combined with available player choices and resources, it acts as an ecosystem of variables permitting the player to achieve success.

Balance, pervasive in gamemaking, is observable at the macro and micro levels of design. It becomes the catchall sum of a game's characteristics; that is, the macro idea of "Yes, player versus player combat is very well balanced." But, it also exists at a level of minutiae (see Economies of Scale).

Scrutinized at a micro level, balance is the quality of suitability for practical elements like spawn rates, outcome tables, or resource economy. Here's an example: "Unfortunately, health pickups are too infrequent in Level X, so it unbalances combat as overly challenging."

As a result of this macro and micro implementation, most aspects of the game implemented by designers and the development team contribute to the overarching concept of balance. However, not every game design component achieves perfect balance, and consequently, balancing the overall game experience is paramount.

Tuning is the process of adjusting variables gradually up or down to achieve specifically desired outcomes when evaluating game content and balance. Designers can tune to make a game harder, easier, faster, slower, and more (see Doubling and Halving).

Tuning can range from modifying a single variable, like the number of lives a player receives at a game's start, to removing an entire feature, like a sprint function. Keep in mind that if a game has too many outcomes or conditions that allow a player to succeed, then it is balanced as being too easy, and, in order to tune that balance, the designer must directly remove one or several outcomes that result in success or add more failure states to create a more difficult implementation.

As another example, in a fighting game like Marvel vs. Capcom, a designer might tune every character by making them overpowered in isolation with infinite combos, high damage moves, and more. Then, since all characters are tuned this way, the game achieves a working balance. Now that's not to say that balance is ever completely permanent. Fighting games are notorious for requiring post-release balancing and patches to tune any overlooked or emergent imbalances. An imbalanced game can ruin the competitive challenge and the audience's enjoyment.

In practice, tuning refines game design on the basis of currently observed results versus the intent of the game's design. The designer must weigh the ideal design against the actual, ongoing manifestation while anticipating the final audience's expectations. Tuning homes in on the model gameplay settings. Remember, as noted, tuning is a continuing process and plays a huge role in polishing a game.

Although balance may seem slightly theoretical, it is made practical through tuning, which refines the desired feel of a game. Thus, balance is an important and complicated aspect of creating video games.

Details

Focusing on delivering "the right" details can make the difference between an on-schedule, polished product and an ill-planned disaster. Deciding *what* the right details are in the first place comes from analyzing what presentational and communicative elements are required to keep the player fully immersed. Although the specific requirements differ from project to project, keeping the following high-level presentational and communicative methodologies in mind ensures a tightly focused game and a smooth production pipeline.

Presentational Details

On the surface, games seem to be judged by how detailed and lifelike they are. Reviews and press reiterate that the more detailed a game is, the more impressive it is; however, no game comes close to accurately modeling reality.

Because they are focused and goal-oriented (see Attention vs. Perception), players process what they see and interact with in games as *whole* compositions instead of a collection of individual elements (see Synergy). Because of this, not every single thing in a given scene needs to be immaculately detailed for it to be perceived that way.

For games that have finite deadlines and an ambitious amount of content, the rule of thumb is to fully detail aspects that the player will closely or repeatedly inspect or interact with. If these are lacking detail, players will be constantly reminded of that fact and quickly lose their immersion. Everything not falling into that category just needs to convey the *illusion* of being highly detailed.

A few examples of elements that need to be highly detailed are

- Guns in a first-person shooter (FPS)
- The player's back in a third-person game
- Environments that players look for or spend a lot of time in such as a) nearby landmarks in massively multiplayer online games (MMOs) and b) locales with puzzles and set-piece combat encounters

A few examples of elements that do not need as much detail are

- Distant, unreachable terrain and architecture
- Articulated hands and feet (unless they're shown in extreme close-up or integral to the game or character design)
- Hallways leading to large environments (see Spatial Awareness). (These are often used as the modern "loading screen" where upcoming content is streamed in behind the scenes and needs all the room it can get.)

Keep in mind that from an environmental standpoint, most engines and tools have become very good at efficiently using instanced objects. This allows designers to place large numbers of identical objects while carrying the memory footprint of a single instance. When designing environments with an artist, come up with a list of reusable objects that can populate the space. Rotating, scaling, and tweaking variables associated with these objects will also help the developer give the illusion of detail without them having to specifically create everything from scratch.

Communicative Details in Games

Communicative details in games are the direction and assistance given to help players solve specific problems. Provide too little, and the player is lost. Provide too much, and the player's intelligence and ability are insulted.

Making sure the player is aware of both their immediate and long-term goal is a crucial communicative detail to uphold. If a player returns to a game months after their last session, they need a readily available, brief rundown of where they are and what they have to do so they understand how to proceed. This is especially important for story-driven games that require memorizing plot points and character arcs. The format of this rundown depends on the style of game and should be consistent with how progress is generally communicated.

On the other hand, forcibly holding a player's hand without them explicitly asking for it constitutes too much detail and can ruin an experience. Once players have gone through in-game tutorials, they should be trusted to use their acquired knowledge effectively. In the case where the player hasn't played in awhile, the tutorials should be available *only* on request through menus or through a separate mode.

Communicative Details in Design Documentation

Everything about a game's design must be thoroughly documented and communicated clearly to every member of the team. This usually means including copious spreadsheets with vast arrays of carefully balanced variables. However, when an individual team member asks a question, hand them one segment or direct them to a single clear, precise page on the dev wiki rather than making them wade through a 400-page universe bible.

Focusing on the correct details is a matter of being in sync with how the game will be played and how it should be developed. It's a matter of scope, project management, artistic talent, and experience.

Careful attention to detail is important for preserving a sense of immersion for players, but the level of detail also needs to be managed to keep the project in scope. Common strategies for this include adding more detail to objects players will focus on, and less detail on background objects.

Doubling and Halving

Game designers apply the principles of Doubling and Halving as a general practice for design discovery, during prototyping, and in order to refine game balance. For game balance, Doubling and Halving involve adjusting a specific, tunable variable or programmable input to elicit noticeable changes in a game's play. Simply put, Doubling means taking a game design variable and increasing its value by 100 percent to observe how this tuning impacts the experience. Halving means taking a variable and reducing its value by 50 percent.

A key factor to the practices of Doubling and Halving is that they involve making extreme adjustments. These extreme adjustments demonstrate whether a variable needs delicate Balancing and Tuning or fundamental reworking. It takes the numbers closer to correct end results faster than a multitude of small, incremental alterations that only yield subtle changes in results. Doubling and Halving involve severe rescaling meant to deliberately stress the game design. Outcomes should highlight deficiencies in existing designs, especially in the game balance elements most strongly linked to the doubled or halved change. The great thing about Doubling and Halving as design techniques is that they expose problems clearly and quickly.

When using Doubling and Halving, the best results come when exposing flaws in balance and design or, by adjusting the tuning of a variable, you gain significant data to help obtain a better-balanced implementation of a game's design. This design method seeks to avoid the circumstance where only slightly augmenting or reducing a variable provides nominal feedback that lacks noticeable or actionable findings. If there is no major change from Doubling and Halving, apply the principle again until there is.

For example, consider a game where the player character's health value starts at a set point value of 200. However, after conducting Play Testing, it is clear that death through combat is too infrequent, and the game's challenge is too low. Following the principle of Halving, the next step would be to divide the health value down to 100, and then retest the design to observe the results. Remember, if the new health level of 100 still proves to be too generous, reapply the principle of Halving and retest with a character health set point of only 50. Halving is often a more efficient way to get definitive results than fine-tuning is, and it can save a lot of time, especially while design changes are ongoing.

Like in the previous example, variables and inputs that are good candidates for Doubling and Halving are those that have a high impact on core game balance. These include, but are not limited to, the following areas: movement options, time limits, resource economies, and health or damage ratios. It's important to note that a key step is to first define the importance of a tunable variable within the context of the play experience before deciding to implement Doubling or Halving. Not all variables that can be tuned will end up affecting gameplay in ways as significant as illustrated above.

When initiated successfully, Doubling and Halving often dramatically impact the composition and application of a game's rule sets. This, in turn, affects the audience's experience of the game and forces designers to evaluate many aspects of the game design. The principles of Doubling and Halving make up a great toolset as part of design (see Iteration).

Consequently, Doubling and Halving are periodically performed during development to establish "work in progress" balance. In addition, Doubling and Halving can be utilized right up until the final moments of game development to test and finalize balancing assumptions made during production. A cautionary note: Doubling and Halving during play testing is often too aggressive a measure for non-developer play testers. Although using it in A/B play testing may produce quick, clear results, it also subjects players to extreme conditions they might be unwilling to tolerate. Doubling and Halving tend to be tools used by system designers who have intimate knowledge of the interrelated aspects of game design features and are prepared to use suboptimal play sessions as a tool for tuning, rather than feeling like their time or money was wasted.

The process of Doubling and Halving applies to more than just play testing. In the course of making game development schedules, it's common practice to double a time estimate for how long a feature will take to develop, just to be on the safe side. Unfortunately, the process of Halving often comes into play when it's time to cut features if needed to re-scope a project.

Doubling and Halving variables during testing can bring numbers into line quickly, as well as demonstrate which variables have a significant impact on the play experience.

Economies of Scale

There are two major ways to look at every economy: on the micro scale and the macro scale.

Microeconomics is the study of economic choices made by individuals. This field analyzes economic situations from the bottom up. It looks at what motivates an individual to behave in a particular way and how that impacts the larger system, following the dominoes where they fall out into wider society.

Macroeconomics studies the economic choices of aggregate economies or countries, taking a look at patterns and influences on the systems from the top down. Macroeconomics looks at large trends and influences on a national or global scale and follows those down to eventually examine how it impacts individuals.

Some games feature these types of differences as well. In The Sims, choices of the individual homeowner constitute the Core Gameplay Loop. Microeconomics are the spotlight in this game as it is a one-person life simulator where choices are very detailed and on a small scale. In SimCity, however, the fun comes from adjusting the ebb and flow of entire industries. Human lives are in the form of neighborhoods and labor pools, not individual agents. Macroeconomics takes center stage. Decisions are on a large scale where success is measured in big numbers rather than personal wins.

Not every game is clearly focused on one scale or the other. To get a clear picture of the economic forces at play in a game without a tight micro or macro focus, developers need to take a look from both directions, bottom up and top down. When considering changes to systems, whether it's as severe as Doubling and Halving or a more subtle tuning (see Balancing and Tuning), the full impact of the changes won't be visible if viewed from only one direction.

Game economies have become quite sophisticated, but they didn't start out that way. In the early days of one of the first truly massive MMOs (massively multiplayer online games), Ultima Online, overproduction of some goods via the crafting system led to hyper-inflation, while players hoarding other goods (ingredients for spells) caused a core gameplay loop to effectively shut down. The developers came to understand that these were natural market forces at work in a closed system and that not every player action could be predicted (see Metagames).

Ever since then, MMOs in particular have worked better in a balance of "sinks" and "faucets," where the wild ups and downs of market forces can be mitigated by setting up systems for the removal of excess resources (sinks) and the replenishing of resources that are in high demand but shouldn't be too scarce either (faucets). Opening up the system in this way allows developers to tune the player experience to be more fun and less punishing (see Experience Design and Punishment).

Nevertheless, some games still allow a great deal of freedom in market forces. One example is Eve Online, where players can (and in some ways are encouraged to) form monopolies and cabals, and employ protection rackets. Design approaches like this, however, are not for the faint of heart. Eve Online's ambitious economic design ideals require the employment of a full-time, purely academic economist and his team of approximately eight people just to help manage, predict, and design the economics of the live game.

Keep in mind that price and availability are not the only factors involved in game economies. For instance, if a game includes a Dominant Strategy of any kind, an object involved in that approach will have inherent value to players that goes way beyond its price in the online store. For instance, when Counter-Strike: Source implemented dynamic pricing on weapons, a Desert Eagle was going for $16,000 while a Glock bottomed out at $1. Both are pistols that would kill a person equally dead in the real world, but they had drastically different values to players in the game economy because one was an ingredient in a dominant strategy and the other was not.

Making economic principles a part of the Core Gameplay Loop instead of hiding them in the background (see Transparency) can lead to challenging, fun games such as the German-style board game Power Grid, which is all about the subtleties of Supply and Demand. Or consider classics such as M.U.L.E., where survival on an alien world depends on trade negotiations, and the desperation of each rival for a particular resource is clear to see.

As players find themselves powerful participants in both the micro and macro economies of games, they see new ways to interact with each other, make alliances, and enact retribution. Although individuals in the real world have to suffer through an economic recession or depression with nowhere else to go, in games the players are free to walk away whenever the game becomes unfun.

Economics can be looked at from two directions. Macroeconomics looks at entire cities and industries and how large-scale systems interact with each other. Microeconomics focus on individuals within those systems and the decisions they make.

Errors Players Make

The types of errors players make can always be categorized as problems in one of two areas: performance or motor control. The simpler of the two is a *motor control error*.

Motor Control Errors

These types of errors may be as simple as the player pressing the wrong button by accident or as complex as failing to master the timing of a boss fight. Such errors stem from a player's difficulty with coordination, mastery, or application that (in video games) usually involves an input device. Accidentally knocking over chess pieces on a game board would also fit into this category.

Designers can anticipate and moderate motor control errors in the design process if they understand their target audiences very well and if they participate in play testing. Keep in mind that some players may be unable to master a certain motor control issue due to age or accessibility. One-inch tall chess pieces may not be ideal if children are going to use them, for instance. Designers of console games must keep in mind that not everyone they may be designing for is intimately familiar with the controllers and may fumble to find the right trigger button.

Performance Errors

The other category of errors is known as *performance errors*. Performance errors can be further broken down into three types.

- **Errors of commission:** In this case, players add extra, unnecessary steps to a process. They may believe they need, for example, to return to the home screen to get to the map while, in fact, they could have accessed the map from the screen they were on already. This may be a case where the interface is confusing or the player is suffering from inattentional blindness (see Attention vs. Perception).
- **Errors of omission:** In errors of omission, the player has failed to complete a required step in the sequence. They simply skipped something important. The key here for game designers is to make sequences that are short and directed in such a way that the player does not fail at completing the steps. After all, no team member will be at the player's side saying, "Oh, you forgot to do X. That's why it didn't work." It needs to be obvious, logical, or ingrained for the player to take action X in sequence Y. If the Learning Curve has been properly balanced, players should not suffer errors of omission (see Balancing and Tuning).
- **Errors of wrong action:** In this case, the player has performed an incorrect action. They were supposed to do one thing, but instead they did something else. This is where Errors Without Punishment come into play. Players should get an interesting failure state or at least a message (preferably witty) that they have performed the action incorrectly.

Keep in mind the types of errors players could make when interacting with a game and plan ahead. Help text will then be honestly helpful, error messages will lead people in the right direction, and a slip-up may even lead to a laugh instead of frustration and anger (see Errors Without Punishment). Anticipating the kinds of mistakes players make can improve the game experience in general.

Errors players make: 1) Motor control error: Oops! Clumsiness can result in broken parts. 2) Error of wrong action: using the wrong tool for the job will never work. 3) Error of omission: Skipping steps doesn't quite work either. 4) Error of commission: Doing the right steps too many times won't have good results.

Errors Without Punishment

One of the most difficult problems to navigate as a designer is how to handle situations in which players are not doing what the design intends for them to be doing. Errors can be classified in several categories and studied individually to mitigate them (see Errors Players Make), but in every case the game needs to do three things:

- communicate that an error has occurred
- redirect players into correct procedures
- convince players not to repeat the error, but to play the game as intended

The first two items on this list are usually handled effectively in Feedback Loops, and sometimes it's appropriate to use Punishment for the third, but many times that has broader effects than necessary and can cause more harm than good. If a player is already feeling frustrated because they haven't mastered a necessary skill, the last thing they need is the pain of punishment. This is not fun.

Instead, the player should encounter what is frequently referred to as an "interesting failure state." The idea behind the interesting failure state is that when a player fails at something, such as combining two items in such a way that they cannot be used or failing at a boss fight, the player deserves an interesting outcome.

Back in the days of text adventure games, for example, it was a point of pride for designers to include responses that were more interesting than "nothing happens" if a player mistyped or took a misstep. The most well known of these was a case where saying "Hello, Sailor!" prompted the game to respond with "Nothing happens *here*." (Italics added.) This signals to the player that there is, in fact, a location somewhere in the game where saying "Hello, Sailor!" will produce some victory condition, puzzle solution, or interesting outcome. So instead of feeling disappointed about making a mistake, the player is intrigued and incentivized to continue testing this behavior in different locations to find said victory condition. (Spoiler: It's a red herring. In no game where this was implemented did it ever result in an actual victory condition, puzzle solution, or more interesting outcome.)

When faced with a daunting challenge, it is best to find a way to communicate to the player that they have failed but still encourage them to try again to master the task. Similarly, if a player is playing a game differently than intended by the designer, rather than punishing the player—which is discouraging and disappointing for the player, who has simply found a new way to entertain themselves with an old toy—it is better to supply the exploring, boundary-pushing player with an interesting outcome. Feel free to make it a less desirable outcome than the "correct" one. Just be sure it's interesting. This increases satisfaction and is more gratifying for players than unvarnished failure or punishment.

Now, this is not to say that players should never fail; only that when they do fail (in the designated play pattern), they should be rewarded with an engaging outcome so as to not feel the sting of defeat so poignantly. Certainly, they should not be discouraged from playing the game and giving up. Rather, they should be encouraged to pursue the desired outcome. In fact, the presence of multiple interesting failure states will encourage players to experiment more, seeking the wittiness of the game designer to see what failure states they've accounted for in the design.

Giving lesser rewards to players who stray from the designated path is another way of handling errors without punishment. Rather than the full reward, these explorers may receive part of the reward and learn that while they did not follow the optimal path, their way of doing things is still valid. This approach encourages these explorers to go back and try again or at least proceed unimpeded by their error. This is not as effective as a more interesting failure state, but it still accomplishes the goal of not punishing the player for being less than perfect.

Punishing players for making a mistake can discourage them from continuing to play your game.

An interesting failure state provides players with enough information to know where they went wrong, but encourages them to continue exploring and playing.

Hick's Law

Hick's Law basically states that when a user is presented with a list of similar choices, with each additional item that is added to that list, the time it takes the user to make a choice increases logarithmically. Hick's Law is evidence of the importance of simplicity in design and it provides guidance for how to organize information to speed learning and use, making the whole design feel more intuitive.

One mathematical form of Hick's Law is: $T = a + b \log_2(n)$, where T is the reaction time, n is the number of choices, and a and b are constants that depend on the specific conditions. The variable a also depends on the user choice of whether to make a choice at all, which in turn is related to how many choices there are, n. The greater the number of choices, the less likely the user will make any choice, in a sense, giving up. The function is logarithmic, base two, because a binary search is implied on the assumption that the search items are similar and/or ordered. Unordered, unrelated choices would have reaction times that are more linear, not logarithmic, and therefore would be even more time-consuming.

The application of Hick's Law can be seen in ultra-simple websites like Google, and in the grouping of similar choices in more complex approaches like Amazon's front page design (see Details). The misapplication of Hick's Law can also be seen in game user interfaces (UIs) where gamers are faced with too many high-level choices in menus, each with too few items listed within each of these choices: longer lists under fewer categories might be considerably faster and less frustrating.

Sheena Iyengar, Professor of Business at Columbia Business School, did an illuminating, often-cited study using jam. In a paper called "When Choice Is Demotivating," she showed that consumers were more likely to purchase jam when they had fewer choices. Faced with 24 different types of jam, 60 percent of customers stopped to sample the jam, but only 3 percent made a purchase. However, customers in the same context who only had to choose between 6 different jams stopped to sample 40 percent of the time, yet 30 percent of those people made a purchase. When the task seemed overwhelming, consumers chose not to choose.

Since choice is such an integral part of designing interactive experiences like games, this tendency for people to abandon the problem when faced with too many options has a broader impact than just on UI design. It comes up regularly in sandbox games, for example (see Sandbox vs. On Rails), where consumers may say they want infinite choices, but in reality, when faced with too many choices, they say they are bored or confused. These same studies show that the optimal range of choices is between three and six—no fewer than three, but no more than six.

The only time a broad selection of choices is an advantage is when the person making the choice is approaching the situation with a very specific need in mind. For instance, if a die-hard fan of a particular jam flavor and brand approached that jam choice with only 6 choices, they would probably be disappointed and would likely not make a purchase. Their preconceived, ultra-specific preference is more likely to appear in the 24 choices. In games, this situation comes up when players are allowed to customize their avatar or personal space. They often have specific ideas of what they want and will try to find it from the choices offered. Just remember to organize the many choices into just a few categories with long lists of related options.

Be careful about taking Hick's Law too literally, however. Another logical conclusion from the formula mentioned earlier is that it would only take a user 30 times as long to choose from 4 billion choices compared to 4 choices. Certainly a computer can do a binary search on 4 billion ordered numbers only 30 times more slowly than on 4 choices (a result of the logarithmic order of execution), but obviously a human couldn't. As in all design decisions, common sense and Play Testing trump mathematics and rigorous formulae.

Temper the menu simplicity called for by Hick's Law with focus group testing and common sense.

Interest Curve

An *Interest Curve* identifies the level of audience engagement and their reaction to stimuli provided by an experience. Interest Curves chart participants' perception of an event; they are not limited to video games or even media but are observable in experiences ranging from sporting events to ergonomic design, or things as pedestrian as a bus ride. Thus, regardless of what type of Interest Curve you are studying, the principle behind using it is to balance and optimize your audience's enjoyment by manipulating design.

To create an Interest Curve, monitor participant experience by plotting a simple graph of Interest, as a value on the y-axis, over the duration of the experience, usually measured as Time along the x-axis. Additionally, points of significance or concern within the experience can be marked along the x-axis so you can figure out their particular impact on the audience. Such points may include general conditions, like starting a new level, or specific ones, like acquiring a new ability.

The big-picture goal behind Interest Curve observation is to learn whether particular stimuli are more or less effective than others within the context and continuity of the overall experience. After gathering data in the form of an Interest Curve graph, analyze the results against the curve your designers anticipated. This comparison between expected design and real practice can identify false assumptions about design, areas for improvement, or even unexpected successes.

Deviations will need to be rectified. Balancing and Tuning an Interest Curve includes, but is not limited to, configuring Pacing and difficulty, cutting content, or resolving outliers. And, although not an exact measure because it is often based on observation rather than reporting, an Interest Curve is able to provide value to the entire development team. The Interest Curve is not limited to design feedback alone; and remember, the Interest Curve and Learning Curve can be very complementary design tools.

Changes in visuals, mechanics, story, and even technical features affect Interest Curves. A consequence of this holistic quality of interest is that you must involve stakeholders from all disciplines when you review Interest Curve outcomes. When you are tuning Interest Curves, keep these guidelines in mind:

- Consider the preconceived notions the audience brings with them.
- Grab the audience quickly. Use a hook that may take the duration of the experience to resolve.
- Avoid stretches of static interest (see Ten Minutes of Sustained Attention).
- Dynamic peaks and valleys help generate interest; an experience needs to seem like it spontaneously ebbs and flows (but designers know better).
- Even within the rising or falling movements, utilize smaller peaks and valleys to prevent staleness.
- Periods of high engagement often benefit from a period of less engagement afterward; this allows the audience to recover or rebuild expectations.
- It's generally a good idea to have at least one or a couple of high peaks to leave the audience with something memorable.
- For example, at the time of its release, Call of Duty: Modern Warfare had a couple of very noteworthy peaks in its campaign design: particularly, the AC-130 Gunship mission and the event of a nuclear bomb detonation. These points of peak interest are still memorable to the audience years later.
- When reviewing Interest Curves, the tendency is to make the primary concern always optimizing the entire experience; however, remember that individual subsets of players have unique Interest Curves, too. A player mostly interested in the story may have a very different curve than a collection-minded player. Within audiences there is variety (see Bartle's Player Types).
- Use variety to spur interest. Music, visuals, story, mechanics, and social prompting are just a few tools you can use to engage the audience.
- Don't be afraid to make cuts in content to streamline and enhance the entire experience.

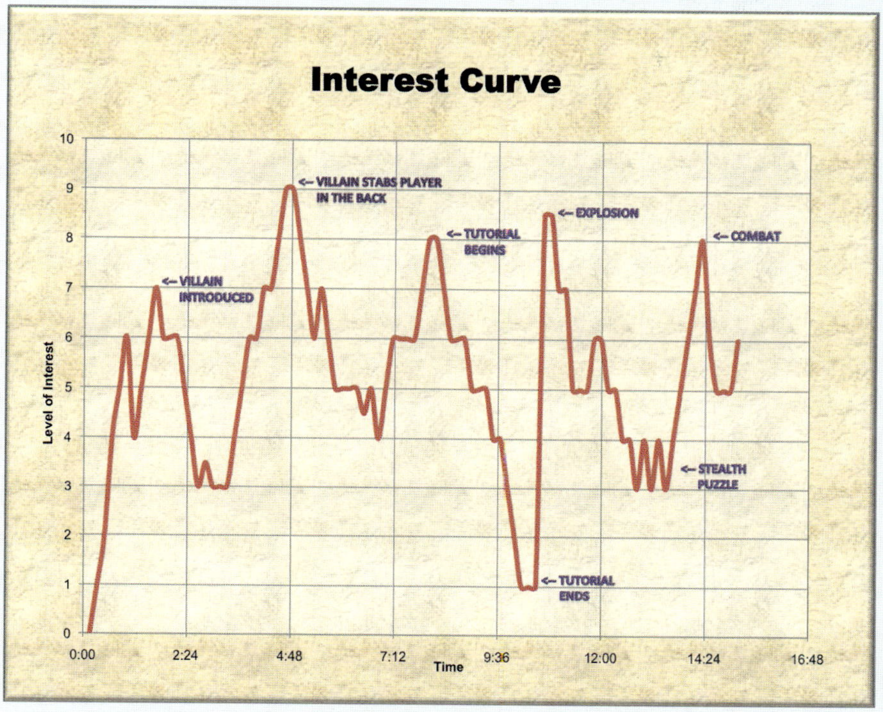
Interest Curve
Level of Interest
Time
0
1
2
3
4
5
6
7
8
9
10
0:00
2:24
4:48
7:12
9:36
12:00
14:24
16:48
<-- VILLAIN INTRODUCED
<-- VILLAIN STABS PLAYER IN THE BACK
<-- TUTORIAL BEGINS
<-- TUTORIAL ENDS
<-- EXPLOSION
<-- STEALTH PUZZLE
<-- COMBAT

Learning Curve

A *Learning Curve* is a visualization of the idea that task completion requires time and effort to understand, and that skills improve as tasks are repeated. The Learning Curve can refer to skill advancement of the individual player (e.g., "Because she's experienced with real-time strategy games she experiences a shallower Learning Curve when playing our game."), or it can characterize the degree of difficulty in getting up to speed with the specifics of a game (e.g., "Memorization of too many button commands steepened the game's Learning Curve in mission one."). Fortunately for game designers, the Learning Curve is a tunable relationship between the player and the game; it can be modified.

Causing further complication is that video games tend to require tasks to be repeated (see Feedback Loops) but also frequently add new tasks. As a result, the Learning Curve of individual tasks may be deemed too shallow or too steep, whereas the entire experience may be tuned just right. So, it is difficult to set Learning Curves so that you can balance individual mechanics while you also preserve the overall design's curve, or vice versa. Choosing which area to favor and when is part of managing proper Balancing and Tuning. And remember, it's important to maintain Learning Curve design with a specific audience in mind.

Learning Curves are customarily described as steep or shallow. Primary factors you should consider when composing Learning Curves are how quickly players learn or improve at new tasks and how much or how many aspects of a task require learning. Too many tasks, too many components to a single task, or a task that is too difficult creates an overly steep curve. Steep curves tend to frustrate players who are more interested in easy fun than fiero (see Lazzaro's Four Keys to Fun).

Conversely, a shallow curve results when the required tasks are too simplistic or there isn't enough novelty or variety for them to maintain player interest. Shallow curves tend to be described as boring. By adding some complexity to these designs, you can avoid them being classified as shallow.

When you are presenting new elements in a game, one way to prevent overly steep Learning Curves is to make sure that each new task at hand is the sole focus of play at a given time. Don't obfuscate key teachings. Let them exist in the spotlight of player attention. Provide familiarity in problem setups, introduce a new pattern, and then apply the pattern through to complete the task. Consider this framework for teaching players a new task:

- Remove distractions from the teaching effort.
- Let the player maintain control and teach them through doing, not by reading or observing.
- Set a clear goal to be achieved.
- Allow for practice without penalty or hindrance.
- Give direct and positive feedback to a successful application.
- Reinforce the ability and lesson by adding an additional degree of challenge, and give it a clear goal.
- Give direct and positive feedback to a successful application.
- When the player completes the task successfully, integrate their behavior with previously mastered tasks to evolve puzzles or scenarios and keep things fresh.

Here are two rules of thumb to smooth a Learning Curve: Set clear goals and provide direct feedback. These are good practices for direct tutorial design, if you want to go that direction, or you can apply them to more general encounter design, which may then provide knowledge transfer without the artifice of a formal tutorial.

In the big picture of game design, remember to consider the link between Learning Curve and Interest Curve. Audiences' sense of mastery, knowledge acquisition, and challenge are all derived from Learning Curve, and this, in turn, affects audience engagement over time, ergo the Interest Curve. Strive to strike a deliberate balance between these two principles that surprises and delights your players.

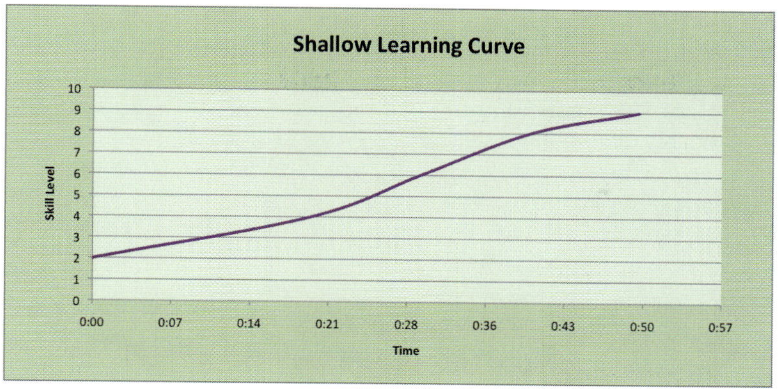

Shallow Learning Curve
Skill Level
10
9
8
7
6
5
4
3
2
1
0
0:00
0:07
0:14
0:21
0:28
0:36
0:43
0:50
0:57
Time

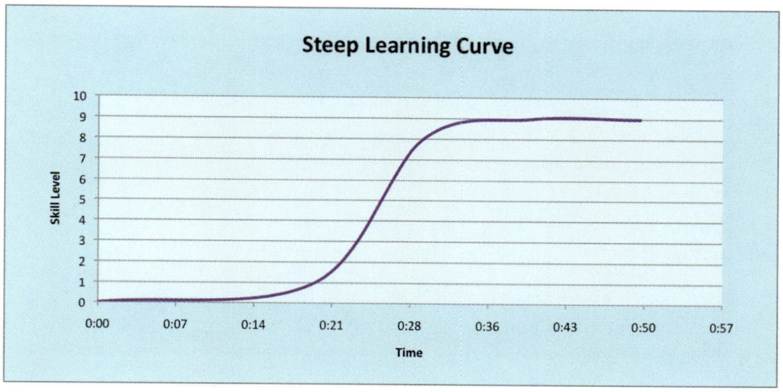

Steep Learning Curve
Skill Level
10
9
8
7
6
5
4
3
2
1
0
0:00
0:07
0:14
0:21
0:28
0:36
0:43
0:50
0:57
Time

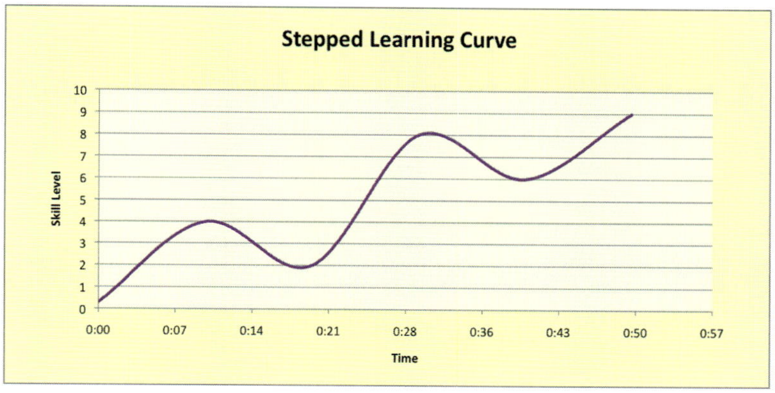

Stepped Learning Curve
Skill Level
10
9
8
7
6
5
4
3
2
1
0
0:00
0:07
0:14
0:21
0:28
0:36
0:43
0:50
0:57
Time

Loss Aversion

Imagine one person offers another a chance to play a game with them. They will only play once. They will flip a coin. If it lands heads, the second person wins a dollar from the first. If it lands tails, the second person wins two dollars from the first. Sounds pretty good right? Most people would jump at the chance to play this game.

Now imagine a second game. In this one, one hundred ping pong balls are in a jar and the player will blindly pick one out. Ninety-nine of the ping pong balls are golden in color. If the player picks one of those, they will win $10,200! The remaining ball is a black ball. If the player picks it out, they will owe the person running the game one million dollars.

Does that game sound as attractive? Sure the upside is much higher and the probability of getting that "good" outcome is higher, but the penalty for the bad outcome is massive! In similar experiments, researchers have found that most people will take a sure thing that is a reasonable outcome over a better average outcome that is risky.

The first game has an expected value of $1.50 for the player. The second game has an expected value of $98 for the player. The second game, on average, is 65.33 times better for the player! But people focus on the extreme negative value if given the opportunity. This is why people buy insurance—the sure thing of a premium payment is much more attractive than the chance of an extreme negative experience that could bankrupt them.

The implication of the principle of loss aversion for game design is clear: The fear of something being taken away is scarier and more motivational than the joy of being given the same amount or more. Look at Farmville. If you do not log in regularly, the crops you have planted will wilt and rot. The time and in-game money spent on planting those crops would be lost. Let's say that time and money is equivalent to 100 in-game credits. The rot mechanic will be more motivational to the player than simply giving the player an extra 100 in-game credits if they log in.

Say a designer has an imbalance in their released game that they want to fix (see Balancing and Tuning). The Sword of Power is just too powerful. *Nerfing* something in your game (decreasing the power of something relative to the power of other available options) is generally decried by players since it is a form of loss. However, if you increased the power of everything else relative to the Sword of Power, it would no longer be imbalanced and the players who want to use other non-Sword of Power weapons will be happier that their favorite items got a "boost."

Maslow's Hierarchy of Needs

Abraham Maslow was a behavioral scientist who developed theories of human needs in the 1940s based on a hierarchy of importance divided into five groups. Although Maslow himself never displayed them this way, the five groups are generally represented graphically by a pyramid. The groups include the following:

- **Physiological:** Food, shelter, clothing, air, water, sleep, and sex form the fundamental physical needs of every person. If any of these needs are not satisfied, achieving this will be the focus of the individual's efforts until such time as they are. These are also sometimes called "biological needs."
- **Safety:** These needs are connected with fear of loss, injury, or death, including financial security, health insurance, and protection from physical and emotional damage for one's self, family, friends, and community.
- **Love and Belonging:** Social needs form this tier of the pyramid, such as friendship, sexual intimacy, family unity, and group acceptance (e.g., clubs, churches, gangs, and sports leagues). Teachers, co-workers, family members, and friends all have roles to play at this stage.
- **Esteem:** These needs include respect, confidence, authority, responsibility, competence, status, reputation, and appreciation. These may be achieved through profession, family, hobby, or social group. The internalization of these values is far more important for success than any formal or insincere external recognition.
- **Self-Actualization:** The highest need, this is the desire for an individual to become whatever they are capable of becoming. When a person fulfills their maximum potential, accomplishing whatever is most wanted, after having mastered all of the lower-order needs, they have *Self-Actualized*. This can even be transcended by pushing the boundaries of their own cognitive and emotional limitations to include the advancement of society and all of humanity in their personal needs.

In general, this hierarchy tends to be used as a barometer of progress, with people meeting their lower-order needs first, then their higher-order needs once the lower-order needs have been adequately achieved.

Clayton Altderfer is an American psychologist who merged Maslow's Hierarchy of Needs with his own ideas, derived partly from Self-Determination Theory, called ERG (for Existence, Relatedness, and Growth). He put Physiological and Safety needs together to make Existence needs, Love and Belonging to make Relatedness, and Esteem and Self-Actualization were combined into Growth. He also added a theory of regression, which states that when needs are unmet in a higher category, greater efforts are made in a lower category to compensate in an attempt to stimulate achievement. Other theorists have postulated more, rather than fewer, needs at the higher orders, replacing Self-Actualization with a combination of Cognitive (knowledge), Aesthetic (appreciation), Self-Actualization (potential), and Transcendence (helping others) needs.

Concerns with Maslow's theories have been raised by later scientists, including individual responses to several needs simultaneously (rather than only one), problems in determining when a need is satisfied, varying behaviors resulting from the same needs, and lack of empirical evidence. Some also oppose specific findings of his, such as the order of the needs and whether lower-order needs must actually be met before higher-order needs can have higher precedence. Likewise, he has been criticized for basing his work primarily on individualistic societies, focusing ethnocentrically on the Western middle class, and studying only the most healthy and intelligent people he could find. It is widely agreed that these needs can vary in importance by circumstances, age, gender, and culture.

It is tempting for game developers to assume this model is only applicable in that it puts games near the top under "hobbies," but this would imply that everything else can be ignored. Looking deeper reveals many ways this model can be used within games. Here are just a few examples to spur brainstorming:

- Simulations feel more realistic when needs are part of the player's responsibility. What would SimCity be if workers didn't need to have housing?
- Artificial intelligences feel more human when they exhibit these needs.
- Players feel more frightened when needs lower on this scale are threatened.
- Complex conflict and choices can be set up when players have to face the tension between needs. This sets up interesting theme and narrative opportunities.

SELF ACTUALIZATION
Hats, Crafting
ESTEEM
Leader Boards, Conspicuous Consumption
LOVE AND BELONGING
Pets, Romance, Friends
SAFETY NEEDS
Armor, Weapon, Health Potions
PHYSIOLOGICAL
Sleep, Food, Water, Mana

Min/Maxing

Not to be confused with Minimax and Maximin, Min/Maxing is a Dominant Strategy that occurs when a player creates an optimal character (in a roleplaying game), an avatar (in a video game), or a unit (in a war game), by minimizing less important factors and maximizing more useful ones. This can result in avatars that are so heavily focused that they are only good at a single technique, which leaves them less flexible, but extremely capable with their chosen ability. Min/Maxing is especially common in tabletop roleplaying games where combat is frequently perceived as the most important part of the game. It results in characters with low social, intellectual, and moral statistical abilities, but with strong sword arms. In military games, units may end up as *glass cannons*—they have very high offensive capabilities and ridiculously low defensive values. Min/Maxing tends to be tolerated in new players and encouraged in groups where roleplaying (acting) is valued less than collecting rewards (treasure, equipment, and/or experience).

Min/Maxing is the subject of a great deal of argument among gamers, particularly participants in tabletop and online roleplaying games. On one side, those in favor of Min/Maxing believe this strategy is legal and viable and contributes to gameplay (they also tend to make that player one of the most powerful and effective in the group). They often point to the fact that nearly all of these games encourage specialization through character classes and they use these specializations as evidence to back up their position—that they are playing in the spirit of the game. On the other side, many roleplayers feel that Min/Maxing violates the social contract inherent in these kinds of games; it is this social contract that allows players to create varied and multifaceted characters with a selection of skills that perhaps even approach a degree of realism that contributes to a player enjoying the game experience outside of combat.

When opportunities for Min/Maxing are designed into a game, it is typically up to the group of players sitting down to each play session to determine the extent to which it is allowed or encouraged. Violating established house rules or guidelines (see House Rules) may get the player ejected from the group or banned from the game.

Game designers use several approaches in an attempt to circumvent Min/Maxing behavior by players:

- Set predefined, carefully-balanced (see Balancing and Tuning) values for units and characters.
- Generate new values randomly at the beginning of each new game.
- Tie some values together into complex systems where increasing one desirable stat decreases another desirable stat. Note: this approach doesn't eliminate Min/Maxing, but it often focuses it into these complex systems.
- Heavily emphasize theme and the lore surrounding the game, providing a narrative structure to encourage role-playing behavior instead of stepping through the game in a purely mathematical approach.

Related game design pitfalls include the concepts of powergaming, rules lawyering, and twinking. *Powergaming* is when dominant players attempt to coerce others into following their lead or bully them into doing what the dominant players want so they can achieve a specific goal, leaving the spirit of the game behind. Similarly, being a *rules lawyer* involves following mechanics pedantically, ignoring the fun of the process to focus on the mathematical/optimizing challenge. And finally *twinking* is when players stack low-level characters (either their own or others') in roleplaying games by giving them unearned weapons, armor, or other items that make it easy for them to dominate their opponents at that level.

Character stats in RPGs are often Min/Maxed by players, as in this example with the warrior and wizard, in contrast to the more balanced rogue. Designers need to be aware of how this strategy will impact the play experience for all players.

Punishment

Often the source of debate in recent years is the concept of negative reinforcement, or *punishment*, within video games. Old-school gamers have grown up with the mentality that games are stern disciplinarians—every intricacy of the game must be studied and mastered in order to progress, and the slightest step off the "proper" path results in the player having to repeat the whole segment or level or even having to start back at the very beginning. Nowadays, many current-gen games are adopting the trend of Errors Without Punishment, a concept in which the game is always there to actively push the player toward the right decision without ever letting them fail or having them repeat segments of gameplay. Traditional old-school gamers would protest that this trend kills the concept of challenge, and the player is merely experiencing the game instead of crafting the skills required to conquer it. The debate over whether this is a cause or a symptom of today's so-called "Entitled Generation" is a topic for a completely different book, so for the time being, take a look at a few models of punishment that video games utilize.

Lives/Game Over/Continue

This model of Lives/Game Over/Continue is the classic construct of video games, and is almost as ubiquitous as video games themselves. Upon reaching a failing condition—running out of health/time, missing an objective's requirements, and so on—a player loses a life. Upon the depletion of lives, a Game Over screen is presented to the player. If the game grants the player Continues, they may then choose to use one. A typical punishment structure in games that utilize the Lives/Game Over/Continue concept is as follows:

- Lose a life: Start from the last checkpoint.
- Continue: Start from the beginning of the current level.
- Don't continue: Start back at the very beginning of the game.

This concept achieved its full potential in the arcades: The player had to make the very grave decision of punishing their pride by not reaching the end of a game (and having to start back from the very beginning the next time), or of punishing their wallet by having to pay to continue; all the while they had to endure an onscreen ticking timer to even further pressure them. This punishment had real-world consequences!

Wither

Plants are living organisms and require attention from time to time. If one were to forget to water their plants for weeks on end, they would start to *wither* (the plants, not the person). This is similar to how *wither* is implemented in video games; the attributes of a game element—say, a weapon's strength, or an animal's health—weaken over time if the player doesn't interact with them. The best possible example of this mechanic is a Tamagotchi. If the player forgets to feed or clean up after their digital pet, the pet's health and happiness suffer as days go by. Examples of *wither* can also be found in Farmville, where the player's crops suffer if they don't tend to them regularly.

Permadeath

Permanent Death, or *permadeath* (or sometimes PD), is a mechanic where a player's character only has one life for the entire game. If the player's character dies for whatever cause, it is forever gone, and the player has no choice but to go through the grieving process, create a brand new character, and start fresh. Diablo II and III have a Hardcore mode where permadeath is implemented: Once the player's character is killed, the game is over, and the player loses all of their items, weapons, stats, and so on. Minecraft has a Hardcore mode that permanently deletes not only the character, but the world as well! This mechanic also shows up in a Tamagotchi, although this seems inappropriately morbid. If the player's creature withers too much from neglect, it can die, forcing the player to raise a new one from scratch. There are constantly "threats" in the massively multiplayer online game (MMO) industry that a new MMO will have permadeath, but it usually gets vetoed before the game's release, as many players really dislike the concept of investing so much time into something that could vanish forever, and lack of player interest usually results in lack of profits.

Sandbox vs. On Rails

Children playing in a sandbox will amuse themselves by reforming sand until they're bored, and boredom does eventually set in. It comes from their perception that there's nothing left to discover. So too it goes for sandbox games, which allow players to explore responsive, expansive worlds with little to no direction from the game itself. The fascination of the virtual sandbox revolves around exploration and experimentation for extended amounts of time, and game designers can never forget that key.

Sandbox Experiences

To promote experimentation, the systems need to allow players to creatively combine individual mechanics and objects. Each mechanic needs to be simple to execute so the player feels comfortable trying it in combinations. The resulting emergent gameplay is a series of chain reactions that rewards the player for their ingenuity. For example, Grand Theft Auto allows the player to combine the driving, combat, and non-playable character (NPC) interaction systems to create seemingly unique reactions from the NPCs each time.

When potentially hundreds of systems work concurrently, however, it's practically impossible for the world to handle each combination uniquely. Developers cover their bases on the obvious combinations and try to anticipate the edge cases players will attempt to see how far they can push the systems. That way, players will grow to trust the game's responsive functionality on common combinations and developers can trust in the charm of unpredictability resulting from the unanticipated cases.

Although all open worlds are sandboxes, not all sandboxes are open worlds. The only things sandboxes definitively require is a room that the player can roam around in freely and modify in some fashion without a specific modification being the explicit goal. So a sandbox can be encountered as a small part of an otherwise differently structured game. On the other hand, open worlds are excellent delivery mechanisms for sandbox gameplay. Recreations of real cities or fully realized, fictional worlds offer the opportunity for tremendous discoveries. Their sheer size also hides the physical edges of the sandbox, which helps players forget that there are limitations to their experience.

As a note of caution, building environments modeled after reality comes with the expectation that everything is handled realistically. For example, a world with only two types of people or a city that doesn't have weather changes requires fictional justification to avoid breaking the player's sense of immersion.

On Rails Experiences

Games that are said to be "on rails" ask players to move through the experience in a more or less linear fashion. These experiences excel at focusing player attention on specific tasks and key moments. It's possible to have a game "on rails" and also have multiple paths, as players are able to choose (consciously or unconsciously through variables set through earlier actions) which fork in the road they will go down.

Retaining player agency is also important for on-rails experiences, as it feels so much less fun to simply watch a movie interrupted every so often with a button-mashing punishment. However, choices can be offered in the complexity of the mechanics or the complexity of the scenarios. Puzzle games like Portal are certainly experiences on rails, but they provide simple mechanics and complex scenarios, whereas fighting games like Mortal Kombat offer simple scenarios with complex mechanics.

Understanding how to pace an on-rails experience is a matter of relating the pacing to two constructs that utilize rail travel: trains and roller coasters. Trains keep the course without dramatic twists, turns, or changes in direction. They do "the same thing" for an extended amount of time to ensure a smooth ride. Roller coasters, on the other hand, build in big thrills by exploiting sudden changes in direction, exciting visuals, and compelling themes. Roller coaster designers strategically manipulate the rider's anticipation of what's coming next so they can execute exciting and surprising twists and turns.

Sandbox or Rails?

Choosing the appropriate structure for a game is one of the first, foundational decisions made in preproduction. As with any design decision, clarity for how to move forward on this one comes from analyzing Game Pillars, target audience (see User-Centered Design), and Theme.

It's important to note that nothing is stopping developers from marrying sandbox and on-rails structures. In fact, most sandboxes start out as on-rails experiences to help orient players, and some on-rails experiences pause for some sandbox play now and then.

Sandboxes and on-rails experiences appeal to different players (see Bartle's Player Types) and solve different engagement and retention problems. They are not mutually exclusive, but combining them can be a delicate operation.

Whether a game is set up as a sandbox or on rails, it can include the same features. The difference is in how and when the player encounters these features.

Ten Minutes of Sustained Attention

Whether playing a game, watching a movie, reading a book, or listening to a speaker, humans have a limited attention span. After 7 to 10 minutes, regardless of how hard they try to pay attention, their minds wander to something else, whether it is the feel of the chair, some passing thought, or other stimuli breaking through their attention barrier.

What does that mean for game designers? It means that the finely crafted 15-minute cutscene they so painstakingly made will not sustain the players' attention. It means that the narrative segments that take 20 minutes to read will lose the player at some point. Finally, it means that as the experience is being crafted, they should think about how long any particular task takes and craft the experience into smaller chunks of 7 to 10 minutes (see Interest Curve). When designers create these easily digestible chunks, the players' attention is not guaranteed, but it is not impossible to maintain.

Many games are designed to deliver a minimum of 4 hours of gameplay. This implies that the player will not be riveted to the screen that entire time but will be distracted by other things. The job of the designer here is to try to constantly engage players and keep their attention for stretches of time.

On the other hand, certain game experiences are crafted to be digested in small chunks; the designers expect that players will enjoy them for 10 minutes of gameplay before they return to another task. Social network games are particularly geared toward this sort of short-play-session experience. Although many people will play a social game for up to an hour a day, they play it in short play sessions, many lasting only 5 to 10 minutes. During that time, the player can be fully attentive to the game but will readily turn their attention elsewhere when the play session is done. When designing a social network game, keep in mind that no task should take more than 10 minutes if you expect the player to complete it. Most play loops last a minute or two, delivering tiny, easily sustainable game chunks.

This does not have to be bad news for the game designer who seeks to deliver more sustained play loops. It simply means that they need to examine and tool their play loops to grab the player's attention again when it starts to flag (see Core Gameplay Loop). This can consist of the game passively introducing new elements to the player after about 7 minutes, such as a reward, or this can be actively accomplished using a timer to detect activity on the part of the player. If the player has been inattentive for more than a minute or two, the designers throw up a help screen or a new quest or some other content that reengages the player.

ENERGY

Variable Rewards

Rewards tell players they have done well and have achieved something. They come in two basic types: fixed and variable.

Fixed rewards are associated with a fixed time, type, and amount of reward. For instance, "Do this quest within one week and get 50 coins." These rewards are clear to the player and they expect to receive them when they complete the task set. Fixed rewards are a way of rewarding players in a specific way for a specific action or for succeeding at a fixed goal.

Why not simply use fixed rewards for everything? The player knows the clear goal and exactly what they must do to achieve it. And the player knows that when they complete that goal, they will get the reward promised up front, no more, no less. However, imagine the player's surprise if a rule has been put in place that says if the player completes the task in half the allotted time (or less), they get a bonus reward, such as an extra 10 coins added on to the 50 in the earlier example. The player then has the incentive to work harder/faster to accomplish other goals since they have been rewarded for this behavior. This is *random conditioning* (see Skinner Box), which strongly influences people to find patterns and match them to succeed in goals. So even if the player isn't explicitly told they will get a bonus if they succeed in half the time, if there is a set pattern to uncover, it is still considered a fixed reward.

Variable rewards, on the other hand, are not set or fixed. They contain a degree of randomness that is tied to the game mechanic awarding the reward. In games, variable rewards are commonly "loot drops" for killing monsters or foes. If the player knows exactly what reward they are going to get for a specific action, it removes any surprise from the equation; removing that emotion and variation in the experience leaves it feeling flat and unengaging (see Interest Curve). A level of excitement and surprise is associated with variable rewards. Sometimes, it will feel completely random to players, or they may attribute complicated, subtle influences, like luck or karma. Of course, variable rewards are usually not random but are dictated by carefully balanced tables. And luck usually has nothing to do with how the code functions.

Variable rewards reinforce the play pattern that they are used for. When developers make a game where the player is primarily killing monsters (see Core Gameplay Loop), the player knows that they will gain some reward for killing the monster (or foe), but often they will not know exactly what that reward will be. In some cases, the rewards are reliable enough to be counted on, but variable enough to require an unknown number of repeated behaviors. For instance, if a monster drops a pelt most of the time when it's killed, but sometimes it drops meat or antlers instead, a player may have a general idea of how many monsters they need to kill and collect pelts from to make a magic robe, but they won't know for sure. The number is even more uncertain if they are trying to collect a certain number of antlers for making a special bow. When the player needs to repeat the same action over and over again, this uncertainty makes things more interesting. It makes the task more enjoyable by providing a quick hit of surprise when the player sees exactly what the reward turned out to be.

Variable rewards also encourage exploration of the play space. A treasure chest, for instance, is an excellent example of a variable reward. Unless the player is on a specific mission to get that particular chest, they will have no idea what it contains and will therefore have incentive to open and investigate it. Who knows what treasure it might contain? This is the same sort of motivation that drives real-world treasure hunters today: the *possibility* of finding something fabulous. Possibility space is very promising and alluring. It will drive players forward to investigate and explore.

To keep players engaged and motivated, use some variable rewards. Players will enjoy a greater sense of accomplishment and surprise from their repeated actions (see The 80/20 Rule).

4

UNIVERSAL PRINCIPLES FOR TROUBLESHOOTING

Advance Organizers

An *advance organizer* is a technique from the field of education which helps students learn faster and better (see Koster's Theory of Fun) The idea is to provide a high-level overview or hook that prepares the student for what they will learn next. It can be designed to help them relate the new concepts to other things they already know and put everything in context. In the case of a player, it lets them know that new information is on the way or that a transition is about to take place. Advance organizers have several forms in video games.

The first advance organizer a player is likely to encounter is Hype. This type includes ads, previews, game press, conventions like E3, trailers, and other similar methods for advertising an upcoming game. The hype could take the form of an Alternate Reality game designed to heighten the player's awareness of an upcoming game. Each time a player encounters an advance organizer, they become aware that a new game is out or is about to be released and new game experiences or new knowledge is imminent. The hype helps players understand how the new game fits in a genre or franchise and provides general expectations for what they should focus on in the game (see Attention vs. Perception).

The next type of advance organizer players encounter is the loading screen. While the game is copying files onto the hard drive and is loading content, players are treated to a screen that introduces them to at least one character from the game or other art that prepares them for the upcoming content, thus setting the tone for the content. The loading screen will also likely have some kind of counter or time indicator to show that something is going on (a spinning ball, a timepiece, etc.) while the game is loading and doesn't appear to be doing anything. All of these cues inform the player that something new and exciting is about to happen, and that they should pay attention and get ready.

When designing the loading screen, make sure it has a consistent art style with the rest of the game. With this advance organizer, the designer emphatically sets a tone for how the game will proceed (see Cognitive Biases).

Frequently, games start with a cutscene to provide a backstory for the player and to provide context for the start of play. The cutscene may be long or quite short but will certainly inform the player that something is about to happen and set up expectations and suspense. Cutscenes can be used throughout a game to inform the players of transitional content or a scene change where they will encounter new content and, hence, new knowledge. The players have been primed by each of these advance organizers to succeed at new challenges.

Many games present the players with a menu to start them out. The menu is another advance organizer that the player knows will take them to a different venue or part of the game, depending on which option they choose. For instance, letting players choose a destination from a clearly laid-out map as a menu sets them up to be ready when they enter a new environment, rather than just a boring list of place names, which provides little information and can result in serious disorientation rather than excitement.

Finally, be careful of using advance organizers in places where new content is not going to be introduced, since this is their role. Games that use excessively long loading screens can frustrate players who are expecting something new but don't get it; this can be the sign of an asset loading/storage problem that a designer can overcome with some clever coding.

Affordance Cues

Remember as a kid pushing all the buttons in the elevator? Finger-sized circles, beveled edges that stick out just a bit from the wall plate, lights that come on . . . those buttons just cried out to be pushed. Their physical qualities communicated how to interact with them without requiring a tutorial or instruction manual. Psychologists refer to these qualities as *affordance cues,* and they are not just useful in elevators. Horizontal bars on doors imply they should be pushed; a vertical handle implies it should be pulled. Affordance works in a virtual environment with just as much power.

The original concept of affordance was introduced in the 1970s and was used primarily in psychology. It was openly adapted to the design process in works like Donald Norman's *The Design of Everyday Things.* Human-Computer Interaction (HCI) and interface design took affordance one step further by making intent central to the principle. Designers need to be aware of the intentional and unintentional affordance cues their products demonstrate and make an effort to use affordance to encourage the intended use—if a button is meant to be pushed, do not use affordance cues that encourage pulling.

This concept is at the root of interface design. When a web interface or game heads-up display (HUD) is filled with buttons that have beveled edges to imply depth, this is affordance at work. Many designers go one step further and try to make their buttons seem edible or tasty, appealing to not only the visual and the sensory (touch) but also the oral. Every sense that is appealed to increases the player's desire to act on the object in question, thus increasing its affordance.

Affordance is key in user interface and user experience (UI/UX) design (see Krug's First Law of Usability). Those HUD elements and interface elements must cue the player into how to interact with them in the game. If the element is a dial, players will expect that they should use their mouse or fingertip to gesture in a circular fashion while interacting with the object. An example of this occurs in a horse riding game called My Horse in which players must mix grain for their horses. This iPad game makes maximum use of affordance here by showing a circular indicator on the screen that the player must then follow with a fingertip to execute the move. Tablets open up new channels of affordance with the gestural systems they cater to naturally. Swiping, tapping, and so on are natural motions games can give easily interpreted cues for, thus optimizing affordance.

And in games, affordance goes even deeper than interface design. Environments and puzzles with appropriate affordance cues can make a game feel more fun and effortless. Affordance can cut down on time players spend in tutorials and draw them into appropriate behaviors without having to enforce those behaviors with rules.

When designing or troubleshooting the UI, it is especially important to keep affordance in mind. What action should the player perform? What path should players follow? Every element placed in the environment will influence the affordance of the player's possibility space. If the player needs to be guided from one location to another, put in a path or carpet between those points to make the path clear. With proper use and care, affordance can make a game eminently playable rather than a logistics disaster.

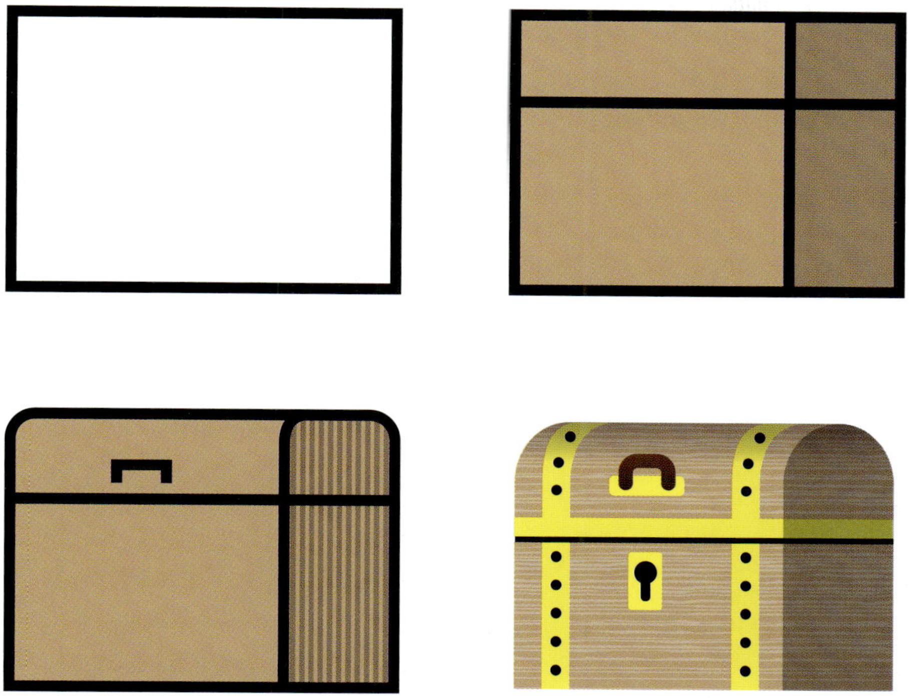

A blank white rectangle doesn't include enough affordance cues to prompt users to take any particular action. As more affordance is added—color, shading, handles—intended action becomes clearer. Instead of a confusing white box, players instinctively know they should try to open the treasure chest.

The Buster Principle

Too often in games, game makers punish players inadvertently by making the game too hard (see Punishment). Obviously, there are cases where making the game hard is in pursuit of *fiero*, or hard fun (see Lazzaro's Four Keys to Fun), but what about the player who is trying hard to play but lacks the motor skills to master the game's demands (see Errors Players Make)? Should this player walk away from the game, frustrated and angry at not being able to complete an experience they were previously enjoying tremendously? How many players fail to complete a game they love because of a boss battle they simply cannot win due to their fingers not moving fast enough? In these cases, even cheat guides are no help. If that player doesn't have a 10-year old nearby they can hand the controller to for a few minutes, they have no recourse but to quit in frustration or simply lose. Frustrated and angry is no way to leave a player feeling. Players should leave a game with a sense of satisfaction at having accomplished something (see Sense of Accomplishment).

The Buster Principle is simple: Be kind to your players. In the event that a player has clearly tried repeatedly to succeed at a task (something easily tracked in modern video games), try making the task just a little bit simpler. It may not even be necessary to change the task enough to be perceivable to the player. A small decrease in the difficulty may be the difference between an unhappy player throwing the controller across the room and an ecstatic player rejoicing and pumping their fists upward with a sense of accomplishment.

The Buster Principle was invented and demonstrated by a Goffin's Cockatoo named Buster Keaton. He played dexterity games with his owner, and kept a sharp eye on how frustrated the human participant was feeling during the whole endeavor. He knew that irritated, annoyed humans tended to walk away from a frustrating activity. The bird wanted the game to continue for as long as possible, however, so when sensing rising frustration in the owner, the bird would back off on the difficulty just a bit to make the human participant feel a sense of success. The adjustments were subtle enough that it took the owner some time and many games to realize the bird was going easy on her at just those moments when she was about to give up.

So the basic concept of the Buster Principle is to allow a game to automatically (and behind the scenes to the unaware player) tune the difficulty level of a particular skill to the ability of the player—or the frustration level of the player.

This is not in any way to suggest all games be made easy. It is simply recognizing that making games inordinately difficult isn't a good experience for players. Creating a good experience for the player should be the goal rather than developing a hard game to prove how clever and smart we are as game makers.

Early Infocom games were well known for how impossibly hard their puzzles were. So hard, in fact, that it led to an entire product line known as *Invisiclues*—books that included a marker with invisible ink the player used to answer a puzzle on numbered clues. The questions in the clues became increasingly direct, the first being obscure (see House Rules). Computer games have come a long way since then, and now that game makers can easily detect how much a player is working at solving a problem, better solutions exist to avoid excessive player vexation. In short, don't torture players. Throw them an easy one now and then to reward them for continuing to try.

Cognitive Biases

Players all bring their own psychological filters to games. These filters skew "what really happened" into "what I *felt* happened." Naturally, each person is an individual with their own filters; different people may perceive, understand, and react to stimuli in different ways. However, certain threads are common to most people. Each of these filters tends to operate in similar ways for all people, affecting their understanding of events and shaping the feelings they get as a result.

Collectively, these filters are referred to as *cognitive biases.* Although there are scores of different identified cognitive biases, some primary ones rear their heads in how players perceive games.

Perhaps one of the most cited is *confirmation bias.* Put simply, confirmation bias sounds a lot like "see! I told you!" People are disproportionately drawn to information that aligns with what they already believe—even if their belief is wrong. For example, when reading news stories, people are more attracted to those that state things they already feel to be true, and they tend to reject those that dispute their notions. In games, people are more likely to notice events that confirm their preconceived notions (positive or negative) about characters, places, or occurrences. Correspondingly, they are more likely to dismiss, ignore, or even not notice things that do not conform to their beliefs.

When searching for information to process a decision or answer a question, people often rely on an *availability heuristic.* Because they usually do not have mental access to *all* the information, they put a disproportionate weight on whatever comes to mind first. The belief is that it must be more important if you can remember it. In particular, emotionally charged events are more "available" to memory than mundane ones.

One type of availability heuristic is the *negativity bias.* Negative experiences are more emotionally charged, and thus they are more easily remembered. Because of this, people tend to put more weight on negative occurrences than positive ones. For example, players of popular word tile games (such as Scrabble or Words with Friends) might form false beliefs about the random distribution of tiles based on how often they draw difficult-to-use collections such as all vowels or all consonants. They notice those groupings more because they are frustrating compared to the (far more frequent) mixed vowel/consonant combinations.

Another type of availability heuristic is the *recency bias* where people put more emphasis on recent events. Because people have a hard time accumulating and analyzing statistics over long periods, they put more weight on things they can remember. More recent occurrences are not only easier to remember, but when combined with other forms of bias (e.g., confirmation or negativity biases), they can lead players to believe that some new trend is developing when, in actuality, they are only random events.

A typical type of recency bias is *anchoring.* When people are given a piece of information about something, they process all subsequent information relative to that initial information—or anchor. For example, if someone was shown an initial price of $80 and a reduced price of $50, they would view that lesser-priced item as a better value than if they had never been shown the initial price. That is, they tend to think, "it's $30 cheaper than it used to be," even when they know the initial price is arbitrary or irrelevant.

People are also very susceptible to having their perceptions of information changed by how the information is *framed* with different words or other delivery mechanisms. For example, when information is presented with positive wording, people infer very different conclusions than when the same information is presented with negative wording. In games, framing comes up in a variety of ways, such as through the user interface, the type of wording selected for the story or dialogue, and even the specific colors and sounds.

Another type of framing is shown in the *Kuleshov Effect.* Originally this term applied to film editing, but it can also be broadly applied to games. The original Kuleshov Effect experiment included a clip of an actor's expressionless face with one of three other images (a bowl of soup, a dead child, a beautiful woman). Despite the face being the same in all three examples, people thought the actor was emoting the appropriate feeling—that is, hunger, sadness, desire—based on which of the three subjects it was shown with. It illustrated that, when asked to make judgments about vague or indistinct information, people look to nearby information to infer what *should* be there, and then they believe that it really *is* there. In games, we can combine pieces of information to make the player believe that something is there that is not. For example, artificial intelligence (AI) characters with a small set of very simple behaviors suddenly take on the appearance of intelligent decision-making with the careful application of audio *barks*—short, often randomized dialogue chunks such as "Hey, is someone there?" or "Oh! I've been hit!"

Images from the film that demonstrated the Kuleshov Effect. Audiences reported that the actor's face showed a different expression when juxtaposed with each of the other images. In reality, the same footage of the actor was duplicated three times. Audiences saw what they expected to see.

Kahneman and Tversky's "Outbreak"

There is an outbreak of a virus that affects 600 people. You have to select which one of two experimental treatments to administer to the entire group. Because you only have the time and resources to administer one solution. The estimates of their efficacy are listed below.

Group 1:

Program A:
200 people will be saved ← 72% chose A

Program B:
A 1/3 probability that 600 people will be saved, and
a 2/3 probability that no people will be saved

Group 2:

Program C:
400 people will die

Program D:
A 1/3 probability that no one will die, and
a 2/3 probability that 600 will die ← 78% chose D

Mathematically, A = C and B = D. However, because of the framing of the words "*will be saved*" vs. "*will die*", people's perceptions are different enough that they will select a different program.

Dominant Strategy

Dominant Strategy refers to a frequently adopted, extremely successful approach to gameplay exploited by players to gain victory in a predictable fashion. A Dominant Strategy showing up in a game can be

- Accidental, due to a designer's inattention to balance
- Emergent, from player behavior or personality
- Deliberate, through a conscious design choice

Dominant Strategies are relevant to single- and multiplayer games. Consequently, it's the designer's responsibility to identify and troubleshoot all play strategies, especially those that negatively impact audience enjoyment.

At least a single Dominant Strategy exists in most games. Thus, you, the game designer, need to be aware of this principle and then decide whether to embrace or reject it in your design. As games seek to preserve an economy of Fairness, and Dominant Strategies threaten this, the solution comes down to balancing. If a game feels as if it has become routine, disinteresting, or too simple, maybe a Dominant Strategy imbalance is to blame.

Problems arise when a single strategy is so potent and so preferred that it leaves no variety to play. For example, if players have access to multiple configurations, yet they always use the same character class, weapon, or play method, then a game's design may feel uniform and stale. In this case, audiences may grow bored and disengaged. If it gets to a point where a single strategy hurts player interest and demotivates learning, engagement, and the Interest Curve, you must redesign or remove it. Doubling and Halving variables may be one of your first steps toward re-balancing strategies and play.

However, this isn't to say that Dominant Strategies can't benefit play experiences. Sometimes designers will nurture a Dominant Strategy, especially if it is only temporarily applicable or not too insurmountable. By providing a balanced Dominant Strategy, you can empower your players with sensations of intelligence, strength, and successfulness. A key to tuning Dominant Strategy is to understand and weigh how powerful the strategy is against existing rules and alternative strategies. So, yes, it's OK to have stretches of play where a Dominant Strategy exists. This can promote a temporary sense of mastery and feeling of omnipotence for your players; but, if this state persists for too long, players may quit because the game has failed to remain challenging.

To create a deliberate and well-designed Dominant Strategy, make sure that the best strategy does not too greatly disadvantage non-adopters of the Dominant Strategy. For example, a Dominant Strategy in competitive first-person shooters may be for players to prefer grenades and close range explosives. Often with these weapons, damage inflicted is high enough to kill at least one or two opponents, splash damage provides for unintended homicides, and lobbing grenades or placing explosives is relatively less skill-driven than precision gunplay. To balance against this strategy and create a counterstrategy, designers can provide measures that reduce the efficacy of explosives. These can involve mechanics tweaks including ways to detect explosives, armor against explosives, or long range weapons that are most effective beyond the distance of grenade throwing and blast zones.

Note that in the previous example, skill level can play a role in which Dominant Strategies are favored. For example, new players may prefer an explosive-based approach to combat while learning maps and other players' behaviors because explosives tend to be easily executed and less precise. Then, as the players gain familiarity, they may abandon the explosive-based strategy in favor of a different skill set that allows for greater precision. Maybe the experienced player's strategy becomes ranged weapons, like sniping. Remember, Dominant Strategies are subject to skill level, players' interaction with Learning Curves, and the strategies the players are competing against.

Despite the risk associated with allowing for Dominant Strategies, it is worth mentioning that certain games benefit from including them. The dominant M6D pistol in Halo: Combat Evolved was imbalanced, but it did not ruin either the single- or multiplayer experience. The Zerg Rush in StarCraft is an effective strategy that can be dominating, but it is not a certainty. In each of these games, a skilled player can circumvent the Dominant Strategy and gain a feeling of mastery and accomplishment, but it does take familiarity and practice. Perhaps you could argue that gameplay in these examples is "fun, but broken," but these are two high-profile titles that thrive with these strategies included regardless.

Another way to use a Dominant Strategy as a design advantage is to capitalize on the fact that the strategy centers on controlling a particular power, weapon, spawn, or specific advantageous location. This can create hot spots and bottlenecks, funneling players without using architecture or level design, but still bringing them together for interactions where conflict, reward, satisfaction, and fun can occur. Again, the key to handling a design that includes Dominant Strategies is in balancing the strategies against one another while leaving the opportunity for slight imbalance and the human elements of play.

Dominant Strategy: bringing a machine gun to a knife fight.

Fitts' Law

In Human-Computer Interface (HCI) studies, the tradeoff between speed and accuracy of aimed human muscle movement is referred to as *Fitts' Law.* In other words, the faster someone moves to point at a target, the less accurate the movement becomes. This can be predicted using a mathematical model. When a human uses a controller (such as a mouse), this tradeoff becomes important to game design. The speed and accuracy with which a player must interact may be set at impossible levels or at least very difficult ones. At its simplest, the larger a target is and the closer it is to the starting point, the more quickly and accurately a person can point to it.

Fitts paid particular interest to the task of pointing, something players do constantly with their cursors, long before the advent of personal computers. In his description of pointing, three parameters are of interest. The first is the time needed to point to the target. The second is the distance that must be moved from the starting position to the center of the target. Finally, the width of the target comes into play. Each of these three factors affects the ability of the player to accomplish the movement.

Though the model only considers the width of the target, it is obvious that the height must be taken into consideration as well. An object may be quite wide, but if it is only one pixel high (a thin line), it will still be harder to click than a more proportional object.

Now, though the obvious application here is in combat and targeting, the less obvious but perhaps more important application is in the user interface (UI). UI elements should be placed close to where the player is enacting pointing behaviors and should be large enough to be easily targeted and clicked when the user desires. If the UI is built such that the player is constantly having to move long distances to get to it, the user will become fatigued and frustrated. The principle is simple: The closer an object is, the easier it is to use.

Grouping objects of similar functionality in the interface will make it easier for the player to access them as it is easier to find similar objects. Also, having shorter distances between similar buttons will make them easier to use. Finally, making UI elements that need to be used often larger will make life easier for the player.

When it comes to combat and targeting moving objects, the designer must take human constraints into account. Of course, if the aim is to make the game difficult, the constraint becomes the fastest tester in the pool of people testing the game. Every test team has at least one super-human tester who can handily rise to the most difficult challenge.

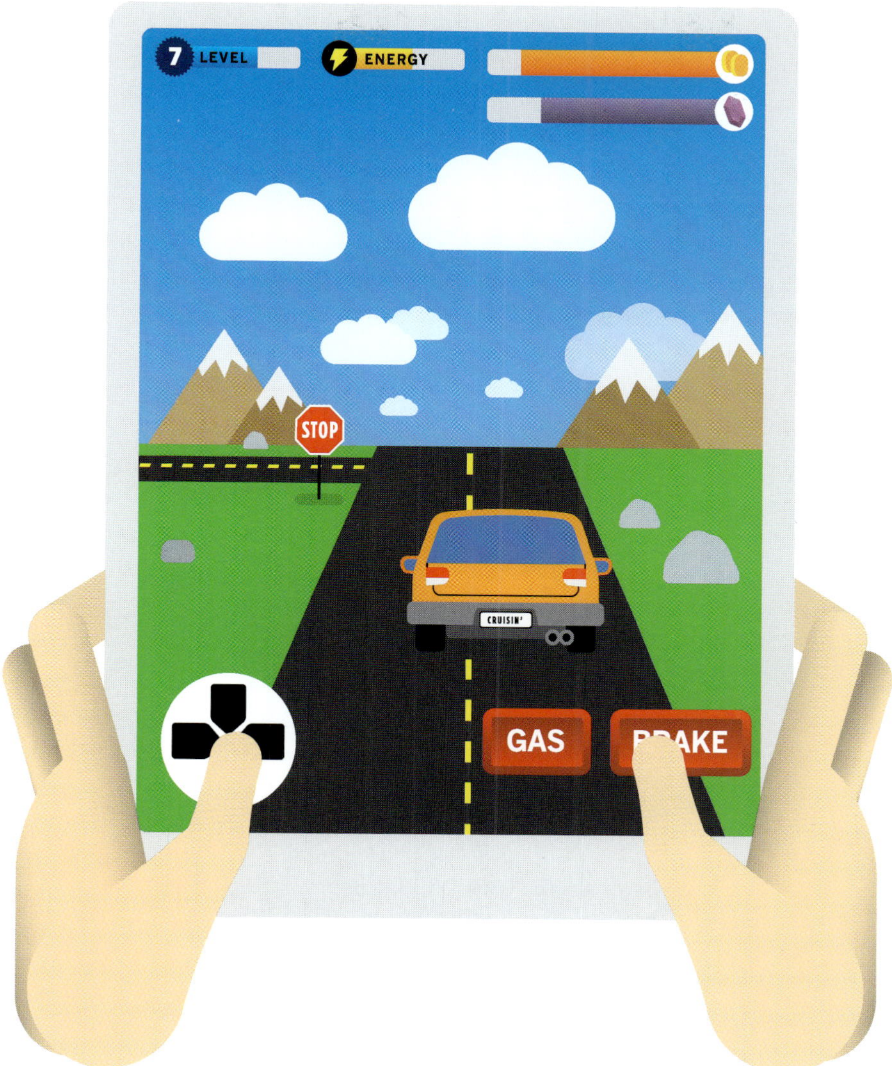

Fitts' Law can be summed up as the idea that the faster someone moves to point at a target, the less accurate that movement becomes. So when the Core Gameplay Loop involves both speed and accuracy, clear and easy controls are essential.

Fundamental Attribution Error

Someone is driving down a busy yet swiftly moving highway. They have a meeting to attend and are running a little bit later than they would like. They see an old Cadillac getting closer and closer in front of them. "Come on, old lady!" they grumble through clenched teeth. They eventually pass the Cadillac; then, just after they reach a comfortable speed, they notice a sports car in their rear-view mirror. It is getting closer and closer to their rear bumper—dangerously close. They shift to another lane and the sports car speeds by at a seemingly breakneck speed. "Maniac!" they yell.

Of course, what they don't seem to realize is that to the Cadillac, they were the maniac. And to the sports car, they were the old lady. When they are told this, they respond, "No! I was late for a meeting. That's why I needed to pass that slow-poke Cadillac. But I'm not going to drive recklessly like that sports car!" They've assigned a situational reason to their behavior. Yet the other cars were driving the way they were because they were "reckless" drivers or "slow-pokes."

In another example, a student fails a test. He complains: "It didn't help that my job made me work overtime every day this week." The instructor has a different view: "I wish my student wasn't so lazy and would just make the time to study." The student attributes his failure to a situation. The instructor attributes it to the characteristics of the student.

This is what psychologists call the *Fundamental Attribution Error.* It is the nearly universal willingness of someone to assign situational reasons for their own behavior while simultaneously treating the behaviors of others as a result of their character and not at all a result of their situation. Researchers have found that even when someone knows they are doing this, it is very hard for them to stop doing so.

This sounds like something that is only applicable in laboratory situations, but it has major implications for game design, as the following scenario shows:

A play tester sits to play a game and doesn't have a good experience.

The play tester blames the system—certainly they won't blame themselves! Maybe they didn't understand how to play because they slept poorly last night, didn't eat breakfast, or were preoccupied with a strained work or romantic relationship. Those reasons will not come up.

The designer will almost unerringly blame the play tester: "The instructions were in the Pause menu! How could they miss the shining tutorial icon?" To the designer, clearly the problem was that the play tester was dumb or bad. Or maybe the designer will blame the situation: "I hate that we have to play test with an unfinished build." The designer's explanation is to assign blame to the character of the play tester or to the situation of the game.

When assigning reasons for human actions, be very aware of the knee-jerk reactions that everyone makes to assign behaviors as coming from the nature of the person rather than external elements. Perhaps in the previous example the tutorial really isn't obvious. Perhaps the game does need work. That's what you play test for in the first place!

All human beings tend to have some trouble attributing blame appropriately when something goes wrong. If the failure is their own, they take into account mitigating factors such as lag or bad controllers. Blame is spread out. But when observing someone else's failure, humans tend to ignore mitigating factors and assign all the blame to personal shortcomings. When I miss an easy shot, it's because of lag. When you miss an easy shot, it's because you're a lousy shot. These fundamental attribution errors need to be taken into account especially when analyzing results from play testing experiments.

Golden Ratio

The *Golden Ratio,* or the Golden Mean, is a term from mathematics and the arts wherein the ratio of the sum of the quantities to the larger quantity is equal to the ratio of the larger quantity to the smaller one. It is expressed algebraically as follows:

$$\frac{a+b}{a} = \frac{a}{b} \equiv \varphi$$

The Greek letter Phi represents the golden ratio. Its value is 1.61803398875. This value is quite common in architecture and is found in nature constantly. Found by the Greeks, the Golden Ratio has been used as a guideline in proportion ever since. The common expression of this is the Golden Rectangle wherein the shorter side of the rectangle equals a, and the longer side equals $a + b$.

As early as 450 B.C., the statues of the Parthenon were made to the Golden Ratio, as were many other features of the structure, and buildings today are still built with these proportions in mind.

Now, what has this to do with game design?

Just as artists use the Golden Mean to proportion their works, designers should keep this principle in mind when building items that rely on proportion. Whether using the Fibonacci sequence (which approaches the Golden Ratio asymptotically) to create a curve in balancing a progression or creating an interface, the Golden Mean should be observed or at least consulted.

For instance, in creating a rectangular game board, the proportions of the board should follow the Golden Ratio. This will provide an innately pleasing proportion for the player. If a designer is constructing a building in a game and wants the player to be inherently attracted to it, they should use the Golden Mean to create the building. Any item in the game that uses proportion in any way can have the Golden Ratio applied to it.

This can, of course, be flipped on its head. In order to make players feel uncomfortable with a building, dismiss or mess with the Golden Mean in creating its proportions. The player will feel discomfort and not even know why. This can be done on the level of the building as a whole, with a single room or with a hallway.

Similarly, when creating a user interface (UI), look to the Golden Mean for proportioning its elements. Elements that use this proportional guideline will feel comfortable and natural to the user. In order to create a sense of unease, create a UI that defies the Golden Ratio. The user will still engage with the UI but will feel uncomfortable without apparent reason.

Griefing

Samaritans are players who intentionally help other players for the social rewards. These players typically reach a mid-level of experience and then focus their time on assisting other players by healing them or helping them battle monsters from a distance. This is a massively multiplayer online (MMO) behavior that is not accounted for by Bartle's types, but it is seen repeatedly. These players are not being rewarded directly by the game for their behavior; instead they are being rewarded by the other players and the social ties and positive strokes the other players provide.

Diametrically opposed to the Samaritan is the griefer. The *griefer* derives pleasure from making life (the game) hard for other players. These players will do whatever they can think of to make other players unhappy and will effectively spoil the game experience for these players. Player killing is one of the original griefer behaviors. In this case, players discovered that instead of killing monsters, they can kill one another, take loot from corpses, and other delightful things like jumping on their corpses.

About 3 percent of all players fall into this category. They block players from entering structures (if collision programming allows this), they kill steal (come in at the last second to deliver the coup de grace and claim the corpse of a monster and the loot thereon as their own), and they go to all sorts of lengths to make other players unhappy.

Sometimes griefing is an art form. Players find an exploit (a loophole that allows them to effectively cheat in the game) and lay a careful path of IP addresses and pointers that lead to the head of a rival guild.

Griefers go to great lengths to cause misery to other players. On a Player Killer server, players may hang out at the spawn point of new players and kill them instantly when they appear in the world. After doing this two or three times, they may offer to let the player join their guild. So much for benign recruiting techniques. Another well-known example involved one group of players inside a walled city who piled up crafter good that could not be removed in front of the main gate. The only other gate, the "traitor's gate," was a single person wide and could only be used by one player at a time. When players tried to leave the city, a second group of players was waiting outside to kill each player as they exited. Thus the city was held hostage.

Occasionally, griefers grief the developers. For instance, in one game, a player found that they could take the moon from the sky, put it in their inventory, and keep it there, which messed with the skybox for everyone in the game and the developers in particular.

Even though griefers constitute a tiny fraction of players, they are still numerous. If a game has 1 million players, 3 percent still equals 30,000 players who are bent on destroying the game experience for the other 97 percent of the players. Strangely, griefers are very busy people and wreak more havoc than one would think could be accounted for in such small percentages.

One of the biggest problems with griefers is how one mitigates their behavior without rewarding them. For instance, giving them a negative reputation score is a reward for these players, like becoming one of the Most Wanted in the Wild West. Many developers agree that the best method for dealing with griefers when it is clear that they have no intention of changing their griefing ways is to simply ban them from the game permanently. While one may question the permanent loss of the player revenue, losing the revenue from griefers constitutes a small percentage of revenue, and letting them stay costs money for developers in the long run when their behavior results in endless streams of customer support complaints. The simplest, most direct, and cheapest way to handle these players is to ban them from the game.

Hype

In general, *Hype* simply refers to "something that the player is expecting based on other information." Similar to Cognitive Biases, the notion of Hype involves what players bring to the game mentally, emotionally, and psychologically. The information can be real or imagined and its delivery intentional or unwitting. Naturally, this can be a factor before the game is ever directly encountered. For instance, players may have a complicated set of expectations for what they will experience in the game as a result of exposure to marketing, prior games in the same franchise, or other games in the same genre. Hype isn't just a principle for use outside a game, however. Designers can also use it within a game to prime the player's beliefs and feelings as well.

The most traditional use of the word is in the purview of marketing. For example, telling people that an upcoming game is going to be a blockbuster is an establishment of Hype. Most people will have expectations of the game's art, complexity, and scope, sight unseen, simply because it is being talked about in those terms. Similar expectations can be adopted from information about genres ("shooter," "dungeon crawl"), settings ("fantasy," "space"), or even development studios (e.g., "a typical [development studio] game"). Saying, for example, "an epic, open-world, fantasy, roleplaying game from [huge studio]" will seed different expectations in a player's mind than "an abstract platformer from [indie startup]." People will likely infer which of the two games will have longer gameplay, better graphics, and a story-based narrative. Then they will bring those expectations with them when they sit down to play the game for the first time.

The key here is this: By simply having an expectation of something, people are likely to genuinely see and feel what it is that they expect—even if it is not there. In psychology, this is called a placebo, but it doesn't just work on sugar pills. If a player is told something in a game is beneficial, they are more likely to experience it as such. If a player's character acquires a magic weapon, for instance, the player may attribute some (or all!) of their subsequent successes to the purported benefits of the weapon over and above the weapon's actual abilities. You can magnify this false belief by including properties that have nothing at all to do with performance or mechanics—for example, impressive graphics, attention-grabbing effects, or in-game narrative mystique about the item.

On the other side of the proverbial coin is "nocebo"—when a player experiences something as detrimental, whether it has the power built into it to be detrimental or not, simply because that expectation was set up for them before they encountered that thing. This nocebo effect can have an impact on specific player experiences: "I am moving more slowly because I am wearing those muddy boots." Or it can impact an entire game experience: "That reviewer really hated this game, and I do too."

Often, aspects of Hype can be utilized by game designers to shunt the responsibility of crafting the player's perception of the world from a mechanic that is difficult to implement onto one that is much easier. For example, realistic combat artificial intelligence for shooter games is difficult to develop correctly. However, players are likely to believe that the AI is "smarter" on higher difficulty levels simply because the designers increase the amount of damage an enemy can take. Nothing changes in the decisions that the AI makes—they just don't die as quickly. The players experience a "smarter" enemy (rather than a "thicker" one, so to speak) because they believe in the Hype that a harder difficulty means more advanced opponents. In this case, the use of Hype would allow the developer to present an experience for the player they may not have been able to achieve through code because of restrictions on time or money.

Naturally, Hype has its down side. If artificially crafted expectations don't hold up, the user experience can come crashing down with surprising force when a player sees past it. At that point, the opposite effect may occur—the player may believe something is worse than it actually is because they are now suspicious or resentful and the placebo has become a nocebo.

Players can experience the same game in entirely different ways depending on what they believe about it. Marketing hype and other factors set the stage before they ever begin playing.

Instant vs. Delayed Gratification

"Mr. Smith, are you sure you want to purchase this video game for $60? Tomorrow, we are having a sale ... buy one get one free!"

People work to earn money. They earn money to pay their bills from consumer purchases they have made. The video game industry is leading the way in profits from such sales. Video games use technology as their platform and it is advancing at an alarming rate, giving the world more content on a daily basis. The content is also getting to consumers faster. Due to this, societies are becoming hungrier for information, living lives faster, and losing interest in their purchases sooner, thus creating an instant gratification society. Prior to the major advances in technology, such as the Internet and smartphones, people were willing to work hard for items that they wanted, and so they gave those items more respect and consideration, and admired them more upon receiving them.

Instant and Delayed Gratification can be found in most parts of our hurry-up-and-wait lives. Hungry people rush to get food, just to wait in lines to order, or to wait at a table to be served, and to wait again for beverages prior to eating. In the game industry, this can be seen as well during the "opening night" a game is sold. If a game is being sold in a store at midnight, a line forms around the store hours before it even opens, just so the customers can be the first to purchase the game the minute it is available. The amount of sales on that opening day (instant gratification seekers) can deter others from purchasing said game (delayed gratification seekers) due to poor reviews, games being sold out, and because the Internet hosts large amounts of screenshots and information about the game almost immediately, thus spoiling it.

From a developer perspective, this behavior is added information they need while designing a game. The instant gratification players tend to rush through the games so they can get to multiplayer modes, unlock more powerful items to sell, or take advantage of newer players. Those players will often either help or hinder sales by promoting the game online with good word of mouth or bad. However, the instant players are usually *extrinsically motivated* and enjoy the game less than the delayed gratification players. The delayed players will make informed decisions based on purchase price, game reviews, and online content. They will also spend more time exploring all aspects of the game due to being *intrinsically motivated* to play the game.

From a game designer standpoint, there is a lot to take away from this difference in behaviors and many game types have been created with it in mind. Multiplayer modes are for people who want to jump right in and play some aspect of the game, while story mode takes a player through a journey. Roleplaying games (RPGs) and turn-based games are tailored to delayed gratification due to players immersing themselves in character customizations, level development, and abilities upgrades, which can take hours to perfect, just so they can experience two minutes of action.

Fun and immersion are other reasons game designers need to take these two types of players into account. If a player obtains an overpowered item too soon, they feel that they did not earn it and will exploit it more often, whereas if a player obtains an item too late in the game, then the game might have been too complicated for them to enjoy. A player may also lose their sense of immersion if they walk through an abandoned and destroyed warehouse and find that all the doors are locked and they have no method to open them. But a player can also lose their immersion if all the doors are unlocked instead. During Play Testing, designers can get a feel for a balanced approach to the instant and delayed game play styles—that is, players who check all doors instantly, those who wait to find the key to unlock the doors, and those who wait for something in the game to tell them that they are able to open the doors. Although finding the perfect balance is hard, there are ways to help balance it.

Visual clues, non-playable character (NPC) dialogue, sound cues, and story lines can set the speed for each level, for quests, item drops, item pickups, upgrading, and more, and it is good to measure and tweak those throughout the game to keep things fresh. This is also where gamification comes into play. When developers add gamified elements such as leader boards, special power-ups after reaching specific item levels, and badge rewards, they help players keep themselves immersed in games so they can unlock achievements, thus adding to their delayed gratification needs and enhancing their gaming experience.

A few gaming traits for each behavior include the following:

Instant Gratification: This type of gamer is aggressive, is fast, dies more in games, likes to upgrade more often, takes the easy route, plays offensively, likes forward moving games, does not like traveling back to areas they have already played, plays more games over a shorter amount of time, makes poor choices in longer games, plays by trial and error, gets frustrated easily when they cannot get past a specific part of a level, and has good reflexes and timing during game movement.

Delayed Gratification: This type of gamer plays defensively, stays alive longer, buys and plays fewer games but plays each for longer periods of time, enjoys working toward a goal, plays most aspects of a game, uses strategy, plans for upgrades, makes choices that affect other parts of the game and not just the level or enemy at hand, and thinks clearly during puzzle elements.

Krug's First Law of Usability

Steve Krug is widely known for his Three Laws of Usability. The foundation of these laws is his assertion that people do not use interfaces the way designers expect them to. Instead of reading directions, or carefully weighing and understanding all their options before making a choice, users scan an interface for the first, most immediately useful-seeming link; then they select it, hoping to get information they can use right away (see Satisficing vs. Optimizing). They may continue down this first, "good enough" path for as long as their actions (often clicking links) appear to bring them closer to their destination. When they no longer feel they are getting what they want, they may back out the way they came in and try another path, or they may simply quit. To avoid frustration and abandonment, design interfaces specifically and games generally with these user behaviors as guiding principles. Designers should prioritize simple navigation and clear feedback so the game leaves a positive, lasting impression.

Krug lays out three laws, but his First Law of Usability is the most profound. He states it simply: Don't make me think.

Since so many people will avoid reading (or even looking for) directions, a good interface must be intuitive, self-evident, obvious, and self-explanatory. There are two keys to achieving this.

- **Simplicity.** Every element of an interface should be boiled down to its bare essentials. Users will simply skip lengthy descriptions, obtuse in-jokes, and clever metaphors (see Details). They want what they want—not what they are told they want by some overbearing designers who think they know better. So focus on clarity and simplicity on heads-up displays (HUDs), scoreboards, rewards, and the Core Gameplay Loop. The places where players directly interface with a game—where they put their hands and their clicks—should be so simple and straightforward that it becomes transparent in the experience. If players have to think about where to click next, or how to hold the cards correctly, or which buttons to use on the controller, they will not be thinking about how fun your game is. Rather, they will be thinking the opposite (see Working Memory).
- **Consistency.** The second hallmark of good interface design is consistency. Although players do crave and appreciate a certain amount of surprise in their game experience, they don't enjoy it in the interface. Buttons with the same function should have consistent placement on the screen, general aesthetics, and affordances (see Affordance Cues). If two things look alike, players will assume they are alike. The corollary to this is that if two things look different, players will assume they are different. So if the Replay button is usually yellow, players will assume all yellow buttons involve restarting the game. Changing the color of the Replay button every time a player sees it will only frustrate them and drive them to quit. This holds true in all aspects of the game, not just the user interface. If two enemies look or act the same, players will assume they are identical (see Gestalt); they won't stop to think about subtle differences or context.

Ultimately, the thing to remember is that designers should not require the player to figure out what to do or where to go; as the rule says, if they have to think about it, they're already gone.

Keep in mind that this does not mean removing challenges, mystery, or puzzles. It merely means clearly communicating to players what the end goals are, making them transparent. For example, a player encounters a room with no obvious exits: Is it a puzzle to be solved, or a dead end to be avoided? Don't make them think. Make it clear which is which. That way they can get to the fun part—either puzzle solving or exploring, depending on the answer to the question.

Krug's other two laws of usability are also important for interface design but have fewer applications in a more general sense.

- Rule #2: It doesn't matter how many times I have to click, as long as each click is a mindless, unambiguous choice (see Risk Assessment and Satisficing vs. Optimizing).
- Rule #3: Get rid of half the words. Then get rid of half of what's left (see Doubling and Halving). Many people feel some friction when encountering words, especially a large collection of them. Reading requires thinking and ... well, see Rule #1.

Music and Dopamine

Many people have experienced chills while listening to a piece of music. It is a strange, yet surprisingly pleasurable sensation. This feeling is brought on by dopamine being released in the brain. Studies have found that listening to music can trigger such a release.

Dopamine is a neurotransmitter that creates feelings of pleasure or enjoyment when released. It ties heavily into the brain's reward system, which releases dopamine as a response to a variety of biologically desired stimuli, such as food and sex, as well as during *reward prediction*—when a person or animal is anticipating a reward (e.g., the feelings of joy you get when you hear you just won a prize, or what Pavlov's dog felt whenever he heard a bell).

As previously mentioned, music can trigger dopamine release; however, not just any beat or melody will do. Dopamine receptors are known to adapt quickly to repetition, which is why a song that is too repetitive can be perceived as boring. The brain can perceive new, exciting changes introduced through a song as a kind of reward. In fact, the brain has been observed releasing more dopamine when the reward is even greater than what the subject expected. Anticipation also helps facilitate a larger reward response. Eating at your favorite restaurant every day is nowhere near as satisfying as when you come back to it after a four-month gap. This same effect is used in music to varying degrees. Classical music often has motifs that appear in a song multiple times throughout a piece—sometimes in a slightly different and surprising way (different arrangement, major to minor, etc.). In modern music, this is most easily observable with a song's chorus, which is often considered the most enjoyable (or catchy) part of a song; the verse, bridge, and other parts are purposely more subdued and less dynamic, so the song can build up anticipation until it hits the listener with the bombastic chorus they've been anxiously awaiting. If a song were only four minutes of the chorus, it would have less of an impact on the listener and less of an effect on their dopamine levels.

How does this relate to video games? A good game designer should be concerned with not only creating robust and interesting gameplay, but maintaining a firm command of the player's emotions. Music and sound design are pivotal components in accomplishing that. Similar motifs (melodies, arrangements, tempos, etc.) can be used to great results if there is enough variation between repetitions of them and/or the tension and anticipation build in the music. Keeping the player's attention is another important aspect of game design, and a dynamic soundtrack can greatly contribute to this.

Although repetition should not be vilified when designing music, the designer should make sure that the composition tries to maintain a balance between small, gradual changes (e.g., the same three-chord progression, but with slightly different accents on the drums, and different instruments chiming in and out), large, drastic changes, and returning to common themes or parts after anticipation builds up. Small melodies or *themes* triggered by in-game events, such as opening a treasure chest in The Legend of Zelda or beating a level in Super Mario Bros., also help these events play into reward prediction. Performing these activities, especially when pleasant music is tied to them, causes the player to associate these events with something highly enjoyable. The release of dopamine and the enjoyable sensations felt as a result are some of the main reasons people play video games, and music is a very integral component.

Pacing

If an experience simply repeats one action over and over again—even if that action is a steady stream of slapstick comedy or shocking scares—the emotion it engenders is only boredom. The best games (and comedians and horror movies) give the audience breathing room between thrills. There needs to be areas of sanctuary where the audience is lulled into a sense of security during a point and has time to breathe before they are thrust into the action once more. This ebb and flow in the low points and high points is what defines *pacing* and can be the key to maintaining an audience's engagement (see Interest Curve).

In Western entertainment, pacing is said to be built upon these basic building blocks:

- **Tempo:** The beat/rhythm/timing of the current level of action being encountered by the protagonist (Player).
- **Tension:** The mood of the level or perceived danger felt by the protagonist (Player).
- **Threat or Suspense:** The threat of danger to the protagonist (Player).
- **Movement Impetus:** The willingness of the protagonist (Player) to continue moving forward.

Each of these elements overlap, but if Play Testing shows there is a problem with a game's pacing, check each of these areas individually for problems.

Frustratingly enough, this is about as far as Western traditions go in describing good pacing. The creator is expected to have an intuitive sense of good pacing, and tune the above elements until it "feels" right.

Fortunately, creative people all over the world have been pondering this problem of pacing entertainment for centuries. Zeami Motokyo, a master of Japanese Noh theatre in the 14th century, formulated an approach for ideal pacing. He called it *Jo-Ha-Kyu* (序破急, literally "start-break-rapid") and it consists of the following:

- **Jo (start):** This is the start of the sequence. Here, the energy of the scene/action/subject is very calm and restrained, but slowly building up.
- **Ha (break):** The energy of the Jo has built up tension, and it finally "breaks" suddenly and rapidly into more intense action. This moment is sometimes called the reversal or main plot twist in Western techniques.
- **Kyu (rapid):** As the energy of the Ha continues on, more tension builds until there is a final motion that dispels all of the energy and tension built up to this point. This can be viewed as the Climax in regards to Western storytelling.

The visual that helps explain this concept is a stream of water. At the beginning (Jo), a stream is small and pretty. It moves along at a good clip, but there is not a lot of pressure. As the stream goes along its way (Ha), it grows and becomes a rushing river. There are twists and turns until finally it breaks over an edge. And then the water rushes dramatically (Kyu) down in a waterfall, inspiring great awe. What's key is the idea that the momentum continues. The water pauses peacefully in a pool at the bottom of the waterfall (Jo), then begins the cycle again.

Jo-Ha-Kyu communicates the sense of movement and the satisfying feeling of a well-paced story or experience. It describes how to avoid getting reviews with vague comments such as, "The game dragged on in parts. I got bored." It describes a dynamic way of moving things along, and not just remaining a static map.

Zeami Motokyo believed that all things in nature exhibit some form of this pattern, and that it should be used extensively within the arts, especially in Noh theatre. There it is utilized in the movements of the actors, the flow of the dialogue and music, as well as the structure of scenes.

Jo-Ha-Kyu is often instinctively implemented within a "level" structure of a video game. The level starts out relatively easy, with introductory opponents (*Jo*). The difficulty in puzzles or opponents increases steadily and plot twists are introduced (*Ha*) until the difficulty significantly jumps up as the player encounters a boss fight (*Kyu*), and once defeated, the level ends, and the pattern begins again in the next level.

One particularly excellent example of *Jo-Ha-Kyu* in games is Space Invaders—the gameplay starts out calm, the difficulty slowly rises in the middle, and the end becomes very frantic before resolving once again (temporarily) into calm.

Just as in Noh theater, even small-scale actions in games demonstrate *Jo-Ha-Kyu* pacing: Mega Man's charge buster, Ryu's hadouken, and many fatalities in Mortal Kombat are paced in this manner. In the NES classic Punch-Out, as the characters waiver back and forth (*Jo*), they perform some form of action or wind up to telegraph their move (*Ha*), and finally release their punch (*Kyu*) on Little Mac. No matter the scale, *Jo-Ha-Kyu* can be the solution to most pacing problems.

"Jo..."

"Ha...."

"KYUUUUU!!!

Problem-Solving Approaches

So much of game design is about solving problems. Whether it's the problem of how to make a functional game into a fun game or how to get a project funded, problem solving is the number one task on the designer's daily to-do list. They tackle problems from the other direction as well—inventing and creating interesting problems (aka challenges) for players to solve and tuning those problems so their solutions relate to each other and have a logical progression (see Balancing and Tuning).

Game designers need to clearly understand how humans go about solving problems. This can help them more quickly write design documents and resolve gameplay problems, but it is essential that they also be able to anticipate players' problem-solving behaviors when they are managing difficulty levels and player engagement. Designers must walk the tight rope of nudging their players into successful problem-solving strategies without being too obvious (see Advance Organizers, Hype, and Cognitive Biases).

See the appendix at the end of the book for an extensive list of problem-solving methods.

For every problem, there are many different approaches to take when solving that problem. Make a list, draw a chart, find the weakest link, writing the problem as numbers. Check the appendix of this book for many more suggestions.

Satisficing vs. Optimizing

Classical economic theory says that people make decisions through a process—either conscious or unconscious—that goes something like this:

1. Make a list of all possible outcomes.
2. Assign each possible outcome a probability of happening.
3. Assign each possible choice a value based on its outcome.
4. Then choose the optimal outcome.

Take buying a dessert as an example. A hot fudge sundae provides $3 of happiness and costs $1, whereas a banana split provides $1 of happiness and costs $2. The sundae is then the obvious choice because it provides more value and optimizes the outcome, where more value is received than is spent. Classical economic theory suggests that people will optimize their options and always choose hot fudge sundaes.

However, real humans don't make decisions this way. It is often too time-consuming, complicated, or inconvenient to gather all the information and appropriately optimize every variable. Maybe in special cases, like a splurge on a dessert, people will weigh everything carefully. But take something that everyone does every day: choosing what to wear. Nobody creates a spreadsheet listing everything in their wardrobe sorted out by temperature appropriateness, fashion trends, a clash matrix, or a list of what they wore for the last seven days before they get dressed in the morning. This kind of labor-intensive, optimizing solving for the perfect solution just doesn't happen most of the time for most everyday decisions.

Instead, people do what is called *satisficing*. They pick the first satisfactory result based on essential rules of thumb, or requirements that get them close enough to the optimal solution. Using the dessert examples, a person might choose the banana split if it is easier to reach or becomes available sooner. It gets the chooser close enough to their desired outcome. In choosing what to wear, people often make their decisions based on a few simple rules, like what is clean and has worked as an outfit in the past.

The benefit of satisficing is that it is so much easier for a person to do than optimizing. When creating games, don't force players to optimize what can be satisficed.

Here are some examples where satisficing vs. optimizing enter into the game design process:

- Players will approach puzzles and challenges in games often using satisficing to find the fastest, easiest solution, rather than optimizing at great length. For instance, if it is easier to look up a walkthrough video on the Internet than to solve an extremely difficult puzzle by themselves, players will often take this shortcut and avoid fully experiencing the game as it was intended. This isn't a matter of cheating, it is simply that the players are weighing how valuable their time and attention are.
- Game developers are always working within constraints (see Pick Two: Fast, Cheap, Good) where optimizing may not be possible, but satisficing is a very good way to decide which features make it into the final game, how much polish a particular element gets, and how much time is spent making the game perfect, rather than just good enough.
- In games involving multiplayer cooperation, players often choose to satisfice rather than optimize their personal outcome if it will ultimately work to improve the chances of achieving the shared goal, especially if it is obvious that there is no way for an optimal outcome for all players (see Nash Equilibrium).

Personality traits do enter into this process. Some players enjoy optimizing (see Bartle's Player Types) and avoid satisficing. So, as always, it's important to understand the target market. Optimizing vs. Satisficing algorithms have been developed in the fields of economics, decision theory, and game theory. It was developed and popularized by Herbert Simon in the middle of the 20th century.

When choosing between two options, such as these desserts, people rarely weigh every possible variable involved to carefully optimize the results. Rather, they rely on rules of thumb and obvious benefits, such as focusing on the cost and happiness variables, which satisfy and get close enough to the optimal result without a lengthy deliberation.

Sense of Accomplishment

Few things in life are as rewarding as a sense of accomplishment. This can be seen on a baby's face when they first pull themselves up to a standing position, or on a Bingo player's when they shout "Bingo!" A sense of accomplishment will drive a player to continue in a game, and the lack thereof can drive them away.

A sense of accomplishment will follow naturally at the end of a task that was satisfying to complete. This may be a task that the player has found to be somewhat difficult or challenging. The extreme example of this is called *fiero,* that feeling of overcoming an obstacle that was a large challenge; it usually results in pumping one's fist in the air or shooting up both fists in victory (see Lazzaro's Four Keys to Fun). These moments in gameplay are key to keeping a player engaged and relating to the game context without getting frustrated, bored, or overwhelmed (see Interest Curve).

Think of the sense of accomplishment as being like rat food pellets. When experimenting with rats, researchers often use food pellets to reward the rats for tasks, such as pushing levers or completing mazes (see Skinner Box). Those small rewards keep the rats motivated to perform the next tasks researchers set before them. Without that regular, positive reinforcement through a sense of accomplishment, players will refuse to continue in a game. When the designer supplies a steady stream of accomplishable goals that are somewhat challenging (see Balancing and Tuning), the player has a sense of challenge and reward that is more satisfying than a simple task that is not challenging, even if it is accompanied by the same reward. The importance of the challenge is key to the feeling of satisfaction (see Koster's Theory of Fun).

A feeling of pleasure and fulfillment is key to the sense of accomplishment, and that requires real effort. A simple, single mouse click for a reward is not very satisfying. A relatively complex task followed by a significant reward will usually deliver where the single mouse click does not. One provides a tension, which is relieved by the completion; the other simply lacks any tension whatsoever.

Balancing simple and complex tasks is part of the art of game creation. If every task is a challenge, the player may get overwhelmed or discouraged. On the other hand, if every task is too simple, the player will grow bored. By supplying a good balance (see Balancing and Tuning) of easy and complex tasks, a sense of accomplishment can be continuous and sustained. It is a delicate process to maintain equilibrium between challenge and boredom (see Flow). If balanced properly, a sense of accomplishment ensues and player engagement increases (see Interest Curve).

One behavioral model often used in teaching (see Koster's Theory of Fun) attempts to dissect exactly how to deliver a sense of accomplishment. It is known as ARCS and is championed by John M. Keller. The letters stand for

- **Attention.** *Attention* in this context refers to the effort and willingness on the part of the audience or student.
- **Relevance.** *Relevance* here refers to the use of terminology and examples the audience is familiar with already. Using elements the audience (or players) is already familiar with to explain the new material or skill demonstrates exactly how the material is relevant to previous experience.
- **Confidence.** *Confidence* refers to the process of providing positive outcomes and feedback so that people understand how well they have succeeded at assimilating the new skill or information.
- **Satisfaction.** *Satisfaction* comes in the form of reward for achieving the learning; this can be as simple as praise or as complex as fiero.

The ARCS model hinges on the idea that people can be motivated to learn because the knowledge is valuable, and the job of the instructor (or game) is to demonstrate that value in easy-to-understand terms. Then when the player (or student) realizes they have acquired this new, valuable skill, they are filled with satisfaction—or a sense of accomplishment.

An easily conquered enemy or effortlessly acquired skill will never provide the same rush that comes from a sense of true accomplishment.

Spatial Awareness

Spatial awareness is being cognizant of one's position in space in relation to the surrounding objects and environment. It mostly comes into play in video games that depict virtual worlds or spaces. Some board games use it as well, but they depend heavily on players' imaginations to make the effects work. The idea that architecture and environment can influence human experience and emotion seems counterintuitive at first, until closer inspection into real examples makes it more clear.

Each of the following categories describes a real phenomenon that people experience viscerally and architects have been consciously exploiting for centuries. What works in real buildings and cities also works in virtual ones.

Positive Impacts on Human Psyche

- **Prospect-Refuge.** Prospect-Refuge is a concept on two sides of the same coin. On the one hand, people show a marked preference for environments with unobstructed views (prospects). Some instinctive part of the human mind feels safer knowing it can see or hear any threat nearby. So encountering a space that has wide-open views, such as the top of a mountain, is deeply appealing and satisfying.

  On the other hand, they also prefer areas of concealment and retreat (refuge). That same deep part of the human mind enjoys "safe" environments like hiding places and dens. If that instinctive paranoia is satisfied by being able to see threats coming from a distance, it is equally happy to find itself in an enclosed area where no threats can get in.

- **Cathedral Effect.** The Cathedral Effect is a remarkable relationship between the height of a ceiling and how people think. People who find themselves in a room with very high ceilings are prone to do more concrete and detail-oriented thinking. They think better, the higher the ceiling is. The effect's name comes from how it has been used over the centuries in the architecture of religious spaces. People feel a sense of elevation and clarity in places with high ceilings.

Negative Impacts on Human Psyche

- **Agoraphobic Spaces.** Agoraphobic spaces are related to the Prospect concept described earlier, but agoraphobia is a pathological fear of such vast, large, open areas. To tap into this feeling of anxiety, provide a sense of vulnerability along with the vast views. Mechanically these environments may have a total lack of, or extremely limited, options for the player in which to seek refuge and take cover from ranged attacks. The dynamics of these spaces set up enemy encounters such as snipers, bosses, aerial attacks, and distant mortars.

- **Claustrophobic Spaces.** Claustrophobic spaces are aesthetically narrow, constricted areas that feed into player anxiety when they perceive that they are trapped in a small space with a serious threat. Mechanically, these environments also usually include multiple hiding places and the potential for secret entrances. Conversely, sometimes the most straightforward approach is the best. This means literally trapping the player in sight of the enemy. Either of these approaches feeds into the fear players feel as the threat is closing in.

Deep and Complex Worlds

Of course, the real world is made up of a variety of these architectural approaches and not just a single, monotonous type of space. Combining a variety of environments can push players through a linear experience (see Wayfinding) in a calculated way and provide interesting adventures. Here are some established tactics for making this variety of environments work together effectively:

- **Defensible Spaces.** Defensible spaces are a balance. They are neither too constricted nor too open. Mechanically these environments provide easy access to both prospect and refuge. Aesthetically, these environments contain architectural features that convey the perception of value and ownership. The dynamics of these spaces afford the player the perception of proprietorship, control, and a sense of empowerment over the enemies in these territories through their easy access to advantageous locations.

- **Lighting Design.** As with all the other principles listed here, lighting design is a discipline with years of research behind it. A short summary here can barely do it justice. Basically, lighting is a powerful tool for manipulating the environment. For example, humans feel safer and happier in lighting that mimics daylight. Yet, they also feel drawn to a warm, yellowish glow similar to fire—especially in an overall darker room. Lighting can also focus attention on a particular corner or space using brightness and color variations.

The human psyche feels relieved, safe, and elated in environments with wide-open vistas of surrounding terrain. This is the "prospect" side of the Prospect-Refuge concept.

Time Dilation

In Einstein's theory of relativity, *time dilation* is the term used for a difference of elapsed time between two events as measured by separate observers either moving relative to each other or differently situated from gravitational masses. Essentially, time is not only *perceived* differently by the two observers, it is actually different for them.

Although literal relativistic time dilation is not regularly experienced by human beings, perceptual time dilation is very real and occurs often in games. This experience can be described as time "dragging" or "flying" during any activity. The expression that "time flies when you're having fun" is an expression of the perception of time dilation. The feeling that the last hour of work on a Friday is dragging is another common perception of time dilation. In both of these cases, time has not changed at all, objectively speaking; an hour still takes precisely one hour to pass. What can change is our perception of how time passes.

Oftentimes, when immersed in a game, a player can look up and be surprised to see that an hour or more has passed when the player feels that only a few minutes have passed. This time dilation experience is similar to that which occurs during Flow. Presumably, the player has even achieved flow, wherein challenge is at just the right level to balance frustration and engagement.

Players of the game Tetris often experience time dilation, accidentally spending hours playing when they only intended to play for minutes. This occurrence of time dilation, where the player perceives time to be passing more quickly than the clock, accounts for what happens in many of the best games. Like any pursuit that is fun, time passes quickly.

When play testing a game, players may find that time drags by; this is, of course, the inverse of what the game maker hopes for when they are designing the game. If the design is good, and is *fun*, time should dilate in a positive way rather than in a negative way.

Many times, when playing a complex RPG, players get bogged down in screens of narrative, pushing the next button with ennui or outright boredom. For these players, time is dilating in a negative way. If players complain of time dragging, this is a sure sign that the game maker has not found the elusive fun game designers seek to create. Time should, in fact, fly if the player is having fun.

Working Memory

Psychologists classify memory into two types. *Long-term memory* is accessed when someone picks up the controls for Super Mario Bros. and flawlessly remembers how everything works even if they haven't played the game for a decade. *Working memory* is the memory we use when someone tells us their phone number or how to use the controls for a new game.

All memories are stored first in working memory; then they are moved to long-term memory if our brain realizes we may need to hold onto this information for more than a few minutes.

Working memory is not very robust. A convenient rule of thumb is that the average person only holds four things at a time in their working memory. This can seem very limiting when introducing players to a new control schema or memory puzzle. Fortunately, there are ways to make the most out of those four items. For instance, when people try to remember a phone number, they don't remember each number individually, but as what psychologists call *chunks*. The area code is one chunk, the exchange is the next chunk, and the last four digits are the last chunk. So the working memory is only holding onto three chunks, plus the name of the person associated with the number. The total amount of information is 10 digits plus a name, but working memory is usually not too tasked.

Another limitation on working memory is time. If new information is not accessed or used repeatedly and quickly, the information will be lost.

When designing games, be cognizant of the limitations of working memory. Attempting to teach players nine new things during a tutorial will probably never work. There simply isn't room in their working memory for them to integrate that much information all at once. Whatever they learned first will be pushed out by whatever they learned last, and when they move from the tutorial to the actual game, they will not have the information they need to feel successful. A better approach is to unveil new mechanics or controls at a regular pace throughout a game. By doing this, the game waits for a player to internalize an instruction into long-term memory before it taxes his working memory with a new idea.

This relates to a concept called the Learning Curve. Games with steep learning curves often push working memory to its limits, asking players to learn many new things before they can feel comfortable in the game. Examples of games with these kinds of front-loaded learning include Dwarf Fortress, Dark Souls, Eve Online, or League of Legends. Games with shallow learning curves do not necessarily have fewer features or depth, but they put less strain on working memory. Examples of such games include most Facebook social games, many racing games, and NBA Jam.

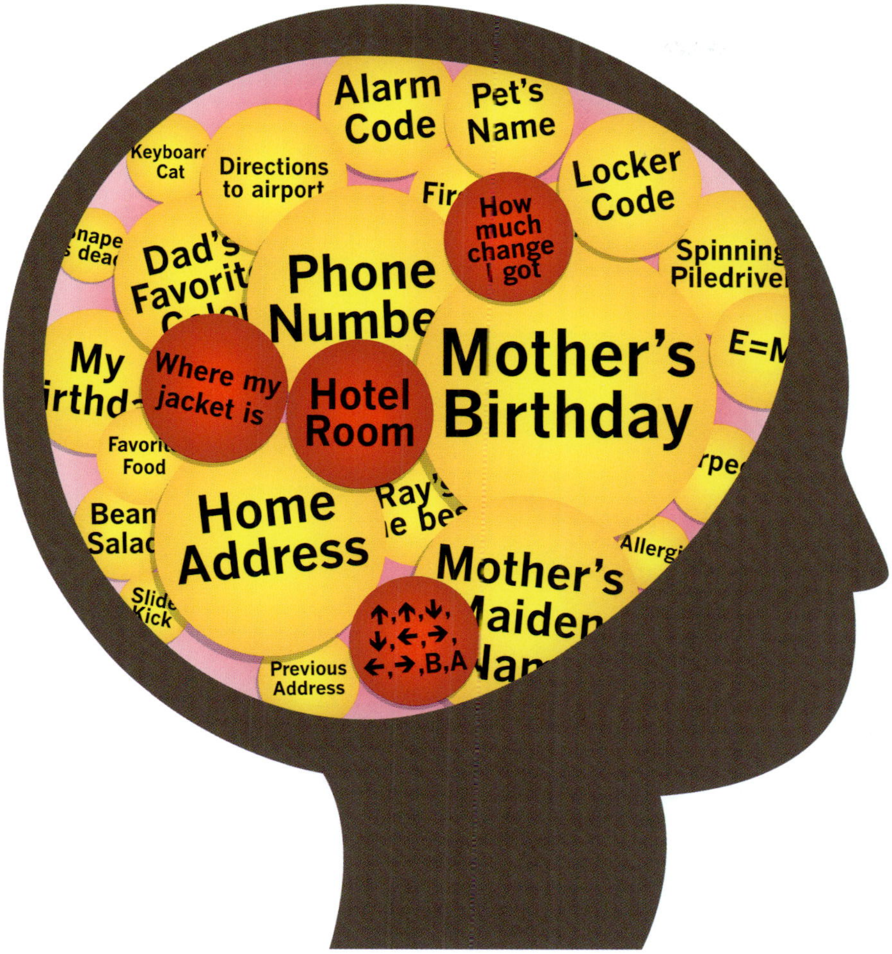

LONG TERM MEMORY

WORKING MEMORY

New information is stored in working memory as "chunks." If it is not used quickly and repeatedly, it will not be moved to long-term memory and will be replaced when additional information is encountered.

Zero-Sum Game

A Zero-Sum Game is one in which winnings are perfectly balanced against losses. If there is a single possible outcome for which the sum is not zero, then the game cannot be Zero-Sum. For example, Poker is a Zero-Sum Game, as every player's winnings are exactly matched by another player's losses. There is no way to win more than the bet amount and no way to lose more than the bet amount. Because the win/loss ratio is fixed, all outcomes in Zero-Sum Games are Pareto Optimal (see Outcomes: Pareto Optimality).

Rock, Paper, Scissors is another example of a Zero-Sum Game; for each throw, exactly one player wins and exactly one player loses (unless there is a draw). This table shows that the total payoff for every game of Rock, Paper, Scissors is equal to zero:

	Rock	Paper	Scissors
Rock	Draw (0, 0)	Paper Wins (–1, 1)	Rock Wins (1, –1)
Paper	Paper Wins (1, –1)	Draw (0, 0)	Scissors Win (–1, 1)
Scissors	Rock Wins (–1, 1)	Scissors Win (1, –1)	Draw (0, 0)

The Prisoner's Dilemma, on the other hand, is not a Zero-Sum Game, since both players may "win" together or "lose" together and the total amount of time spent in prison does not average zero (in fact, a result of zero years spent in prison is only ever possible for one player):

		Prisoner B	
		Cooperate	**Refuse**
Prisoner A	**Cooperate**	Each receives 6 months (–1, –1)	A goes free; B serves 5 years (0, –10)
	Refuse	B goes free; A serves 5 years (–10, 0)	Each receives 2 years (–4, –4)

Zero-Sum Games may be solved with a Nash Equilibrium, or a *mixed strategy* can be used. The mixed strategy overcomes the inherent balance in Zero-Sum Games played one time by increasing the minimum payoff amount over a series of plays. In the example of Rock, Paper, Scissors, a mixed strategy would be to randomly select a throw for each game, resulting in an average of 1/3 wins, 1/3 draws, and 1/3 losses. This is superior to the minimum average value of –1 for each individual game, so the advantage goes to the mixed strategy in the long run, which allows both players to achieve success a minimum of 33 percent of the time. This type of strategy is also called a *minimax*, since it increases the minimum payoff that the player will receive (see Minimax and Maximin).

Non-Zero-Sum Games are not as clean as Zero-Sum Games because multiple players may win or lose, or all players may win or lose. Strategies for Zero-Sum Games may not apply well to complex Non-Zero-Sum Games, such as economic or psychosocial models. Global thermonuclear war is a good example of a Non-Zero-Sum Game in which all participants are likely to lose and none to be better off than they were before the "game" was played.

John von Neumann and Oskar Morgenstern's research in the mid-20th century showed that every Zero-Sum Game has a minimax solution, and that a mixed strategy of randomization always improves the minimum payoff, even if there is no Nash Equilibrium.

Appendix: Methods to Solving Problems

Methods for solving problems have been studied in many different fields. Here is an extensive list, but it is not comprehensive. It draws from a variety of fields and disciplines and is meant to serve as inspiration for further study of problem solving as a discipline as well as to suggest specific approaches to solving the problems of an in-progress game design.

Also keep in mind that many of these approaches are best used when combined or iteratively. For instance, once a problem space has been defined, sometimes it becomes clear that the next step is to find an expert who can help. Or, if following the money turns up nothing but dead ends, perhaps try this method again, but this time, follow the thread of who is exerting power to get the answer.

Make a list.

A common way of tackling a large project or problem is to break it down into sections or steps, list these steps in order, then simply start crossing things off the list as they are accomplished or solved.

Find a pattern.

Many problems include hidden patterns within their structure or echo patterns found elsewhere. If these patterns are identified, they can often be analyzed and managed, mitigating, if not solving, the problem.

Work backward.

Without a clear vision of the destination, it is extremely difficult to reach it. So sometimes the best problem-solving approach is to clearly define what an ideal "solved state" looks like; then deconstruct and reverse engineer it, connecting it back to the original "problem state." This way a roadmap to success has been clearly laid out, and no one has to cast around blindly from the middle of the problem.

Make a table.

If a problem or the data involved in it can be rephrased or reorganized into a table, often solutions become clearer. Tables force elements to be classified as they are grouped together into rows or columns, and relationships between elements can become clear as they are juxtaposed or juggled. This can take a simple form, as in speeding up a too-slow shopping trip by grouping items together that are likely to be found in the same aisle, or it can be as complicated as deductive logic puzzles. These puzzles use specific types of tables to identify missing information, as in truth tables and solution matrices where relationships become clear as roles are matched to individuals. Think of those word problems where someone's child's brother is John Doe's uncle, and your job is to figure out who owns the parrot based on how John is related to Eli, who sold the parrot to his niece.

Draw a picture.

Looking at a problem in a new way can often bring solutions to light. Sometimes making the problem into a concrete thing, using images, is all it takes to identify a solution. Other times, detailed schematics can help create efficient plans, as in technical blueprints for a new building, which can solve the problem of how much brick to purchase. Either way, the act of translating a problem into a new system of thought or a new way of communicating about it can be a powerful problem-solving approach.

Guess and check, aka the scientific method.

The heart of the scientific method is the same as a more casually named problem-solving approach known as guess and check. That is, make an educated guess about what the solution to the problem will look like, then run experiments to find out if the guess is close to correct or invalid.

It's important to note that this method is iterative. Almost no guess (or hypothesis) is absolutely correct. Usually when it is measured something is missing or confusing, and the process can be used again to make a new guess, which can once again be checked for accuracy.

Follow the money.

When faced with a mystery or confusing event in the real world, the problem-solving approach used by detectives and journalists is often some variation on "follow the money." That is, carefully analyzing who benefits from the problematic situation as it stands often sheds light on any mystery and suggests ways to root it out. Money and motive don't always have to be the thread, though. Often the act of focusing on one element and clearly defining that element's position throughout the problem space can help untangle otherwise jumbled disasters.

Make a flowchart.

Most useful when trying to solve a dynamic problem or to hit a moving target, flowcharts help clarify and visualize process and causality. No game design document is complete without at least one flowchart.

Reword the problem.

Sometimes cognitive biases can lock us in to one way of viewing a problem, thereby obfuscating the solution. Simply finding new words to describe the problem can be enough. This is essentially the definition of a riddle—a simple statement reworded into something obscure and surprising. And in this case, if it works one way, it often works the other. Things that look obscure and surprising can sometimes become mundane and eminently solvable when put into simpler or clearer words.

Define the problem space.

Going off on tangents and ending up in dead ends can seriously delay or impede problem solving in general. After they clearly define what exactly the problem is, and what it is not, those working on the problem can focus their efforts in useful directions rather than wandering off down unrelated though interesting paths.

Solve a similar problem first.

Sometimes there can seem like no way to solve a problem, but if the team tackles a related problem instead, an approach for the insolvable problem will present itself. For instance, balancing a national budget can seem like an impossible task, but balancing a household budget with fewer zeros appended to the end of the numbers is easier to grasp. Balancing the household budget uses similar principles on a smaller scale and can suggest methods for tackling the larger problem.

Brainstorm.

This classic problem-solving technique involves coming up with as many solutions as possible, whether they are viable, likely, or even especially relevant. The act of random creativity can generate surprisingly useful results (see Brainstorming Methods).

Come at it sideways.

Humans instinctively approach things from the ends: They look at the beginning of creation or the last sputtering moment. Especially when problem solving, it is easy to get hyperfocused on the point of the spear or the most exciting or inflammatory part of the problem. Yet, if an attack is made on the middle of the problem, sometimes the whole thing crumbles. Similarly, a stealth approach is sometimes better than tackling something head-on. Try getting to know more about the problem, and even try looking at it as if it is not a problem, to at least begin to see how it functions. Remember the adage "Keep your friends close and your enemies closer."

Create something a little closer to solved, then repeat.

This approach is at the heart of the Agile Development methodology. If a perfect solution cannot be created overnight (or at all), sometimes the best approach is to make something that is a "close" solution, without being a complete solution. This method works especially well iteratively, as in Agile sprints, where each burst of effort improves and refines the existing solution, bringing it asymptotically closer to perfect.

Try combining two unexpected elements.

This is the "salted caramel" solution. These two culinary ingredients don't sound appealing as a combination. They are an unexpected pairing that solves the problem of how to make caramel taste even better than usual. Unexpected combinations are not always successful (chocolate and bacon is unreliable as a taste sensation), but when a problem seems insoluble, this approach can yield good results—or at least suggestions for new avenues of discovery.

Add an unexpected element.

This is a trick used by authors who are facing writer's block. They solve this debilitating problem by adding some unexpected element—a cat, for instance. If writing on a novel or nonfiction project ever stalls, a writer might get herself going again by throwing in something silly, random, or at least unexpected. They may go back and delete that section later, but the creative juices get flowing again simply because the problem has been shaken up and they can take a fresh look at it.

Take a step back.

Many problems are solved in the subconscious before that solution ever bubbles up to conscious awareness. Sometimes that intuitive leap is blocked when too much time is spent consciously focused on the problem. Taking a break or stepping away from the problem often lets a person relax enough to hear what their subconscious is trying to say. This is what happens when a solution "just comes to mind out of the blue" while someone is standing in the shower or looking at a sunset. These moments of inspiration can never strike if breaks are never taken.

Solve in parts and combine.

Sometimes the principle of synergy is detrimental, as a combination of factors can result in a problem that is larger than the sum of its parts. This can result in what seems like an insolvable problem. Yet, if the parts are addressed individually, they will stop working together and the huge problem will evaporate.

Try to prove it can't be solved.

This approach is often used in the field of mathematics, but it applies to any problem. If it can be definitively proved that a problem can never be solved ... well, it usually can't, but along the way to finding out why it can't be solved, several options for potential solutions will usually be uncovered.

Simplify elements until the problem resembles a previously solved problem.

The problem of landing a person on the moon may seem overwhelmingly complex, but it is essentially the same thing as shooting a bullet and hitting a target. Although this is a great oversimplification, the bulls-eye on a gun range is a solved problem. The math, methods, and materials all exist. Looked at in this light, the problem of a moon landing becomes much more manageable, as existing tools can be used, at least to get the solution process started.

Solve the opposite problem.

The problem of cooling a house can seem insurmountable, but the problem of heating a house, while technically the direct opposite problem, can result in clear solutions for cooling. For instance, insulation is key in both cases, as is air flow. Both solutions rely on most of the same principles, and the solution for one type of problem often suggests the solution for its opposite.

Has anybody else solved a similar problem?

This approach relates to the idea of "don't reinvent the wheel." Sometimes a solution that seems impossible has already been solved by someone else, and proper research will uncover it.

Prototype.

See Prototyping and Paper Prototyping.

Think out loud.

Often the act of putting thoughts into words, rambling and strange as they may be, will help organize them in ways that suggest solutions.

Get help.

This one is simple. In many situations, an expert can be brought in to provide guidance or an outright solution. For instance, health problems are often best solved by doctors rather than the patient who has the problem. Similarly, cooperation among peers can result in quick solutions.

Act it out.

Actively roleplaying or paper prototyping can bring to light solutions that are not obvious when the pieces are not in motion.

Explain it to your grandfather.

Similar to thinking out loud, this approach doesn't actually require a relative. It's the act of explaining the problem to someone who is not an expert that sometimes illuminates solutions. Whether the listener has suggestions or questions or no input at all, explaining things in their simplest forms can help clarify the problem.

Look at it from the other side.

Turn the puzzle upside down. Look behind the curtain. Try to look at the villain as a hero instead. A fresh perspective often reveals approaches for solutions.

Measure and write it in numbers.

Sometimes a lack of clarity and definition can result in a moving target that is always out of reach. It's hard to know when something is "better," but it is easy to know when it has improved by two percentage points.

Turn numbers into words.

The inverse of writing a problem in numbers is to translate the numbers in a problem into words. For instance, math equations or flowcharts can seem hopelessly confusing, but if spoken or changed into a relatable situation like taking apples off a table, the answer can be more obvious.

Try on a solution for size.

When facing big decisions in life, like which college to attend or which job to take, psychiatry suggests "trying on" a solution—that is, pretending that one or the other decision is the one and behaving as if this were the true plan for a while. Often, this approach reveals problems with the temporary solution (Oh, our budget doesn't fit that pay cut.) that were not obvious before, or it confirms that this is the correct solution.

Watch out for ultimatums/ dichotomies/negatives.

This is another problem-solving approach from the soft sciences; examine the problem statement for ultimatums (always, never), dichotomies (black or white), and assumed negatives (Are you sure there really is no budget for this bug fix?). The real world is usually full of shades of grey, exceptions to the rules, and incorrect assumptions; yet, if the problem statement is built on these unreal expectations, potential solutions may be ignored.

Check for neutrality.

Is a solution being ignored because of personal bias somewhere? No one is perfect.

Use Judo.

The essence of Judo is to use the opponent's strengths against him, and conversely, to find ways to make weakness into a strength. Sometimes the best solution to a problem is to retreat and simply not solve it, and sometimes the problem can be reframed into an asset. Sometimes its big, overwhelming nature can be used as a distraction while the core of the problem is eaten away bit by bit.

Find the weakest link.

Analyze the relative strengths and weaknesses of each part of the problem; then focus attention on the weakest point. Often, breaking this one element can cause the whole problem to collapse, but if it doesn't, this is another case where iteration works. When the weakest/easiest part of the problem is solved, move on to the next easiest/weakest, and so on until all parts are solved. Often the mental practice and incremental development of tools at each step of the process means that the solvers are better equipped to tackle the next section as it comes along.

About the Contributors

Keyvan Acosta is continually developing his talents and passions as game designer, musician, writer, and teacher, sharing it all as a course director in the Game Design department at Full Sail University. In recent years, he's also participated in various industry conferences as a contributor, speaker, and judge, including Art History of Games, Game Developers Conference, Project Horseshoe, Siggraph Bogotá, and SXSW Interactive. Keyvan's credits include game designer at ZeeGee Games, programmer, and creative consultant for various companies like CyberMedia (PR), IGDA Global Game Jam, Mekensleep, and MuninuM.

Liz Canacari-Rose was born and raised in Denver, Colorado. She has studied and worked in the IT industry since 1997, from hardware support to web development to software and game development. In 2000, she had the rare privilege of working with a company to create interactive, 3D training solutions for the medical industry. This, along with a lifetime passion for video games, piqued her interest in the game industry. She went on to receive two degrees from Full Sail University—a BS in Game Design and Development in 2006, and an MS in Entertainment Business in 2009. She continues to develop her own games through her small business, in addition to teaching Game History at Full Sail University.

Michael Deneen has been a professional game designer for over seven years. He most recently designed and implemented levels for PlaysStation All Stars: Battle Royale, God of War: Ghost of Sparta, and God of War: Chains of Olympus. Previously, Michael worked in various roles on the Fantastic Four, Sopranos, Medal of Honor, and James Bond franchises.

Zack Hiwiller is a game designer, educator, and writer who lives in Orlando, Florida. He is the department chair for the Game Design degree program at Full Sail University and the lead designer at Sky Parlor Studios. Previously, in addition to his independent projects, he was a designer at Gameloft and Electronic Arts (EA). His writing, at hiwiller.com, has been reposted by Kotaku, GameSetWatch, and others and has reached over a million readers.

Dr. Jeff Howard is an assistant professor of Game Development and Design at Dakota State University, where he plays a key role leading the narrative focus area in the Computer Game Design program. He is the author of *Quests: Design, Theory, and History in Games and Narratives* (A K Peters Ltd., 2008) and the program committee chair for the Workshop on Integrated Design in Games (IDIG). He continues to develop his transmedia work, Arcana, while filling the quiet moments by researching and writing for his book on magic systems in games.

Christina Kadinger is currently a professor at Full Sail University in the Game Design program. She has a BA in Economics from Rollins College and a Law Degree from Barry University. She enjoys playing games, seeing live bands, and playing ice hockey in her spare time.

Chris Keeling is a video game industry veteran; he first worked on Panzer Elite in 1998, followed by America's Army, Twilight War, Order of War, and other military titles (which probably has something to do with his 23 years of service in the US Army and Army Reserve). He is currently chained to a desk in Eastern Europe at Wargaming.Net, where he is a senior producer on the highly successful World of Tanks, as well as on the forthcoming World of Warplanes, World of Warships, and several unannounced projects. Chris has also worked as a game writer, game designer, and game educator, and until recently, as Program Manager for the Game Design program at Full Sail University, where he still serves on the Program Advisory Board. He also volunteers on the Executive Committee of the International Game Developers Association's Game Writing Special Interest Group and blogs about his tedious life at www.aconnecticutyankee.com.

Casey Kuczik is a senior producer at Ubisoft Entertainment in Paris, where he is part of a team responsible for advancing mobile game development and publishing. During his career, Casey has held the roles of head of mobile, producer, designer, writer, and tester at the companies Bigpoint, Electronic Arts, and Seven Studios. Since 2009, Casey has been an instructor at Full Sail University, where he teaches Design and Development Analysis, a course focused on deconstructing video games with a critical perspective; this is an original course of his creation. Casey graduated from Yale University in 2003 with a BA double major in American Studies and Film Studies, and in 2010, he completed an MBA from Loyola Marymount University.

Nicole Lazzaro is a world-renowned game researcher, designer, and speaker who makes games more fun. Nicole discovered the Four Keys to Fun, a model used by hundreds of thousands of game developers worldwide, in 2004. She used this model to design the iPhone's first accelerometer game, now called Tilt World, in 2007. Nicole is referred to as one of the 100 most influential women in high-tech, one of the top 20 women working in video games, and one of the top 10 women in gamification. Nicole's work has been widely cited by global news media such as CNN, *Wired, Fast Company,* CNET, the *New York Times,* the *Wall Street Journal,* the *Hollywood Reporter, Red Herring,* and the *Boston Globe*. She has advised the White House and the US State Department on the use of games to unlock human potential to improve our world. For the past two decades, as the CEO of XEODesign, she has improved hundreds of millions of player experiences for companies such as Ubisoft, EA, Disney, and Cartoon Network; as well as worked on best-selling franchises such as Myst, Diner Dash, Pogo, and The Sims. One of the pioneers in applying game design outside of games, she designed game-inspired UI for Oracle, Cisco, Kaiser, Sun, Roxio, and others as early as 1992.

Tom Long is an award-winning game studies educator and game designer. He has worked in the game and simulation industry for more than 15 years. During those years, he has twice judged the Front Line Awards for *Game Developer* magazine, has won the Unity Great Education Giveaway Contest, and has contributed to many published game titles. In his spare time, he can be found at the local hacker space, FamiLAB, working on his Maker Faire project. Tom currently teaches Level Design II at Full Sail University in Winter Park, Florida. Follow him on Twitter at @tomlong74.

Michael Lucas was a gamer before the advent of video games; he played tournament Chess and Backgammon and worked to develop one of the best Chess-playing software systems in the world by 1979: DUCHESS (for Duke University Chess). As a National Master of Chess out of college, Michael continued in competitive gaming and worked in war-game simulations for the Navy. Michael later trained artists on *Monster House, Open Season, Beowulf, Surf's Up,* and many other films at Sony Pictures Imageworks and Sony Pictures Animation. His areas of expertise there were in hair and cloth simulation, Python and Maya scripting, and stereoscopic 3D. He has also worked in TV and on documentaries. He was the postproduction supervisor in 2010 on Mark Kistler's *Imagination Station,* and helped the show win an Emmy Award. He is now a course director at Full Sail University and teaches Level Design with UDK, Usability, and The Game Industry.

Dave Mark is the president and lead designer of Intrinsic Algorithm, an independent game development studio and AI consulting company in Omaha, Nebraska. He is the author of *Behavioral Mathematics for Game AI* (Course Technology PTR, 2009), has written for numerous other industry books and *Game Developer* magazine, and is a frequent speaker at industry conferences on the topics of game AI, game theory, and psychology. Additionally, he is the co-founder of the AI Game Programmers Guild and is the co-advisor of the GDC AI Summit. Dave continues to further his education by attending the University of Life. He has no plans to graduate any time soon.

Doug Oberndorf has a BA in Art with a focus in 2D & 3D Animation, and an MFA in Special Effects Animation. Doug is a course director at Full Sail University and teaches courses about the game industry. He owns the indie game development company Tropic Mods

Development and volunteers at events for the National Kidney Foundation (NKF).

Patricia Pizer debuted in the gaming industry at Infocom in 1988, where she made games back when you didn't even need graphics. Over the next decade, she worked at such studios as Boffo Games, THQ/GameFX, and Harmonix Music. Patricia moved into massively multiplayer online (MMO) games as Creative Director at Turbine Entertainment before she worked on MMOs at Ubisoft and Disney's VR Studio, the makers of Toontown. After applying her design skills to alternate reality games for 42 Entertainment, she returned to Disney Interactive Studios, where she designed DGamer, a DS online avatar SNA service, and worked on the Club Penguin Elite Penguin Force. Most recently, Patricia was Creative Director for ZeeGee Games. Mostly, though, Patricia just likes to play games.

Michael Pynn is a creative writing instructor at the college level as well as a game designer. He has taught numerous subjects relevant to students of game design, including composition, professional communication, narrative development, analog game design, game documentation, and more. As a designer, Michael has produced multiple alternate reality games and interactive story experiences. A member of the International Game Developers Association, he holds a BA from the University of Central Florida and an MFA in Creative Writing for Entertainment Business from Full Sail University.

Brian Stabile is a game designer/programmer, musician, audio engineer, teacher, and linguist. In addition to teaching online classes at Full Sail University, Brian is the drummer for Yogurt Smoothness, a nationally touring indie rock band, and co-owner of Astro Crow, an independent game developer best known for their iOS title The Last Ace of Space. He worked as a programmer and Japanese translator for the PC title Three Dead Zed, and worked with the University of Central Florida's RETRO Lab programming "serious games" for clients such as the Robert Wood Johnson Foundation, the National Science Foundation, and the Defense Acquisition University.

Jason VandenBerghe has been making games for 17 years, and is currently a creative director at Ubisoft (most recently on Far Cry 3 and Ghost Recon: Future Soldier). In his career, he has been a programmer, producer, designer, and director. He has worked on bad games, good games, hard-to-make games, and, er, less hard-to-make games, and he intends to keep on doing that for as long as they will let him.

About the Illustrator

Raymond Yuen is an illustrator and designer from New York and is currently living in San Francisco. His love of comics inspired him to work through the caricature ranks at Six Flags Great Adventure and in the colorful offices of Pokémon USA. Currently, he is the cofounder and art director at Suspended Belief Studios, his game design company. You can find him at www.rayuen.com.

Index

10 minutes of sustained attention, 162
"30 Seconds of Fun," 70
80/20 Rule, The
  Legend of Zelda, 64
  WOW (World of Warcraft), 64

Abe and Zac, relationship to time and money, 122
accomplishment
  ARCS, 200
  attention, 200
  confidence, 200
  fiero, 200
  fulfillment, 200
  pleasure, 200
  relevance, 200
  satisfaction, 200
  sense of, 200
accuracy and speed, tradeoff between, 178
Aces High; Jokers Wild, 6
action games, 85–86
Addiction Pathways, rewards, 130
Advance Organizers
  cutscenes, 168
  Hype, 168
  loading screen, 168
  menus, 168
adventure games, 85
advertising, using to capture attention, 102
aesthetics as focus in flow, 80
Affordance Cues
  HCI (Human-Computer Interaction), 170
  HUD (heads-up display), 170
  illustration, 171
  My Horse game, 170
alien world, survival of, 140
Altderfer, Clayton, 154
Alternate Reality games, 98
anchoring recency bias, 174
anger, 48–49
Animal Crossing, 10
animation workload, including in pillars, 86
arcade games, coin crunchers in, 32
ARCS (attention, relevance, confidence, satisfaction), 200
artificial intelligence, 154
A/Symmetric Play and Synchronicity, 4
attention, sustaining for 10 minutes, 162
attention of players, capturing, 102
Attention vs. Perception, 132
attributes, 100
availability heuristic, 174
Axelrod, Robert, 42

Backward Induction, 28
Balancing and Tuning, 134
balancing games, 152
Bartle's Player Types
  Achievers (Diamonds), 8
  Acting On, 8
  Explorers (Spades), 8
  Interacting With, 8
  Killers (Clubs), 8
  Socializers (Hearts), 8
behavior of actors, 30
Behaviorism, 50
Big 5 psychological system
  Agreeableness, 58
  Conscientiousness, 58
  Extraversion, 58
  Neuroticism, 58
  Openness to Experience, 58
Billiards as game of skill, 32
black box testing, 108
bombs, relationship to risk assessment, 114
Brainstorming Methods. *See also* Prototyping
  freethinking, 66
  physical techniques, 66
  structured techniques, 66
  word bubbles, 66
Brooks, Fred, 106
The Buster Principle, 172

Call of Duty: Zombies, 94
Cardinal Payoffs, 40
casual games, 85
character design, including in pillars, 86
character development, supplementing, 76
Chess
  positive feedback loops in, 14
  as symmetric game, 4
choices, difficulty of, 54
chunking, process of, 22
circular chain of supremacy, 46
Civilization, 38
Cognitive Biases
  anchoring, 174
  availability heuristic, 174
  confirmation bias, 174
  framing, 174
  The Kuleshov Effect, 174–175
  negativity bias, 174
  recency bias, 174
coin crunchers, 32
Colossal Cave Adventure, 126
combat design, including in pillars, 86
communicative details, 136
confirmation bias, 174
consequences, lack in fantasy play, 96
Consumer Surplus
  F2P (Free-to-Play) models, 68
  pricing games, 68
contempt, 48–49
Cooperative vs. Oppositional, 10
Core Gameplay Loop
  "30 Seconds of Fun," 70
  elements, 70

Halo games, 70
prototyping, 70
repetition, 70
scope, 70
Super Mario Bros., 70
creativity
cognitive, 82
emotional, 82
flow, 82
forms of, 82
methods, 82
Croft, Laura, 102
crossword puzzles, 44
Csikszentmihalyi, Mihaly, 80
cutscenes, starting games with, 168

D

Dark Souls, 18
Dead Space, 78
Deadly Premonition, 18
Death Race 2000, 30
decision making, process of, 198
demand. *See* Supply and Demand
Demon's Souls, 18
design, simplicity in, 146
Design by Committee. *See also* Environmental Storytelling; Experience Design
best practices, 74
common vision, 74
diagram, 75
vs. leadership, 74
team positions, 74
The Design of Everyday Things, 170
Details
communicative, 136
presentational, 136
disgust, 48–49
DM (Dungeon Master), 4
Dodgeball, positive feedback loops in, 14
Dominant Strategy
accidental, 176
deliberate, 176
emergent, 176
Donkey Kong, iteration in, 94
DOOM, emotions related to, 48
dopamine and music, 192
Doubling and Halving, 138
Dresher, Melvin, 42
Dunbar's Number, 52
Dungeons and Dragons, 16
Dyson, Freeman, 42

E

Easter Eggs, 18, 98
Economies of Scale
Eve Online, 140
microeconomics, 140
M.U.L.E., 140
ecosystem of games, 100
Einstein's theory of relativity, 204
Ekman, Paul, 48
emotional output, 30
emotions
anger, 48–49
contempt, 48–49
disgust, 48–49
DOOM, 48
fear, 48–49
focusing on, 78
HUD (heads-up display), 48
interest curves, 48
joy, 48–49
L.A. Noire, 48
maintaining command of, 192
sadness, 48–49
seven universal, 48–49
surprise, 48–49
enjoyment, creating feelings of, 192
Environmental Storytelling. *See also* Design by Committee
character development, 76
world building, 76
ERG (Existence, Relatedness, and Growth), 154
Errors Players Make
commission, 142–143
motor control, 142–143
omission, 142–143
performance, 142
wrong action, 142–143
Errors Without Punishment, 144
Eve Online, 16, 140
Experience Design. *See also* Design by Committee
creating tension, 78
Dead Space, 78
focusing on emotions, 78
focusing on players, 78
vs. game design, 78
experiences
on rails, 160
sandbox, 160
Extensive Form, 28

F

F2P (Free-to-Play) models, 68
faces, using to capture attention, 102
Fairness
in game design, 12
Rabin's model of, 12
fantasy play, lack of consequence, 96
Farmville, loss aversion in, 152
fast, cheap, good
prototyping, 106
sacrifices, 106
fear, 48–49
Feedback Loops
negative, 14
positive, 14
fiero, relationship to accomplishments, 200
Fitts' Law
combat and targeting, 178
speed and accuracy, 178
task of pointing, 178
UI (user interface), 178
fixed rewards, 164
Flood, Merrill, 42
Flow. *See also* gameplay
aesthetics, 80
beginning levels of play, 80
in creativity, 82
individual concentration, 80
mastery phase, 80
phases of gameplay, 80
task management, 80
flow charts, using in brainstorming, 66
fluid navigation pillar, 86–87
"fog of war," 56
football, negative feedback loops in, 14
Four Keys to Fun, Lazzaro's, 22, 24
Four Ways to Be Creative, 82
FPSs (first person shooters), 32, 85
free rider problem, 60
freethinking, 66
fun. *See* Koster's Theory of Fun; Lazzaro's Four Keys to Fun
Fundamental Attribution Error, 180

G

Game design vs. Experience Design, 78
game ecosystem, 100
game elements
attributes, 100
objects, 100
states, 100
game experience, 100

Game Genres
action, 85
adventures, 85
casual, 85
FPSs (first person shooters), 85
MMO/MMORPG, 85
niches, 85
overview, 84
puzzles, 85
RPGs (roleplaying games), 85
RTS (real-time strategy), 85
simulations, 85
sports, 85
strategy, 85
Game Pillars
action games, 86
animation workload, 86
branching storyline, 87
character design, 86
combat design, 86
crafting, 87
creating tension, 86
exploration, 87
fluid navigation, 86–87
illustration, 87
perspective, 86
using, 86
world design, 86
game state, information about, 20, 56
game structure, information about, 20
Game Tropes
Crates, 88
Free Health, 88
murder, 88
Stealing, 88
gameplay. *See also* Flow
asymmetric, 4
beginning levels of, 80
flow, 80
vs. living, 58
mastery phase, 80
phases, 80
repetition, 70
symmetric, 4
synchronous, 4
task management, 80
games. *See also* Metagames
balancing, 152
casual, 85
classification, 56
concealed structure of, 56
of imperfect information, 56
iteration of, 36
as low-risk learning tools, 22
of memory, 32
Sequential, 28
Simultaneous, 28
of skill, 32
Gardner's Multiple Intelligences
Bodily-Kinesthetic, 16
Interpersonal, 16
Intrapersonal, 16
Linguistic-Verbal, 16
Logical-Mathematical, 16
Musical, 16
Naturalistic, 16
Spatial, 16
genres of games. *See* Game Genres
Gestalt
art examples, 90
Closure/Reification, 90
Continuance, 90
Figure-Ground, 90
Invariance, 90
mathematical example, 90
Proximity/Common fate, 90
Similarity, 90
skill free, 90
story aspect, 90
Symmetry, 90
Golden Ratio
applying to UI (user interface), 182
value of, 182
good, relationship to fast, 106
gratification
extrinsic motivation, 188
fun and immersion, 188
instant vs. delayed, 188
griefer
mitigating behavior of, 184
vs. Samaritan, 184
Griefing, 184
guns and wands, impact of, 96

Halo games, 30 Seconds of Fun in, 70
Halving and Doubling, 138
Hardin, Garrett, 54
Hick's Law
choices, 146
simplicity in design, 146
House Rules. *See also* rules
guidelines, 92
suggestions, 92
Howard's Law of Occult Game Design, 18
HUD (heads-up display)
affordance cues, 170
emotional expressions, 48
Huizinga, Johan, 26
human actions, assigning reasons for, 180
human emotion. *See* emotions
Hype
advance organizer, 168
down side, 186
expectations, 186
as marketing terminology, 186
"nocebo," 186

Imbalance in games, fixing, 152
inattentional blindness, 132
Infocom games, 172
Information. *See also* Transparency
amount of, 20
complete, 56
game state, 20
game structure, 20
imperfection, 20
incomplete, 56
nature of, 20
perfection, 20
Intelligences, Gardner's Multiple, 16
Interest Curve
creating, 148
emotions, 48
guidelines, 148
vs. Learning Curve, 150
rectifying deviations, 148
Iteration. *See also* repetition in gameplay
Call of Duty: Zombies, 94
Donkey Kong, 94
game concept, 95
Metroid, 94
The Street Fighter series, 94
tower defense games, 94
Iyengar, Sheena, 146

J*o-Ha-Kyu*, 194
Joker as wildcard, 6
Jones, Gerard, 96
joy, 48–49

Kahneman and Tversky's "Outbreak," 175
Killing Monsters, 96
Kim, Scott, 44
Kivetz, Ran, 50
Kleenex test, 108
Koffka, Kurt, 90
Kohler, Wolfgang, 90
Koster's Theory of Fun, 22

Krug's First Law of Usability
clicking, 190
consistency of interface, 190
Doubling and Halving, 190
interface qualities, 190
simplicity of interface, 190
The Kuleshov Effect, 174–175

L.A. Noire, 48
lag, impact on gameplay, 4
The Law of Occult Design, 18, 20
Lazzaro's Four Keys to Fun
Easy Fun, 24
feeling of winning, 24
hard Fun, 24
People of Fun, 24
Serious Fun, 24
leadership vs. Design by Committee, 74
Learning Curve
describing, 150
feedback loops, 150
vs. Interest Curve, 150
relationship to working memory, 206
setting goals, 150
steep vs. shallow, 150
teaching tasks, 150
learning tools, games as, 22
Legend of Zelda, 16, 18
load testing, 108
loading screen, designing for advance organizer, 168
Loss Aversion
Farmville, 152
fixing imbalance, 152
nerfing, 152
Sword of Power, 152

Macroeconomics, 140
Magic Circle, 26
Magic Wand, 96
main character, story arc of, 120
Making Moves, 28
Mario Kart, negative feedback loops in, 14
Marvel vs. Capcom, tuning, 134
Maslow's Hierarchy of Needs
artificial intelligence, 154
complexity of conflicts and choices, 154
concerns about, 154
esteem, 154
fear, 154
love and belonging, 154
physiological, 154
self-actualization, 154
simulations, 154
MDA: Mechanics, Dynamics, and Aesthetics, 30
memory
Learning Curve, 206
long-term, 206–207
vs. skill, 32
working, 206–207
menus, starting games with, 168
Metagames. *See also* games
Alternate Reality, 98
Easter Eggs, 98
The Gathering, 98
World of Warcraft, 98
Metroid, iteration in, 94
microeconomics, 140
Minimax and Maximin, 34
Min/Maxing
powergaming, 156
rules lawyer, 156
twinking, 156
MMO, threats in, 158
MMO/MMORPGs, 85
money and time, 122
Monopoly, feedback loops, 14
Morgenstern, Oskar
Rational Self-Interest, 28
Zero-Sum Games, 208
Zero-Sum strategies, 36
Motokyo, Zeami, 194
movement
communicating sense of, 194
using to capture attention, 102
moves, making, 28
MUD (multi-user dungeon), 8
M.U.L.E., 140
murder trope, 88
Music and Dopamine, 192
Musical Chairs, 16
My Horse game, 170

Nash Equilibrium
Minimax and Maximin, 34
Players, 36
Prisoner's Dilemma, 42
negative feedback loops, 14
negativity bias, 174
NES (Nintendo Entertainment System), 18
niche games, 85
"nocebo," relationship to Hype, 186
Norman, Donald, 170

Objects, 100
Occult Game Design, Howard's Law of, 18
O.C.E.A.N., 58
on rails vs. sandbox experiences, 160
oppositional vs. cooperative, 10
optimizing vs. satisficing, 198–199
Ordinal Payoffs, 40
"Outbreak," 175
Outcomes: Pareto Optimality, 38

Pacing
beginning, 194
break, 194
feeling of movement, 194
Jo-Ha-Kyu, 194
movement impetus, 194
rapid, 194
suspense, 194
tempo, 194
tension, 194
threat, 194
Paper Prototyping. *See also* Prototyping
advantages, 104
drawbacks, 104
flow, 104
play testing, 104
Pareto Optimality
Dominant Strategy, 38
improvements, 38–39
Pareto's Principle
Legend of Zelda, 64
WOW (World of Warcraft), 64
Payoffs
balancing, 40
Cardinal, 40
maximizing, 40
motivations, 40
Normal Form tables, 40
Ordinal, 40
perception vs. attention, 132
perspective, including in pillars, 86
Phi, representing golden ratio with, 182
pillars. *See* Game Pillars
play space, exploration of, 164
Play Testing
black box, 108
Kleenex test, 108
load testing, 108
Quality Assurance, 108
white box, 108

players
  being kind to, 172
  capturing attention of, 102
  errors made by players, 142
  focusing on, 78
  griefing, 184
pleasure, creating feelings of, 192
Poker, Deuces wild in, 6
Pong as symmetric game, 4
Pool
  as game of skill, 32
  negative feedback loops in, 14
positive feedback loops, 14
power weapons, relationship to risk assessment, 114
powergaming, 156
presentational details, 136
Press, William, 42
Prisoner's Dilemma
  balancing payoffs in, 40
  chart, 43
  described, 42
  Forgiving, 42
  Nash Equilibrium, 36, 42
  Nice condition, 42
  Non-Envious condition, 42
  rational decision, 42
  Retaliating, 42
  Tragedy of the Commons, 42
Problem-Solving Approaches, 196
Problem-Solving Methods
  acting it out, 213
  adding unexpected element, 212
  almost solving and repeating, 212
  approaching from other side, 213
  brainstorming, 211
  check existing solutions, 213
  check for neutrality, 214
  combining unexpected elements, 212
  defining problem space, 211
  drawing pictures, 210
  explaining to non-experts, 213
  finding patterns, 210
  finding weakest link, 214
  following money, 211
  getting help, 213
  making flowchart, 211
  making lists, 210
  making tables, 210
  measuring in numbers, 214
  proving impossibility of solving, 212
  rewording problems, 211
  scientific method, 210–211
  sideways approach, 211–212
  simplifying elements, 213
  solving in parts and combining, 212
  solving opposite problem, 213
  solving similar problems, 211
  stealth approach, 211–212
  stepping back, 212
  strength from weakness, 214
  thinking out loud, 213
  trying solutions, 214
  turn numbers into words, 214
  ultimatums/dichotomies/negatives, 214
  working backward, 210
  writing in numbers, 214
Problem-Solving Obstacles
  assumptions, 110
  functional fixedness, 110
  irrelevant information, 110
  mental sets, 110
  overcoming, 110–111
problem statement
  common vision, 72
  communicating, 72
  defining, 72
  focusing, 72
  narrowing scope, 72
  testing, 72
Prototyping. *See also* Brainstorming Methods; Paper Prototyping
  data collection, 112
  process, 112
  and testing, 112
psychological filters, 174
Punishment
  Lives/Game Over/continue, 158
  permadeath, 158
  wither, 158
puzzles
  described, 85
  development, 44

Quality Assurance testing, 108

Rabin's model of fairness, 12
random conditioning, *164*
rational self-interest, 28, 40
recency bias, 174
Red Light, Green Light, 16
repetition in gameplay, 70. *See also* Iteration
Resident Evil, 30
rewards
  and addiction pathways, 130
  expectation of players, 50
  fixed, 164
  providing, 14
  variable, 164
Risk Assessment
  bombs, 114
  designing scenarios, 114
  power weapons, 114
  practicing, 114
  principle of, 114
  triangularity, 114
Rock, Paper, Scissors
  circular chain of supremacy, 46
  Normal Form table, 40
  symbolic gestures, 46
  tabletop card games, 46
  winning, 46
  as Zero-Sum Game, 208
RPGs (roleplaying games)
  description, 85
  memory vs. skill, 32
  Pareto Optimality, 38
  positive feedback loops in, 14
RTS (real-time strategy), 85
Rubik's Cube, 16
rules, 30, 92. *See also* House Rules
rules lawyer, relating to Min/Maxing, 156
Rules of Play, 26

Sadness, 48–49
Salen, Katie, 26
Sandbox vs. On Rails, experiences, 160
Satisficing vs. Optimizing, 198–199
Scavenger Hunts, 16
Schell, Jesse
  The Art of Game Design, 100
  risk assessment, 114
Sequential games, 28
sex, using to capture attention, 102
simplicity in design, 146
simulations, 85, 154
Simultaneous games, 28
skill free, relationship to Gestalt, 90
skill vs. memory, 32
Skinner Box
  goal-gradient effect, 50
  variable ratio, 50
Social Ties
  active, 52
  passive, 52
  Dunbar's Number, 52
  effectiveness, 52
  social mechanics, 52
Solitaire, 16

solving problems. *See* Problem-Solving Methods
Space Invaders, 194
Spatial Awareness
- Agoraphobic Spaces, 202
- Cathedral Effect, 202
- Claustrophobic Spaces, 202
- deep and complex worlds, 202
- Defensible Spaces, 202
- impact on human psyche, 202
- Lighting Design, 202
- Prospect-Refuge, 202

speed and accuracy, tradeoff between, 178
sports games, 85
states, 100
storytelling, environmental, 76
strategy games
- Civilization, 38
- described, 85

The Street Fighter series, iteration in, 94
Sudoku, 44
Super Mario Bros., Core Gameplay Loop, 70
Supply and Demand
- as economic component, 116
- providing in games, 116

surprise
- of synergy, 118
- as universal emotion, 48–49
- using to capture attention, 102

symmetric gameplay, 4
Synergy
- combining mechanics, 118
- crafting system, 118
- excitement of, 118
- in games, 118
- surprise of, 118

Tasks, teaching, 150
teaching tasks, 150
Ten Minutes of Sustained Attention, 162
tension, creating, 78
testing. *See* Play Testing
Tetris
- fairness in, 12
- time dilation, 204

Theme
- finding, 120
- main character's story arc, 120
- relationship to narrative, 120
- specifying, 120
- targeting, 120

threats in MMO, 158
Three Laws of Usability, 190
Tic-Tac-Toe
- Koster's Theory of Fun, 22
- Nash Equilibrium, 36

Time and Money, 122
Time Dilation
- play testing games, 204
- Tetris, 204

Tomb Raider, 102
Tragedy of the Commons. *See also* Volunteer's Dilemma
- communism, 54
- government control, 54
- Nash Equilibrium, 36
- shared resource, 55
- solutions, 54
- theory, 54

Transparency. *See also* Information
- involuntary, 56
- voluntary, 56

triangularity, visualizing, 114
tropes. *See* Game Tropes
Tucker, Albert, 42
tuning and balance, 134
twinking, relating to Min/Maxing, 156

UCD (User-Centered Design)
- ISO keys to, 124
- personas, 124
- scenarios, 124
- use cases, 124

Urminsky, Oleg, 50

Van Vugt, Mark, 54
VandenBerghe's Five Domains of Play
- Adventurousness, 58
- Agreeableness, 58
- Artistic Interest, 58
- Conscientiousness, 58
- degree of detail, 58
- Emotionality, 58
- Extraversion, 58
- Imagination, 58
- Intellect, 58
- Liberalism, 58
- Neuroticism, 58
- Openness to Experience, 58

Variable Rewards
- exploration of play space, 164
- random conditioning, 164

victory, thrill of, 24
video games, cooperative play in, 10
vocabulary of games, 100
Volunteer's Dilemma. *See also* Tragedy of the Commons
- vs. free rider problem, 60
- payoff matrix, 60

von Ehrenfels, Christian, 90
von Neumann, John
- Minimax and Maximin, 34
- Rational Self-Interest, 28
- Zero-Sum Games, 208
- Zero-Sum strategies, 36

Wands and guns, impact of, 96
Wayfinding
- birth canals, 126
- breadcrumbs, 126
- Colossal Cave Adventure, 126
- as environmental puzzle, 126
- landmarks, 126
- lighting, 126
- process, 126
- weenies, 126
- well-structured paths, 126

Wertheimer, Max, 90
white box testing, 108
wild card
- designating, 6
- Joker as, 6

winning, feeling of, 24
word bubbles, using in brainstorming, 66
Words with Friends, 4
work in progress, balancing, 138
Working Memory, 22, 206–207
world building, 76
world design, including in pillars, 86
WOW (World of Warcraft), 64, 98

Zac and Abe, relationship to time and money, 122
Zero-Determinant Strategy, 42
Zero-Sum Game
- with Cardinal Payoffs, 40
- Poker, 208
- Rock, Paper, Scissors, 208
- solving, 208

Zero-Sum strategies, 28
Zheng, Yuhuang, 50
Zimmerman, Eric, 26
Zubek, Robert, 30